Montana's Best Fly Fishing

Montana's Best Fly Fishing

FLIES, ACCESS,
AND GUIDES' ADVICE
FOR THE STATE'S PREMIER RIVERS

Ben Romans

HEADWATER BOOKS

STACKPOLE BOOKS

For Heather and Samuel

Published by
STACKPOLE BOOKS
Headwater Books
5067 Ritter Road
Mechanicsburg, PA 17055
www.stackpolebooks.com

Printed in the United States of America

First edition

Main cover image by Jay Nichols; cover design by Wendy A. Reynolds
Maps by Brian Goudreau

Library of Congress Cataloging-in-Publication Data

Romans, Ben.
Montana's best fly fishing / Ben Romans. — 1st ed.
p. cm.
Includes index.
ISBN-13: 978-0-8117-0726-8
ISBN-10: 0-8117-0726-1
1. Fly fishing—Montana. I. Title.
SH456.R633 2010
799.12'409786—dc22

2010004634

CONTENTS

Whether you fish on foot or from a drift boat, fly fishing in Montana's waters is a treat. The following pages have tips from some of the state's top fly shops, outfitters, and guides to help anglers of any skill level experience all the state has to offer. Couple this book with other resources and maps and fish with confidence. NICK ROMANS PHOTO

ACKNOWLEDGMENTS

I put a lot of work into this book, and nobody knows that more than my dear wife. Whether I was gone for weeks at a time or sitting at the keyboard for hours on end, she encouraged me to do whatever needed to be done while she kept us in tune with life's other little tasks (like taking care of our newborn son). She is the most patient and understanding person I know.

I also need to thank the rest of my family. My brother and my dad are two of the best fishing partners I could have, and I'm glad we've been able to share so much water together. Behind the three of us are my mother and sister—always eager to bake us treats to enjoy on our next outing and unwearyingly awaiting our return.

Also, thanks to my friend Dominic. I appreciate your help and willingness to go through hell and high water on some of our insane adventures.

Thanks to Jay Nichols for allowing me to give this project my best shot. I appreciate your confidence, patience, friendship, and mentoring.

Lastly, I want to thank everyone who helped me piece together the information contained in these pages—all the fly shops, outfitters, guides, and friends that let me rack their brains for the seemingly minute details about Montana's rivers. Thank you Kelly Galloup, Jim Cox, Mike Gerhart, James Anderson, Chris McCabe, Joe Sowerby, John Herzer, Chuck Stranahan, and Joel Silverman.

I know I say it often, but the people quoted in this book are the experts. They live and work on Montana's rivers year-round and are the window to learning more than you ever thought possible. Book a day with one of these outfitters or patronize their fly shops. I guarantee you it is worth the time and money.

Montana has something to offer anglers of all skill levels—from challenging tailwaters to small, easygoing tributaries—but sometimes returning to the basics, like casting a Woolly Bugger on an easygoing freestone, makes fishing in Big Sky Country so special.

INTRODUCTION

I don't profess to be an expert. The guides, outfitters, and fly-shop staffs that spend every waking moment possible on the waters described in this book are the experts. From the word go, my goal was to provide more than a snapshot of Montana's finest rivers. I tried to provide deep, detailed information that only comes from spending years learning a river's temperament, thresholds, and nuances—things the average Joe can't possibly gather from summer vacations and weekend jaunts. So I went to the seasoned veterans and fishing junkies that see the good, bad, and ugly season after season, and I asked them what people should know about this state's great waters. Not only did the individuals quoted on the following pages respond in spades, they reviewed the chapters for accuracy.

Montana has thousands of miles of water. Attempting to include them all with any significant level of detail is undoubtedly a lesson in frustration. I settled on the rivers in this book because they have something to offer everyone—wading anglers, floaters, dry-fly purists, and streamer swingers can all find something to suit their niches in some corner of the state.

Second, for as well-known and famous as some of these rivers are, they can be intimidating, which is why, I think, many anglers just fish the same rivers year after year. They become comfortable with a particular piece of water. But the state offers a broad range of experiences, and learning about the when, where, what, and how of unfamiliar rivers might give anglers the confidence to explore them. Read what the experts have to say about these rivers, visit their shops, or book a guide for a day. Learn from what they have to say and fish with confidence. I guarantee you'll see your angling résumé grow exponentially. That said, there is so much out there remaining for anglers to unearth. If you're visiting the state, do yourself a favor and take a day to explore waters that are off the beaten path. The feeling of self-discovery from investigating water on your own often outweighs any big-fish gratification you'll experience on the big rivers.

I took the same approach with fly patterns as I did with the text. I included some recipes because of my own partiality, but I selected the majority of them after recommendations from outfitters and fly shops. These patterns are hot-sellers and solid producers. Most fly anglers already know about flies like a Parachute Adams or Beadhead Prince Nymph, and I wanted to

While the scenery and quality insect hatches are highlights of fishing nearly any river in Montana, the abundance of public access points is the icing on the cake. The state has one of the best stream-access laws in the country, so use the public pullouts, parking areas, and boat ramps to access the water, and then stay below the high water mark and work up- or downstream.

highlight something fresh. Bring the old reliables, but also consider these newer patterns.

When it comes to fishing, there aren't many absolutes. If you want to experience Montana's grandeur during one of its prime hatch events, spread your visit out over a few days. Mother Nature can be cruel, and for some reason she takes particular pleasure throwing a wrench in my gears whenever I set foot in the water. No matter the weather forecast, be prepared for everything from high water to high winds. You may come for Salmonflies and instead be treated to a rare June snowstorm. Allow a few days to explore a river to increase your odds of seeing some decent conditions.

Come to Montana with a plan but also be flexible. Changes in weather and water conditions can be abrupt and extreme, despite what the five-day forecast or fishing reports tell you. Be prepared for anything. Even if it's warm, bring a set of cold-weather clothes to layer. Raincoats, sunscreen, mosquito repellent high in DEET (the Jefferson, Big Hole, and Beaverhead are particularly bad), backup rods and reels, and any other emergency items you can squeeze into your luggage can pay huge dividends if things go sour. Even if you never have to bust out the backup gear, you have the peace of mind knowing you're prepared for whatever comes at you. It takes a lot of time, effort, and expense to fish in such a wonderful state. Don't shortchange your experience by skimping on the essentials or planning poorly.

Drought is another issue. In the early part of the decade, low-water years weren't kind to western Montana rivers. Below-average snowfalls, virtually no summer precipitation, irrigation withdrawals, and skyrocketing temperatures prompted full and partial closures on several of the state's most notable waterways. While fishing closures ruin vacation plans, they are necessary to protect the future of fisheries. But there are other things responsible anglers can do to help decrease trout mortality in dry years. Try to limit your fishing to the early morning when water temperatures are low, and don't fish for trout when water temperatures average 65 degrees Fahrenheit or above. Always land fish quickly to avoid exhausting them, and try to keep them in the water when dislodging the hook. If you notice fish congregating around an underwater spring, this is a sure sign the river is becoming too warm, and you should leave them alone.

Hatch charts, like the ones included, are not carved in stone or comprehensive. They're more like fine-tuned, educated guesses. I focus on the major players. There are simply too many bug species to include on a comprehensive list for each watershed. For example, various species of small black stoneflies are plentiful in the early season on many rivers, but in my experience fish tend to prefer Blue-Winged Olives and midges, so I opted not to include them in some charts. Also, emergences vary depending on weather and water conditions, but by knowing the typical window of opportunity, you're better equipped to decide when and where you want to fish. Expect to encounter bugs both big and small. Montana's rivers have overlapping hatches, and though fish may key on stoneflies one minute, they can easily switch to Green Drakes the next.

No single book is all things to all people. Time, money, and resources simply won't allow it. The maps of each river, for example, are great for reference, but they are not designed to be used if you are driving around western Montana trying to pinpoint an access. Use this guide with other tools like a DeLorme *Montana Atlas & Gazetteer,* Google Earth, Montana Afloat maps, or the new River Rat maps.

Without question, one resource you should have on hand is the state fishing regulations. Consult the rulebook before you fish no matter the time of year or river. Some waters have a closed season, and rules change from year to year depending on factors like fish populations, weather, and streamflows. While entire rivers might not see a change in regulations, specific portions within a watershed can.

Fishing access is always a hot topic in Big Sky Country, especially with court battles over places like Mitchell Slough and the bridges on the Ruby River highlighted in the news over the last few years. Certain landowners and an array of organizations continually attempt to punch holes in the state's stream-access law. Don't give the sport a black eye by trespassing. Enter the water on public land and stay below the mean high-water mark. There's plenty of water for everyone to spread out and find solitude without walking on private property.

That said, some rivers in the state seem more crowded each year, and remembering a few rules of etiquette can go a long way. If you're floating, give other anglers elbow room (especially those on foot), and don't cast in their vicinity or into water they're fishing as you drift by. Also, raising anchor and shuffling immediately in front of oncoming boat traffic to beat another party to an area is no different than cutting off another automobile on the highway. Lastly, whether you're packing out or putting in, don't block the boat ramp—especially if others are waiting to use it. Prepare or unload your gear in the parking lots, and only use the ramp for launching or unloading your boat.

With that, I hope you enjoy this book as much as I did preparing it, and that the information, directions, and anecdotes I've compiled help you get more out of your next fishing trip. Tight lines.

Bighorn River

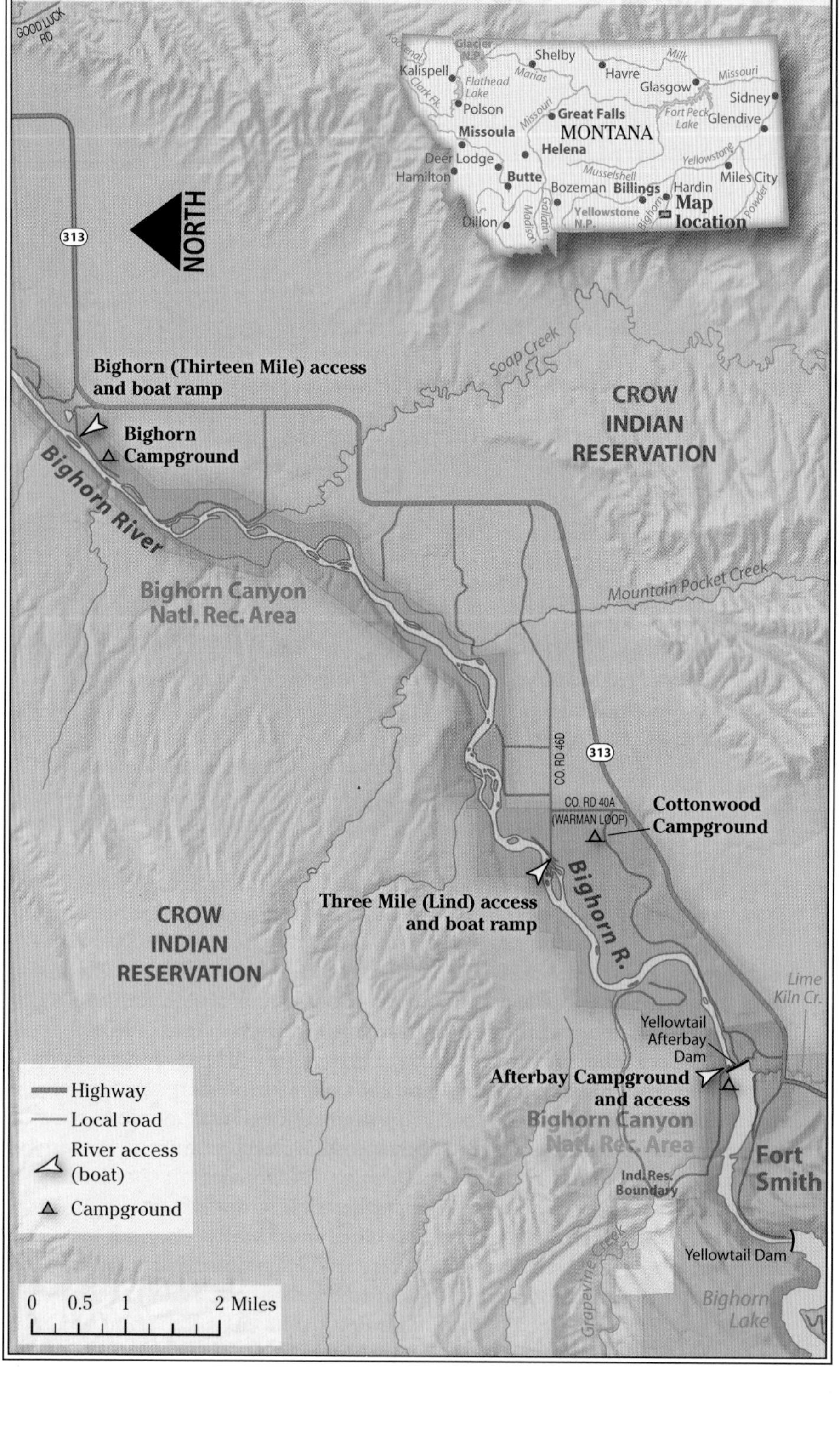

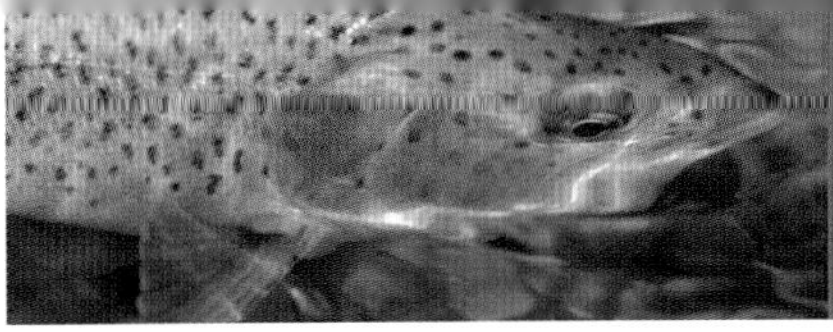

CHAPTER 1

Bighorn River

For those who have never visited this oasis in the sweeping, sagebrush-laden plains of the eastern third of the state, it's an overwhelming experience. It's an area rich with history, from the days of Lewis and Clark (who named the river after the numerous resident bighorn sheep herds) to the mountain men who constructed the state's first trading post on its banks to the gruesome deaths of soldiers and Native Americans at the nearby Battle of the Little Bighorn. But more than the history, the Bighorn draws anglers because you can come to it on virtually any day of the year—even in the middle of winter—and you'll likely see rising fish.

With its headwaters buried deep in the northeast corner of Wyoming, and a majority of its volume stocked up in a reservoir that spans the state border, Montana visitors concentrate their efforts on the water below Afterbay Dam. Built in 1967, Afterbay Dam acts as a buffer when releases from Yellowtail Reservoir dramatically spike or drop. After the construction of Afterbay Dam, the state immediately stocked the river with rainbow trout that reproduce naturally, though early on the river contained predominantly brown trout. "Right now, there's a good 50-50 split of rainbows and browns. You would think during drought times, the predacious browns would fare better, but the rainbow population is in great shape," Bighorn Fly and Tackle owner Duane Schreiner says.

The river garners a reputation for phenomenal fishing and incredible hatches. In years past, anglers commonly brought two dozen or more fish to the net daily. The past decade, however, the Bighorn went through a slump. "The Bighorn is still a relatively young fishery, so it's still evolving," Bighorn Trout Shop co-owner Hale Harris says. "But increased sedimentation from low-water years, combined with low water temps, is tough on the fish and some of these hatches. Low-water years give us low water temperatures because the dam is letting that coldest (bottom) layer of the reservoir pass through. This never lets the river warm up enough to drive some summer hatches. If we get several high-water years in a row, the water is a little warmer, and things will return to the way people remember it."

Winter snowfall amounts in recent years are helping the reservoir rise, and the river is rebounding. While trout may not populate the river as they

Given the number of fish in the river and their willingness to feed near the surface, sight-casting to fish in shallow water is not uncommon. It's a tricky game, however, and requires skillful casting and the proper fly selection. NICK ROMANS PHOTO

once did, the fish are longer, thicker, and stronger than their predecessors. It's hard for them not to be—the Bighorn is a trout factory.

The limestone canyons of the upper river mineralize the water with the nutrient content and alkalinity the lower river needs to sustain insect life. Consistent cold, clean water flowing from the dam and aquatic insect hatches that border on insane help the river produce nearly twice the number of fish per mile on other Montana rivers. Veteran Bighorn anglers say this is mere child's play though, and fish counts during the river's heyday were probably twice as robust. But with numbers like these, many anglers are not complaining.

"Back in the late 1980s, our average fish was just under 17 inches," Forrester's Bighorn River Resort's director of fishing operations Don Lyman says. "But after that, our numbers of fish skyrocketed, and the average size went down. We actually climbed up to about 10,000 fish per mile at one point. The state moved in with new regulations and water flows to balance things out and brought things back down to about 7,500 fish per mile, with the average returning to two-year-old, 17-inch fish, and a good number of three-year-old, larger fish hanging around." This amazing growth rate is due to the great habitat and nutrient-rich water. On average, Bighorn trout are between 12 and 16 inches, but the likelihood of catching a fish that stretches beyond that is better here than probably any other river in the state.

That's all the good news. The bad news is the fish don't always come easy. Bighorn trout see many anglers, many flies, and just about every type of presentation possible throughout the year. Fooling them into striking requires long leaders, delicate casts, and precisely timed, dead-drifted presentations.

The first 13 miles below the dam make up the Bighorn Canyon National Recreation Area, open for public and commercial use. It's also where you'll find the river's three most popular access points—Afterbay Dam, Lind (Three

Mile), and Bighorn (nearly 10 river miles downstream from Three Mile). Outside that, private ownership and Crow Reservation land surround the Bighorn. With such tight quarters, guides, outfitters, and locals know the pools and runs by name.

The fish don't seem to mind the crowds. Time and time again I've seen fish spook, scurry, and then pod up again in a matter of minutes and resume feeding. "The Bighorn is busy with people trying to figure out where to fish. But if everyone has an easygoing attitude, there are no problems. Everyone is on the river for the same reason, and there's enough water to spread out. Most people that come here end up leaving happy with their experience," Harris says.

Unfortunately, the Bighorn's character and distance between access points do not lend themselves well to wading anglers, even at low flows. A boat makes it easier to reach feeding fish and provides the ability to anchor up and work specific pools or runs. You don't have to float the entire time. In fact, get out and wade-fish any side channels or shallow riffles where you see fish. Just remember there is a $5-per-vehicle fee (or $30 annual fee) for anyone using the Afterbay, Three Mile, or Bighorn accesses. Purchase permits at

The Bighorn is a wide and relatively featureless river, so anglers need to pay attention to what's going on under the surface and look for any shelves, trenches, or other structures that break the flow and offer fish a place to rest and feed. NICK ROMANS PHOTO

The three miles between Afterbay Dam and Lind are some of the most popular on the river. Be mindful of other anglers when you're rowing or wade-fishing, and make sure you're allowing others significant space to fish.

a fly shop in Fort Smith or the park service station near Afterbay Dam. There are several places to rent drift boats in Fort Smith, and it's an easy river to float, even for beginners.

At first glance, the Bighorn looks like a flat, uncharismatic piece of water void of any riffles, eddies, or fast-water chutes favored by fish on some of the state's more popular freestone rivers. Look for underwater troughs, undercut banks, overhanging vegetation, or swirling pockets where insects and foam swirl into a froth.

"The flows are pretty much consistent and the holes remained fairly unchanged from year to year," Lyman says. "Now as the flows change—say for some reason they're jacked up to 5,000 cfs (cubic feet per second)—they'll change their location in that area. It's more about the water type and speed than it is the location. As you get to know the holes year after year and see them in different water conditions and temperatures, you get a better grasp of where to be fishing. This is one reason why it sometimes pays to hire a guide if you've never fished the Bighorn before. They can show you some of the nuances of the river."

Where and When

The smooth character of the water, swaying underwater weed beds, and skinny side channels look more like the famous springs in Paradise Valley than a large river. Typical flows on the Bighorn range from 2,000 to 4,500 cfs and are ideal for fishing and floating. If the flows are higher than 5,000 cfs, the river is moving much too fast for fishing to be productive or safe, and you're better off waiting or rescheduling a trip when flows are lower.

Afterbay Dam is the uppermost access point on the Bighorn's 13 miles of prime trout water. From here, the river flows approximately three miles to Three Mile (sometimes called Lind or Lind Ranch). These two points, and the water in between, are by far the most popular. In the prime months, this stretch can be crowded because the perception of visiting anglers is that the upper river contains the highest concentration of fish, as well as the highest percentage of fish over 18 inches, though I think the river downstream offers equal opportunities at both sizes and quantities of trout.

"You hit the Afterbay access too late in the morning, and it can be standing room only. It takes a while for people to disperse. From that point, expect to be in crowds the rest of the day," Lyman says. "If you fall back and let the crowds go ahead, or get on early, then you can avoid it. This works best if you're chasing fish on dry flies, especially for early-morning midges and evening caddis."

Scuds and sow bugs cling to the moss and grasses along the stream bottom and are the most significant food source for Bighorn River trout. Using a simple imitation like a Ray Charles as part of a two-fly nymphing rig is one of the most effective techniques.

CAST AND BLAST

One of the nice things about the Bighorn River's location in the state is its proximity to great upland bird hunting, and an early-fall trip is a good way to mix a little water time with some wingshooting. Nick Forrester, owner of Forrester's Bighorn River Resort, specializes in such trips and says they're a terrific option for outdoorsmen with two passions in life.

"I lease land that's away from the river, and clients fish one day and then hunt another day. If somebody comes out for a longer stay than that, they can mix and match the days," Forrester says. "We have a wide variety of birds such as sharptails, pheasants, huns, and chukar. I've got four to five guides and each one carries five to ten dogs, but we invite guests to bring their own dogs if they want to work them."

If upland isn't your game, and you'd rather try your hand at waterfowl, consider a trip later in the fall around late October and into November. Flights of ducks and geese are scanning for open water, and the river's sloughs and islands become attractive when other open water is freezing over.

"The best times for upland birds are in late September and October. But, in November, you can get some good fishing because the browns are spawning. There's some great streamer fishing and hardly anyone on the river," Forrester says. "We hunt pheasant then, but ducks and geese come into play as well. You can float the river and fish, and then get out in a couple areas, set up, and shoot ducks and geese." For more information visit Forrester's Bighorn River Resort at forrestersbighorn.com or call (800) 665-3799. ■

Many of the river's anglers are guests at neighboring lodges, and most guides and outfitters cater to the whims of their clients—people on vacation that want to eat a hefty breakfast and be back in time for predinner cocktails and hors d'oeuvres. If you're willing to be on the water at dawn, pull out around lunch, and revisit from the late afternoon until nightfall, you can have prime fishing conditions and relatively light river use.

On one particular trip to the Bighorn my brother and I refused to fish through the core of the day to avoid the late-July heat. We were consistently the first boat to put in at Afterbay, and nary saw another angler until midmorning. We took a long afternoon break for a nap and lunch, and then after dinner we fished until we couldn't see our flies, using headlamps to guide us home. It was some of the best dry-fly fishing we ever experienced.

Three Mile is, in my opinion, the busiest site on the river. If someone isn't taking out his boat after floating from the dam, he is putting one in to float to the Bighorn access. The parking lot is large enough for dozens of cars and trailers, but there is only one boat ramp, so be patient and courteous when traffic is heavy. If you've never floated the Bighorn, and plan on taking out here, a series of small islands just upstream of the boat ramp creates a few channels in the river. Stay river right to avoid missing the take-out.

Bighorn (sometimes called Thirteen Mile) is the final pit stop on the upper Bighorn's 13 miles of fame and used mainly as a take-out for those making their way downstream from Three Mile. The water between Three Mile and Bighorn is loaded with braids, channels, and islands that allow you to get out of the boat and fish on foot. Pace yourself if you want to fish the entire portion before running out of daylight. It's easy to lose track of time.

No matter what stretch you choose to float or fish, don't neglect side channels, sloughs, or other water outside the main stem's borders, no matter how skinny or shallow it looks. I've found that fish work into some unique, unconventional holding areas on the Bighorn—places floating anglers never get out of their boat to investigate. Work these areas stealthily, especially when it comes to casting and delivery. The fish are incredibly spooky and sending a shadow over a run or lining a fish shuts things down.

After Bighorn, the number of trout per mile begins to decline, silt replaces the river's fine-gravel bottom, and the warmer water temperatures aren't conducive for trout. "Once you get past Thirteen Mile [Bighorn] the number of trout per mile drops slightly, but the river is still classified as a blue-ribbon trout stream," Lyman says. "That stretch of river is somewhat of an unsung

Depending on water flows, the Bighorn has several shallow side channels and sloughs worth exploring. Approach them with caution—big fish sometimes linger in unusually shallow areas and spook easily.

hero. I wouldn't say you get bigger fish, but I think they fight a little better because the water is slightly warmer than it is close to the dam. Past Thirteen Mile, the water is closer to 58 or 59 degrees. This is optimum for rainbows, and there seems to be more of them here than in the upper end.

"I also don't think they've seen every fly known to man and are a little more eager to accept something. You can get away with a heavier tippet. The issue down there is water quality. There's a return ditch past the Bighorn access that dumps silt in the river after a heavy rain. This stretch of water is awesome when it's on, but it can be a nightmare when it is not. You can't just say 'OK, I'm going to go pound below Thirteen.' You have to watch the weather and conditions. Besides the rain, the moss and grass that breaks off from the upper river can gunk up your flies on every cast."

You can float down to St. Xavier Bridge (MT 91) or Mallard's Landing if you're willing to put in a long day, but don't expect the trout fishing to be on par with anything upriver. There are a few incredibly large brown trout down to St. Xavier, Mallard's Landing, and Two Leggins accesses. These sections are good options for streamer anglers in the early fall. Keep in mind you are drifting through Crow tribal lands until Hardin. Be respectful of private property and stay below the high-water mark.

Downstream of Hardin, as the Bighorn flows to the Yellowstone River, there are a few good places to fish, especially when browns make their way up from the Yellowstone in the fall as spawning season commences. Working downstream from Hardin is Arapooish, Grant Marsh, General Custer, and Manuel Lisa fishing access sites. Aside from a few diversion dams past Two Leggins and the General Custer access, the entire river is easy to row.

"The lower river has more isolated riffles. You'll have a riffle followed by a long, broad flat versus the upper river where there's a riffle around every bend. I think silt is also an issue since there are so many irrigation issues. From Mallard's to Two Leggins, it's more streamer water and the trout numbers really drop off. It's where you go for the big browns and maybe only catch one or two fish a day, but beware of the diversion dams," Lyman says.

Hatches and Flies

Like many other Western tailwaters, nymphing is extremely effective and popular on the Bighorn. And what better way to tip off a nymph rig than with a San Juan Worm. The Bighorn is loaded with aquatic worms and the fish feed on them nearly year-round. If you're using a two-fly rig, vary one pattern to see what the fish prefer, but keep some form of a San Juan Worm as part of the lineup. I recommend trying a string of sizes (#8-16) and different color combinations based on red, such as wine, pink, and bubblegum.

When nymphing, make sure you're getting deep and in front of the fish. Most guides start with a strike indicator near the butt section of the leader. From there is a 9- or 10-foot taper to 3X or 4X tippet and the first fly. Pinch weight a foot or so above this first fly. Tie 1 to 2 feet of tippet to the eye or the bend of the

The Bighorn has one of the highest fish-per-mile counts of any river in the state, and while there are some bruisers in the river, most of the fish are between 14 and 18 inches.

first fly (depending on your preference), and attach a dropper nymph with an Improved Clinch or Eugene Bend.

"Our general nymphing leader is a 9-foot, 3X, and then we tie down to 4X or 5X tippet if necessary. Start with the stout stuff. If you don't get a strike within 15 minutes, you're either at the wrong depth, have the wrong fly, or your tippet is too large," Schreiner says.

Though dry-fly fishing on the Bighorn is the exception and not the norm, especially if you're on the water through the heat of the day when the sun is high and air temperatures are blazing, when conditions are right these fish have no issue rising for midges, mayflies, or caddis.

Midges and Blue-Winged Olives are the mainstay through the shoulders of the season when cold weather and wind make the Bighorn a place for diehards. At this time of the year, it's normal to see pods of rising fish through the warmest parts of the day. "We start fishing in April when the water temperatures are 39 or 40 degrees and the fish are stacked in select holes. Typically, conditions put fish off the edges of seams, in deep water, and not in the shallow riffles and the heavy troughs. They like the methodical, lethargic, slow water. They're not aggressive when it's this cold," Lyman says. Midges are a staple food for Bighorn River trout. One of the most impressive hatches I've ever seen was just below Yellowtail Dam at sunrise. Heavy, dense masses of these bugs made the surrounding landscape look like a grainy photograph, and pods of fish fed on the surface with abandon for the next three miles.

Midge clusters work well on top, but a few shops say pupae patterns that sit in the surface film work better, especially if you can use something like a larger, easier-to-see *Baetis* as an indicator point fly. Size 16-20 Griffith's Gnats are a good start, as are Zebra Midges, Yong Specials, Disco Midges, and Brassies. Look for sippers in the slow water where many of the bugs collect and the even flows can make it easier to present such minuscule representations. But, like any other time of the year, make sure your presentation

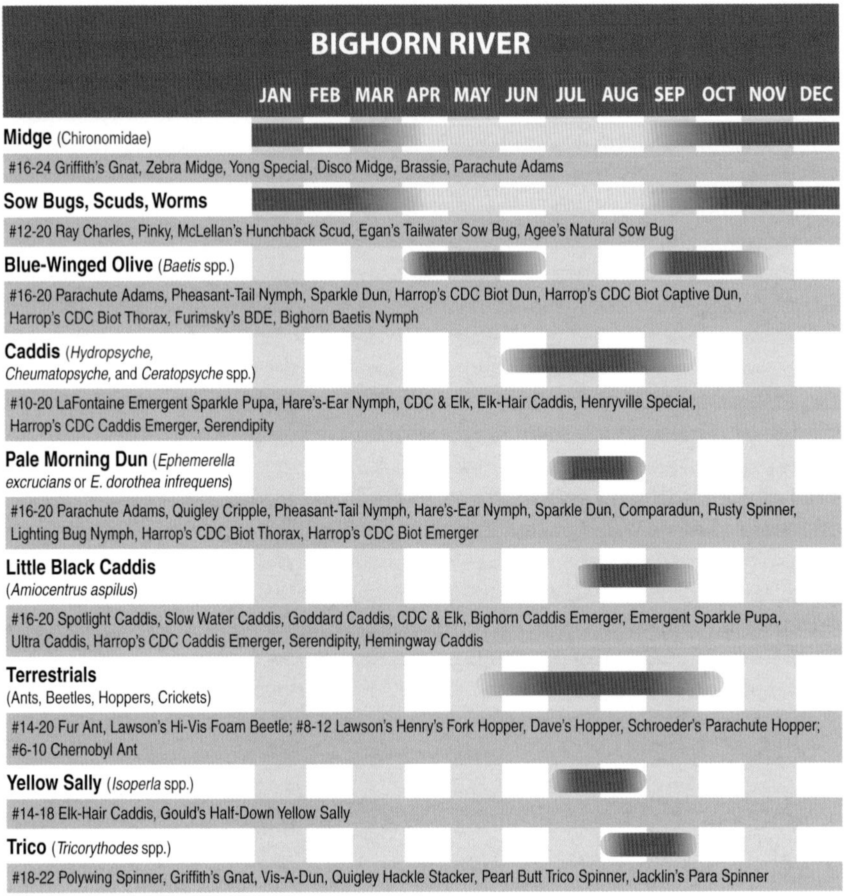

is on the money. There is far too much food on the Bighorn to make a fish want to travel even two inches if it knows another tasty morsel is only seconds away.

"I tell people they have to put their fly in that fish's feeding lane. If you're sitting on a street corner and someone is bringing you hot dogs all day long, you're not going to go across the street to get a hamburger. The fish get in a zone and will sit there and keep feeding," Schreiner says.

Baetis can appear on the river nearly any time of the year, but they are most prevalent from late April through early July and again in October and November. Basic patterns like #18-22 Parachute Adams are reliable, but with so many naturals available, it pays to have other more imitative patterns in your boxes, such as Harrop's CDC Biot Dun, CDC Biot Captive Dun, CDC Biot Thorax, and a Bighorn Baetis Nymph. In the spring, when the adult 'bows are making their way up the tributaries and side channels to spawn, you will catch mostly browns.

Scuds and sow bugs are the most abundant and popular food sources for Bighorn River trout. Fortunately, they're also easy to tie, and the simplest patterns are the most effective. If you're going to the Bighorn, make room in your boxes for a few #16-18 color variations of the Ray Charles, a simple pattern made with ostrich herl and Mylar, as well as any standard #14-20 orange, pink, or gray scud and sow bug recipes you have.

"The limestone leaching in the upper reservoir promotes the grass growth along the streambed and gives our bug life a shot in the arm. So after these fish hatch, they grow roughly one inch per month. Lift up a fistful of grass and it's just teeming with bugs, scuds, and sow bugs. I call it a protein shake. The fish sit in and around the grass and feed on this stuff all day long," Schreiner says.

When the summer season takes over, look for PMDs around July and August. Though they were once a banner hatch on the river, Schreiner says that natural factors such as increased siltation inhibited their progress in recent years. But with the flushes of new water, a lot of people remain optimistic they will return in droves.

Fishing early or late provides the best opportunities to find fish rising to hatching PMDs. Aside from timing, it's crucial to carry a selection of patterns to match whatever stage the fish are keying on—typically emergers and duns in the morning (#14-20 Sparkle Duns, Comparaduns, pale Parachute Adams; #16-20 Lightning Bugs and Pheasant-Tail Nymphs) and spinners (#14-20 Rusty Spinners) before the sun goes down. My personal favorites are ties by René Harrop like the CDC Biot Thorax and CDC Biot Emerger.

This is also a perfect time of year to do some sight-fishing. Many times I have found myself concentrating on the river's deepest runs, only to turn around and see nice fish holding in 1 to 3 feet of water along the shoreline or under overhanging vegetation. They're incredibly spooky, but catching them is a pleasant challenge. Be patient and observant. Sometimes the key to catching a fish isn't the fly you select, but how you fish it.

"People get switch happy sometimes when it comes to flies. I give a fish at least five good casts before I change things. I need that many good presentations to dispose of feeding rhythm, tippet shine, and other factors. After that I'll start digging in my boxes," Lyman says. "Make sure your presentation is floating right before mixing things up. You can present the right fly wrong all day and not get a fish."

I love the summer evening caddis hatches on the Bighorn. The fish are up (in some places you can see them hovering just under the surface, waiting for a bug to pass by), and you can get away with some swinging and twitching techniques. The splashy rises of trout chasing fluttering bugs definitely stand out on this river's flat surface. The trick is finding a pattern they're interested in. Start with a sparsely dressed fly like a CDC & Elk before moving to a more buoyant tie like a small, dark-haired Goddard Caddis. If they don't hit on the dead-drift, slowly raise the rod tip so the fly skates and swings on the surface, creating just the slightest wake behind it.

To avoid crowds on the Bighorn, either go early or stay late. Many visiting anglers arrive after breakfast and return to their cabins or lodges in the late afternoon when the river's hatches often kick-start the action. NICK ROMANS PHOTO

Last season I was using this technique and a fish I estimate at 24 inches hit it like a ton of bricks. I lost the fish at the boat, but I will always remember that strike. Other tricks up your sleeve should include simple #14-18 Elk-Hair Caddis in a variety of colors, Henryville Specials, dark Stimulators, Ultra Caddis, and Harrop's CDC Caddis Emergers for the surface. Under the surface, try #14-20 Serendipities and Bighorn Caddis Emergers.

"Black Caddis are generally a late-summer hatch, emerging in the afternoon and laying eggs in the evening. If the fish are boiling, bulging, making splashy rises, or showing their backs and tails, they're probably taking pupae. Fish feeding on egg-laying caddis may also feed energetically, but usually the activity is more subdued with classic head-and-tail rises. The splashy rises often indicate smaller fish during the evening. A lot of times I'll fish a black CDC Caddis with a Hemmingway Caddis trailing behind it," Harris says. "The CDC Caddis has a great look to it, but the Hemmingway is just a great fly for selective fish."

The grassy banks of the river are hopper heaven, and the midsummer terrestrial fishing is good. "You can always raise fish with hoppers and Chernobyl Ants regardless of how many naturals you see on the banks," Lyman says. Fishing hoppers, crickets, and beetles, in my opinion, is better if you're blind-casting on the lower river between Three Mile and Bighorn where there are deeper runs and undercut banks. The "plop" of a big bug doesn't play well when you're trying to hunt spooky trout in shallow water.

Tricos hatch in mid August through early September, and on some mornings the surface of the water shimmers from a blanket of freshly fallen spinners. Unfortunately, according to some area shops and outfitters, the hatch over the past few seasons hasn't measured up to what it was in the late 1990s. "Tricos used to be a consistent, knock-your-socks-off hatch. But since the high-water event in 1991, the hatch has gone downhill," Lyman says.

If you are fortunate enough to find Trico spinners, it's one of the toughest times to fool a Bighorn fish. But, it can be done. Try a #18-22 spent pattern like a Pearl Butt Trico Spinner and Jacklin's Para Spinner, but also go underneath with sunken spinners.

Later in the season, as the summer turns to fall, it's time to break out the heavy stick and pitch some heftier flies along the banks and near the weed beds. At this time of year brown trout are on the prowl and jiggling a streamer in front of their noses sometimes yields big results. Woolly Buggers in olive and black are the streamers of choice around here, but a Barr Slumpbuster and other leechy-looking flies are often just as effective.

The downside to late-season fishing is the turnover in the reservoirs. This natural occurrence typically happens in the fall when the temperatures between the surface and the bottom flip-flop. The process kills off mass quantities of moss and other plant life around mid-October, which washes downstream into the river and sticks to flies like chunks of green snot. This shuts down the fishing, so call a Fort Smith fly shop before you come to the river.

If you're fishing dry flies, a 4- or 5-weight rod should suit you well. A lighter-weight rod typically makes it easier to delicately present dry flies or small patterns and protect light tippets when you set the hook. If you're throwing heavy nymph rigs or searching for a fall brown with streamers, a fast-action 6-weight is a better tool.

Tippet sizes vary depending on what you're using—the smaller the fly, the lighter the tippet. However, don't go lighter than the situation requires. For one it can help you land the fish of a lifetime, and it prevents overplaying fish to the point of exhaustion. Sizes in the 4X and 5X range are the most common, but if you're drifting nymph rigs, you can sometimes get away with 2X or 3X—especially if you're pinching on additional weight.

"I don't use a lot of long leaders, but I use light tippet. Nine-foot, 5X or 6X is pretty standard," Lyman says. "It all depends on the person I'm guiding. In most cases, casting accuracy trumps tippet sizes. Do not 'flock shoot' when casting to a specific fish working an area. You have to put that fly in a specific place in front of the fish. If you say 'that's good enough,' chances are it's not."

Because the Bighorn is a fickle river, be prepared to change your flies and tactics often until you find what works. Also, be flexible and willing to experiment. Something that works one day may bring nothing but refusals the next. Some outings I've found that I have better results if I study the water more than I fish it.

"There are times when you'll have two or three different hatches going on at once. When this happens, you really have to study the water not only to tell what bug they're keyed in on, but what stage. Figuring out it's *Baetis* might be easy, but whether it's a dun, emerger, or nymph is the riddle," Lyman says.

Directions

From Billings, take I-90 east to the town of Hardin, and then head south on MT 313. This route will take you straight into St. Xavier, past Two Leggins, Mallard's Landing, and St. Xavier bridge access points, and straight into Fort Smith and the Bighorn Canyon National Recreation Area. Bighorn access is clearly marked from the road only a few miles south of St. Xavier. There are public restrooms, a boat ramp, plenty of parking, and a small campground on the southwest side. Three Mile is not as plainly marked from the road as Bighorn. Heading south on MT 313, turn right near mile marker 38. The road will cross an irrigation canal, and Cottonwood Campground is on the left, but continue to the next intersection. At the intersection, turn left and proceed a short distance down the dirt road to the parking lot.

The Afterbay access is north of Fort Smith. From Three Mile, drive through town on MT 313 and take the first right (north) as you exit town. A park service station near the turnoff is a good landmark for remembering where to turn (remember to pay the $5 use fee). The road drops into the river canyon and crosses Afterbay Dam. After crossing the dam, Afterbay Campground (a public-use site with spaces for RVs or tents) is on the immediate left and the access and boat ramp to the right.

Fort Smith is the end-all, be-all trout town. Other than hosting select groups of wingshooters, the town's livelihood depends on anglers coming to fish for Bighorn River trout. You won't find a better source for fishing information than the resident fly shops and outfitters. Each one is unique in its own way, but they'll give you the straight scoop on what you should expect from the river. There are also some great lodges if you're looking for a more regal experience. But, if you're like me and simply need a place to lay your head between hatches, there are options in that range as well—but bring the mosquito spray.

For local flavor, you can't go wrong with Polly's Place—a favorite eating establishment among anglers. You can pick up supplies in town, but liquor is not available on Crow tribal lands, making Hardin the closest place to purchase it.

Black Caddis Sparkle Pupa

Hook:	#16-18 Dai-Riki 075
Thread:	Black 8/0 Uni-Thread
Abdomen:	Olive UTC Sparkle Braid (Midge)
Thorax:	Black Wapsi Life Cycle dubbing

CDC Black Caddis

Hook:	#14-16 Dai-Riki 305
Thread:	Black 8/0 Uni-Thread
Head:	Black Wapsi Life Cycle dubbing
Wing:	Black CDC

Pinky

Hook:	#14-16 Dai-Riki 075
Thread:	Fire-orange 8/0 Uni-Thread
Body:	Medium pink rabbit
Hackle:	Light-dun hen hackle

Ray Charles

Hook:	#14-16 Tiemco 3761
Thread:	Red 6/0 Danville
Tail:	Brown hackle fibers
Rib:	.035-inch-diameter copper wire
Body:	Pink, tan, gray, or olive ostrich herl
Back:	Pearl Flashabou

Yellowstone River (Upper)

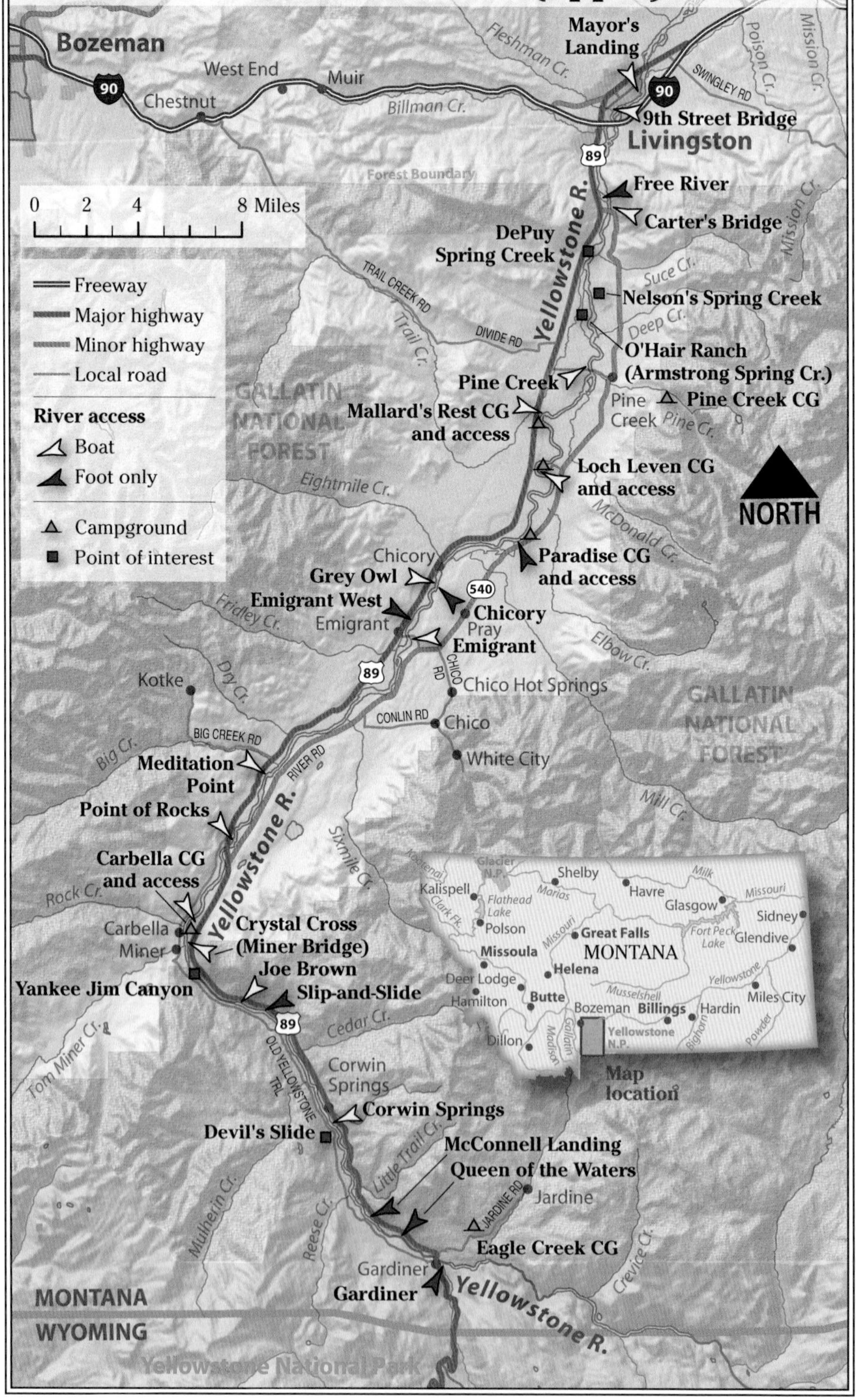

CHAPTER 2

Yellowstone River

Despite the many other notorious rivers in the state, I don't think there is one name that resonates more in the fly-angling community than Yellowstone. In the time it takes to mumble those three syllables, visions of green valleys, snowcapped peaks, sparkling water, and the big trout that reside underneath explode through my head like the burst from a camera flash.

The Yellowstone is also a river of many parts, each section slightly different than the water upstream with different challenges and nuances—something you don't find on every water. "If you've got a guy that's never caught a cutthroat—boom, you're going upstream where you'll catch a lot of fish and not be too worried about size. If you want to do an easy float with some scenery, you do the bird float (Grey Owl to Mallard's Rest). Then right through town you get a mix of both. There's good numbers of decent-size fish. Below town to Big Timber, that's where the guys go for big browns, but you better be happy with catching only one or two fish," Yellowstone Angler guide James Anderson says.

Beginning deep in the heart of America's first national park, the first few miles of water inside the borders are known more for waterfalls, canyons, white water, and other obstacles that keep anglers at bay. There is some fishing in the short area at the outflow of Yellowstone Lake to Yellowstone Falls, but it's often crowded, so unless you like company, leapfrog to the Black Canyon.

The canyon water stretches from inside the park to the east side of Gardiner and is accessible by trail only. If you're in the park, look toward Tower Junction where the trails follow both the Lamar and the Yellowstone. If you're in Gardiner, look on the east side of town near Jardine Road and White Lane. There is plenty of water to fish, and because of the commitment it takes to fish it, there isn't as much pressure here as downriver. Just be mindful of the time of year should you decide to brave this part of the river. Dirty, high-water flushes from tributaries like the Lamar can make a muddy mess of your plans.

After the canyon, the river makes its way into the Paradise Valley and becomes the familiar force most visiting anglers recognize. But it's a big river that can be more intimidating than inviting, depending on flows. And as dis-

Yellowstone River (Lower)

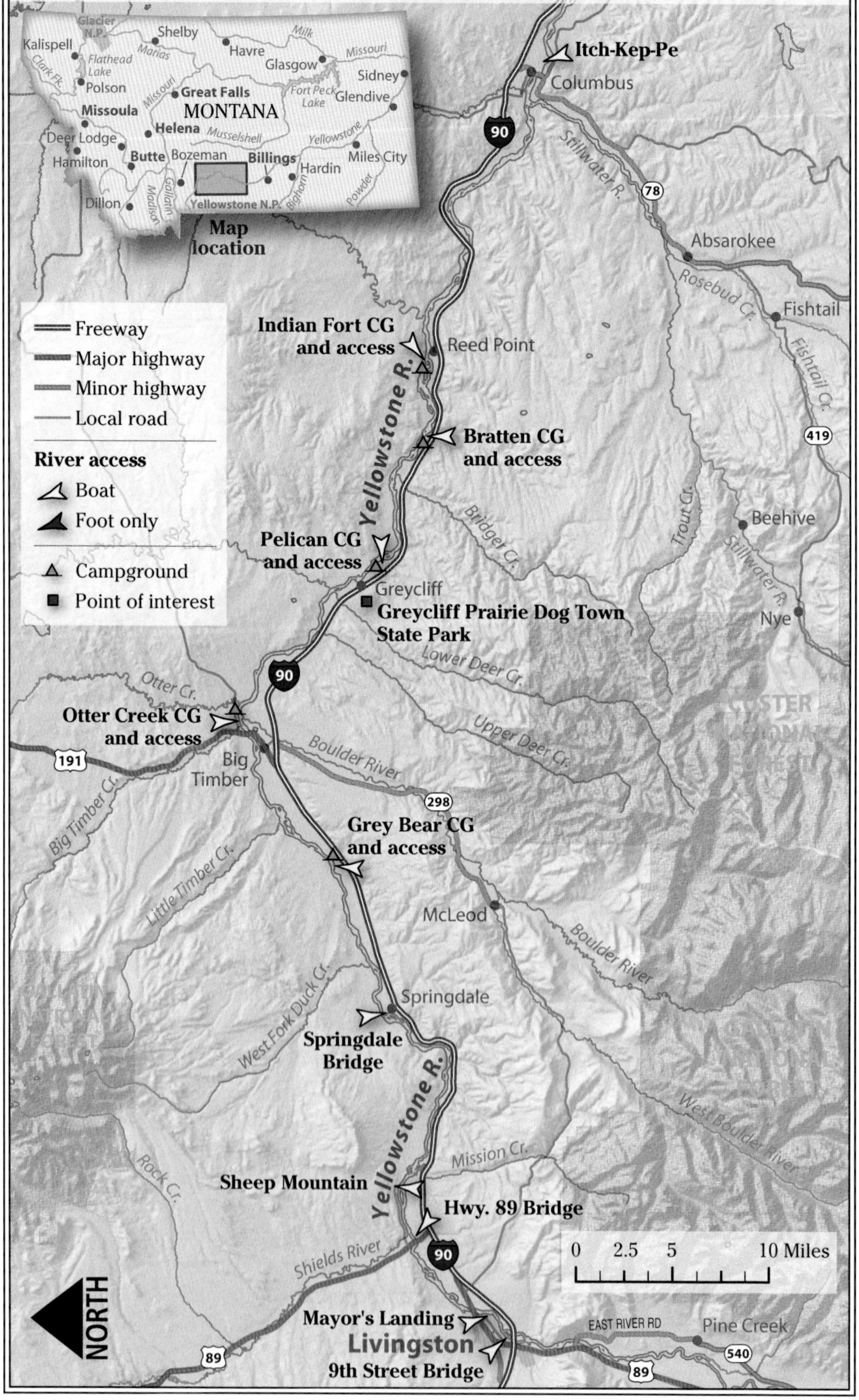

appointing as it may be to wading anglers, it's typically better to float the river than work it on foot.

"You can do it on foot, but it's quite a bit of work and you might not get the angle from shore that a boat can give you," Anderson says. "Some of the really good holes might be a couple miles apart, and a lot of times we'll just push between them."

Adding to the challenge is the Yellowstone's ever-changing facade. Draining such a large region, the river is susceptible to incredible runoff surges in the early season—migrations of water that move trees, cut new channels, create new islands and gravel bars, and destroy old ones.

"We've had some great recent runoff years. The best we've had since the floods in the late 1990s," Angler's West fly-shop owner and outfitter Matson Rogers says. "The fishing after big floods is tough because the ridiculously huge flows change things, but I think freestone rivers need that shift now again. They need new channels scoured out, new banks created, and new

Many regard Paradise Valley as one of the most scenic regions in the state. If you want to see for yourself, consider the "bird float" from Grey Owl to Mallard's Rest. Most locals agree this offers the best views of the mountains in the east. JAMES ANDERSON PHOTO

The upper Yellowstone is suited more for wading anglers than floaters. Trails both inside and outside Yellowstone National Park can lead to isolated pieces of water for anyone willing to put some miles behind them. JAMES ANDERSON PHOTO

cover and new pools. It helps maintain the health of the fishery."

Not only does the high water change the river's façade, it shifts the trout hot spots. "The high water flows from the past few seasons cut new channels, so even though you get keyed in on where fish are hanging out one season, it doesn't mean they're going to be there next year," Anderson says. "It's kind of cool because even the old-timer guides have to go out and figure things out all over again."

Of course, the other side of the coin is where to find fish when the water is lean—something that was all too common during the years of drought. "In low-water years, I think the browns move out of the deep pools and into the shallow riffles because that's where the water is a little cooler and more oxygenated," Anderson says. "In this shallower water, their heads are a foot or two away from our hopper patterns, and they go up and eat them like Milk Duds. So it may seem like the fishing is better in low-water years because the fish move out of the pools earlier. In a normal year, they might not move around until mid-August."

Where and When

Outside the borders of Yellowstone National Park, the river has dozens of access points as it works northward. Despite the sprawl and booming real-estate market, the river remains dam-free and access is abundant. With so many areas to choose from, it's easy to plan a short or long float.

"The one thing the Yellowstone has going for it is access. There are great points between the Park and Big Timber. But most of them are good for boat access and not necessarily wade fishing," River's Edge Fly Shop owner and outfitter Steve Summerhill says.

Around Gardiner, the upper river is mainly a cutthroat fishery with a few rainbows. The landscape is steep, though not as treacherous as the canyon sections, and as such the water is rough. Wade with care and don't go into the middle of the river looking for that special pocket. Work the likely holding spots from shore and move up- and downstream at a decent pace so you can cover water in a timely fashion. If there are cutthroat underneath your fly, they'll generally hit it. If they don't, move on.

Queen of the Waters, McConnell Landing, Corwin Springs, Slip-and-Slide, and Joe Brown are five access points downstream from town all easily reached via US 89. Since floating is outlawed in Yellowstone National Park, these areas are the uppermost floatable sections. The water is swift, so watch your footing. However, as water levels drop after runoff, this is a terrific haunt for Salmonflies. It's also a great area for winter or early-season fishing. Geothermal warm springs like LaDuke pump enough warm water into the system to trigger midge hatches.

Joe Brown is the last take-out before Yankee Jim Canyon, another rough piece of water most floating anglers avoid. If you're inexperienced, or value your boat, skip these few miles and consider accessing at Carbella or Crystal Cross (sometimes called Miner Bridge). There is still some fast water here, but nothing close to the hazards in the canyon upstream. If you are capable of navigating Class III rapids, however, you can proceed through Yankee Jim with caution.

"Some of the biggest fish we catch are on the inside of water that's almost too dangerous to float next too," Anderson says. "Most people shy away from areas like this. So we go through them and the fish hang just on the inside of the chop. We take a safe line and you only get one or two casts, but we usually do really well in water like that."

Point of Rocks is just downstream on the east side of US 89 near the juncture with Donahue Creek, and the water between here and Meditation Point (a large rest area and picnic site neighboring the highway) is considerably tamer than upstream.

I like the water between Meditation Point and Emigrant. There is a diversion canal on the west side of the river three miles upstream of Emigrant, and while you won't necessarily end up in the canal, there is a small diversion dam to avoid. The first half of this section is relatively featureless, but the second half has several islands, braids, and channels. It's a great opportunity to break up the day with a little wade-fishing.

When the heat of summer relegates other hatches to the early morning and evening hours, hoppers keep Yellowstone River trout looking up throughout the day. Cast patterns close to overhanging grass and other vegetation to simulate a natural falling into the water. JAMES ANDERSON PHOTO

The lower Yellowstone is known for holding trophy brown trout, but anglers often have to put in some time before they find one. Trout populations downstream of Livingston slowly taper off, but those fish that remain are typically larger than average. JAMES ANDERSON PHOTO

Emigrant access is on the east side of the river near Murphy Lane east of the town of Emigrant. Another access, Emigrant West, is on the downstream side of the bridge, but it's for foot traffic only, so don't miss the ramp upstream on river right if you're floating.

Grey Owl and Chicory are three miles downstream of the town of Emigrant and a good option if you want to do a short float with some wade-fishing or anchor up over pods of feeding fish. Grey Owl is accessible from US 89, but you need to be on the east side of the river to reach Chicory. It's directly across stream from Grey Owl but access is by foot only.

Grey Owl marks the starting point of what George Anderson once referred to as his favorite float—the bird float—since the take-out has another "winged" moniker, Mallard's Rest. Not only does this stretch offer solid fishing, Anderson said it offers the best scenic views in the valley. There are two other access points in between, Paradise and Loch Leven (both on the east side of the river). Paradise doesn't have boat access, so plan accordingly.

"In the early season, I like the water from Mallard's Rest downstream," Rogers says. "The upper valley has less good corners and deep holding pools. From Mallard's, through town and below town, I think the water is warmer. I think the spring-creek influence from Nelson's, DePuy, and other natural springs in the river helps. During the winter, that slightly warmer spring water tempers the colder river temps. It may only be one or two degrees, but it helps."

Closer to Livingston, Pine Creek access is on the northwest side of the bridge of the same name (it connects US 89 to East River Road). This water to Carter's Bridge (where East River Road crosses the Yellowstone) has plenty of nice channels, seams, and islands that I love to work streamers around and through. For reasons I can't explain, I consistently catch larger and longer browns in this areas than I do upstream. Carter's Bridge is only three miles south of Livingston, so it is perfect if you're in a hurry to get in or out of the water. If you're traveling sans watercraft, hit Free River fishing access a mile or so north (downstream) of Carter's.

After Carter's, the river winds through Livingston, hitting 9th Street Bridge and Mayor's Landing access sites along the way. Downstream from Livingston the river morphs. There aren't as many fish per mile and fishing access points are sparser than upstream, but the average size increases by a few inches. From town to Big Timber is where many guides go on their days off with streamer gear in tow looking for that one (or hopefully more) fish over 20 inches. There are a few modest rainbows strewn throughout to keep things interesting, but it's the brown trout that most anglers set their sights on.

Because of the size of the river, wading is a little tougher downstream from Livingston, but you can give it a shot (or launch a boat) at the US 89 Bridge, Sheep Mountain, Springdale, Grey Bear, and Otter Creek access points.

Hatches and Flies

If you can stand the cold and sometimes-windy days, good fishing on the Yellowstone starts as early as late February. Small nymphs drifted slow and deep and possibly a few midge dry flies for those warmer afternoons are two popular strategies. While you won't see the Yellowstone in all its glory at this time of year, you won't see many people either.

As winter transitions into spring, things pick up in a hurry. *Baetis,* more midges, March Browns, and possibly some small early-season black stoneflies and *Skwala* pop up here and there. Warmer days also bring more people, so be prepared to share the water with other folks trying to shake cabin fever. Nymphing is the most productive technique, but there is always the chance of seeing a window of dry-fly activity. "Some of the pockets are very deep and I think most people don't get enough weight on their nymphs. It's like the old saying, the difference between a good nymph fisherman and a great nymph fisherman is one more split shot," Anderson says.

The action really picks up in late April with the arrival of the Mother's Day Caddis. On the right day, at the right time, these bugs dominate the water, and there's nothing you can do but sit back and watch in awe. Unfortunately, the Mother's Day Caddis flirt with the inevitable rush of runoff, and some years, despite millions of bugs in the air, the river is unfishable. Stay in touch with an outfitter or guide if you're concerned about fishing conditions.

The DePuy, Armstrong, Nelson's, Benhart, and Thompson spring creeks are some of the most famous in the world. Consistent water temperatures, abundant insect life and hatches, and quality fish make them a popular choice for anyone looking for a reprieve from the big river or anyone craving the intimacy of smaller water.

Though anglers know these areas for their tranquillity and solitude, they also regard them as some of the most technical waters in the state, and it's not unusual to head home without catching a thing. Those that watch, listen, and study the waters can unlock their secrets. In either scenario, the fishing is addicting, and once you visit, you may find yourself returning annually.

Although they run exclusively through private property, the landowners grant access through a rod-fee system. The cost varies depending on the season, but the owners regulate the number of anglers allowed to fish on a given day, which helps preserve the experience. The creeks are so popular that I recommend making reservations well in advance. Here is a quick overview of the spring creeks and contact information.

Armstrong Spring Creek

With just over one mile of riffles and long, flat pools to fish, Armstrong (also called O'Hair Spring Creek) has something to offer any angler whether your preference is dry flies or nymphs. While you can encounter a variety of different insects on the water depending on the time of year, PMDs, Blue-Winged Olives, and midges are the bread and butter. But, ask anyone who's fished this creek before and he'll tell you the real challenge is sight-fishing to these wary fish. Visit armstrongspringcreek.com or call (406) 222-2979 for information on rod fees and reservations.

DePuy Spring Creek

At nearly three miles long, DePuy Spring Creek (pronounced Dee-pew) picks up where Armstrong leaves off, and is the longest of the famous spring creeks. But it's the spectacular scenery and hearty fish, not the amount of water, that draws many anglers. Situated in the heart of Yellowstone's Paradise Valley, the views of the mountains are unmatched, as is the fishing—regardless of skill level—because of the copious PMD, midge, Blue-Winged Olive, and caddis hatches. Visit depuyspringcreek.com or call (406) 222-0221 for information on rod fees and reservations. The website has some terrific information on the hatches and seasons of the creek.

Nelson's Spring Creek

What originally started as a source for stock water is now one of the best spring creeks in the state. Nelson's is on the east side of Paradise Valley, and

Paradise Valley spring creeks offer a more intimate alternative to the big waters of the Yellowstone, just be sure to make reservations in advance. Each operation has a daily capacity that can fill up fast depending on the time of year and other conditions. JAMES ANDERSON PHOTO

though it's only three-quarters of a mile long, it has hundreds of fish measuring in the high teens. While hatches of mayflies, caddis, and midges pop throughout the season, terrestrial fishing also has its place. Lodging is available on the property, but the owners only allow six rods on the water a day, so make reservations early. Visit nelsonsspringcreek.com or call (406) 222-6560 for more information.

Milesnick Recreation Company

The Milesnick family ranch actually has two options for spring-creek anglers: Benhart and Thompson creeks. Benhart is nearly three miles long with several twists, turns, and braids. Thompson is closer to one mile long, contained exclusively on the property, and empties into the East Gallatin River. Many regard both creeks as the most technical spring waters in the state. Visit milesnickrecreation.com or call (406) 388-7001 for more information. ■

Next to the Salmonflies, the Mother's Day Caddis hatch is one of the most celebrated on the Yellowstone. The downside is their emergence flirts with the onslaught of runoff. However, even with marginal water clarity, trout waste no time getting their fill of these tent-winged morsels. The hard part for anglers is fooling the fish when so many naturals are available. JAMES ANDERSON PHOTO

High water isn't the only hurdle to overcome. With so many bugs on the water, getting a fly to take your pattern over a natural is a seemingly impossible proposition. If the fish get picky, stay away from high-riding caddis patterns like Elk-Hair Caddis or small Stimulators. Instead, use flush-floating flies like Mathews' X Caddis and LaFontaine pupae patterns.

"You've got to have something that you can see, or something that stands out. Otherwise, you can't tell your fly from the millions of other bugs on the water. A Trude, Goddard, or an Elk-Hair Caddis work, but tie them with a piece of fluorescent foam or something that you can see," Anderson says.

While some argue the hatches aren't as good as they used to be, Salmonflies (nymphs and adults) are still one of the dominant forces on the Yellowstone. The trout keep a sharp eye out for the large nymphs every day of the year, especially in the upper river where June hatches sometimes feel heavier than areas downstream. "Stonefly patterns are key," Rogers says. "The river is just loaded with Golden Stones in particular."

Like on other Montana freestones, Salmonflies generally appear as runoff tapers off, and you can bet Golden Stones aren't far behind. This is a structure-fishing game—bounce flies near and around rocks, trees, brush, or anywhere else a bug can haplessly fall into the water. Depending on streamflow, this is easier in some years than others. "Salmonflies are great as long as you get some cooperation with runoff. Otherwise, the high water pushes the bugs and the fish up into the willows so you can't even cast to them. The Yellowstone is typically the last to clear and the last to get the Salmonflies compared to the other rivers in the state," Anderson says.

Yellow Sallies and Green Drakes sometimes coincide with the larger stoneflies, but most of the time they appear as the big bugs taper off. When water conditions settle back to normal, Pale Morning Duns keep fish feeding on top for a few weeks.

In an especially wet season, the river might not come into shape until late July or even August, and though this means you'll miss out on some of the Yellowstone's iconic hatches, clear water typically arrives when hoppers start making their leaps of faith. "During midsummer, the bulk of what we do is hopper fishing—hoppers and big attractor dry flies. There are other good hatches like Salmonflies, PMDs, March Browns, and caddis—especially the Mother's Day Caddis. Occasionally you'll get Green Drakes and other hatches, but they're not major hatches," Summerhill says. "Because the river flows through so much ranch land, the hopper fishing is the highlight."

In the late summer and early fall, there are a few Tricos dancing about and the *Baetis* return. The fishing is somewhat more technical than the early season, but you won't have to deal with the traffic that comes with the river's other more famous hatches like the Salmonflies.

To me, a sculpin's existence and sole purpose is to satisfy the gluttonous impulses of monster trout. I can't think of a place where that is more apparent than on the Yellowstone. "You take big fish, say around six pounds, and it takes a lot of little bitty insects to fill them up. If they can grab another fish or something big like that, it can satisfy them instantly," 48-year veteran Yellowstone guide Don Williams says.

There are dozens of great sculpin and streamer patterns out there today, so experiment with colors, shapes, sizes, and presentation, especially in the fall when the big browns of the lower river are all juiced up in preparation for spawning. Put a streamer into their territory, and they'll crush it.

"Sculpin patterns are good if you dead-drift them (with or without an indicator). They're weird because they stick to the bottom and scurry from rock to rock. There's no way you can strip one and make it look normal. I tell people to fish it like it was bonked on the head and is drifting down lifeless. It's basically just nymphing with a big streamer," Anderson says.

If you're looking to fish dry flies or moderately light nymph rigs, a fast-action 5-weight rod is perfect. If you are using a double-nymph rig with heavy stoneflies, a 6-weight would be better. For streamers, I like to use a 7-weight rod with a sinking-tip line. When you're throwing around the weight of a streamer and a sinking line (possibly in the wind), you quickly learn to appreciate a heavier rod.

Yellowstone trout aren't particularly leader shy, so there are many days when you can get away with 2X and 3X tippet. Fishing midges, *Baetis*, or

Because there are usually so many naturals on the water during the Mother's Day Caddis hatch, it's sometimes tough to distinguish an imitation from a natural. Use a pattern that stands out from the crowd to make it easier to track on the water. JAMES ANDERSON PHOTO

smaller patterns requires lighter gear, of course, but with most flies it's rarely necessary to go below 4X. "Tippet size isn't a big issue because the current is moving at a good clip. Usually if a fish isn't taking what you're throwing, it's a result of fly-pattern selection," Anderson says.

Directions

US 89 follows the river from Gardiner, through Emigrant, and downstream to Livingston. For access points on the east side of the river, use East River Road, which connects on the south end between Miner and Emigrant, and ends near Carter's Bridge , just south of Livingston.

US 89 (Park Street in Livingston) also connects anglers with other access points in Livingston. Just south of the I-90 intersection, turn southeast on 9th Street to reach 9th Street Bridge. A few blocks north of the interstate, turn south on Main Street, then merge onto View Vista Drive to reach Mayor's Landing.

The US 89 site is five miles east of Livingston off I-90. Drive north on US 89 for approximately a mile. The access is near the southeast corner of the

Sculpins are plentiful in the Yellowstone and one reason why streamer fishing is so effective. Because these small fish don't swim well, a dead-drift or slow-strip presentation typically draws more fish than a fast retrieve. JAMES ANDERSON PHOTO

bridge. Take this same route to reach Sheep Mountain access, but continue over the bridge and turn east on Convict Grade Road for about three miles. The access is on the right.

Take I-90 east from Livingston and exit at Springdale to reach the access of the same name. After exiting the interstate, take the frontage road west, then follow the county road north for .5 mile. The access is near the southeast corner of the bridge.

Farther east is the Grey Bear access. From I-90, take exit 362 and connect with the frontage road on the north side of the freeway. Follow the frontage road northwest, then take the first left. The access is .5 mile down the road on the south side of the bridge. Camping is available at this access.

The Otter Creek site is close to Big Timber. From I-90, take US 191 northeast through town and over the river. Turn east on Howie Road and travel for 1.5 miles to the access on the south side of the road.

There are other access points downstream of Big Timber, and some anglers looking to get away from the crowds fish for trout as far downstream as Columbus. However, the habitat and water temperatures transition from a trout's world to one suited for walleye and other species. If you decide a trip this far downriver is still in your cards, look to the Pelican, Bratten, Indian Fort, Buffalo Mirage (also known as Sportsman's Park), Duck Creek Bridge, South Hills, and East Bridge (close to Billings) access points.

Delektable CDC Elk-Hair Caddis

Hook:	#14-16 Tiemco 100
Thread:	Olive 6/0 Danville
Body:	Olive Holographic Dubbing
Rib:	Fine copper wire
Underwing:	Dun CDC
Wing:	Light bull-elk hair
Hackle:	Brown furnace hackle
Legs:	Pumpkin/green-orange Barred Sili Legs
Head:	Olive Holographic Dubbing

Trina's Carnage Hopper

Hook:	#6-14 MFC 7022
Thread:	Tan 6/0 Uni-Thread
Abdomen:	1 mm tan foam
Wing:	Mottled web Flex Wing
Legs:	Natural latex Centipede Legs (#2)
Thorax:	Golden-tan Antron dubbing
Indicator:	White Widow's Web
Head:	5 mm tan foam
Eyes:	Black #1.2 mono

Bow River Bugger (Brown)

Hook:	#2-8 Mustad 39841
Thread:	Brown 6/0 Uni-Thread
Tail:	Brown marabou
Body:	Brown chenille
Hackle:	Brown hackle palmered over body
Legs:	Brown rubber legs (round)
Head:	Natural deer hair spun and trimmed

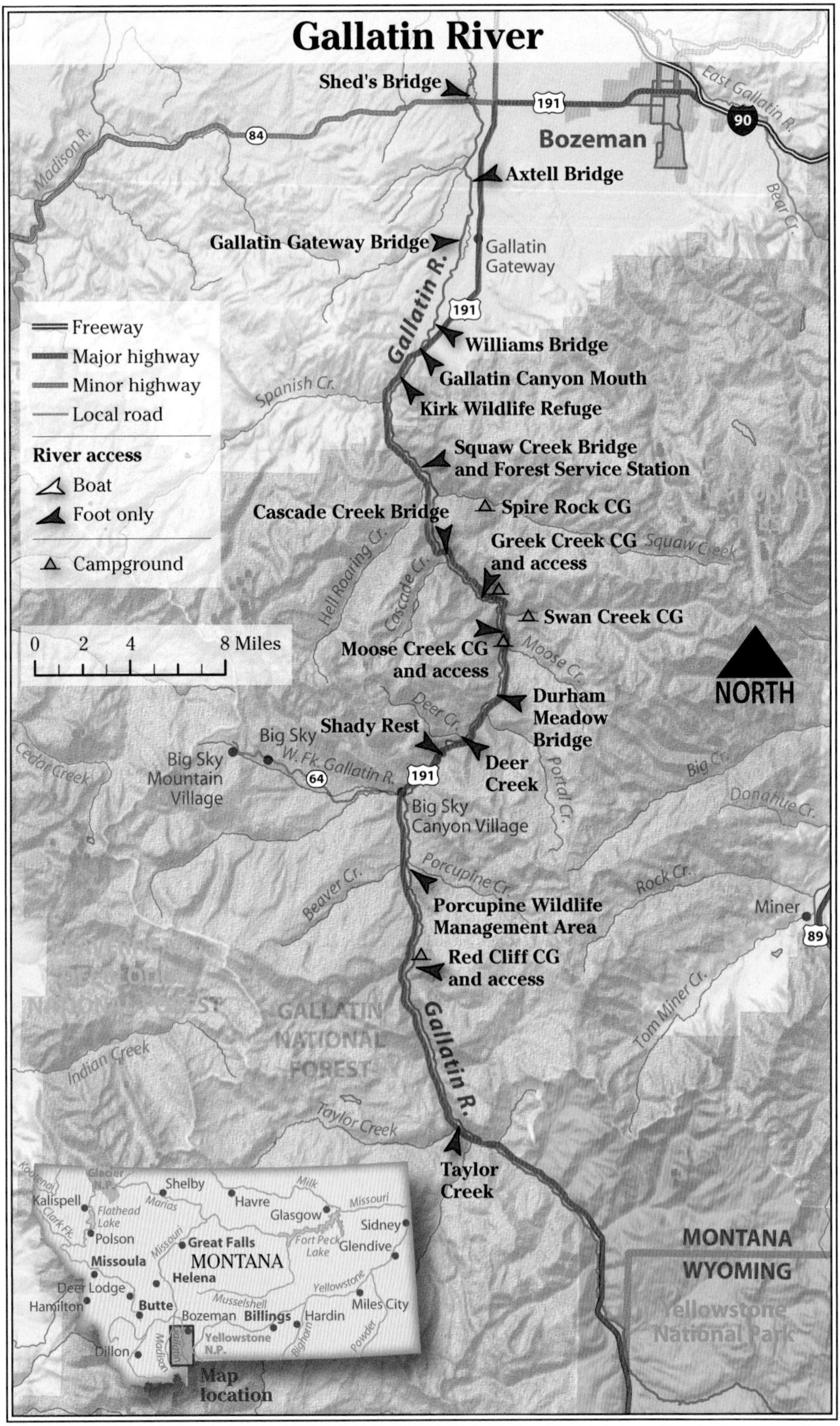

Gallatin River
Shed's Bridge
191
Bozeman
East Gallatin R.
90
84
Madison R.
Axtell Bridge
Bear Cr.
Gallatin Gateway Bridge
Gallatin Gateway
Gallatin R.
191
Freeway
Major highway
Minor highway
Local road
River access
Boat
Foot only
Campground
Williams Bridge
Gallatin Canyon Mouth
Kirk Wildlife Refuge
Spanish Cr.
Squaw Creek Bridge and Forest Service Station
Cascade Creek Bridge
Spire Rock CG
Greek Creek CG and access
Squaw Creek
Hell Roaring Cr.
Cascade Cr.
Swan Creek CG
0 2 4 8 Miles
Moose Creek CG and access
Moose Cr.
NORTH
Durham Meadow Bridge
Deer Cr.
Shady Rest
Big Sky
Big Sky Mountain Village
W. Fk. Gallatin R.
64
191
Deer Creek
Portal Cr.
Cedar Creek
Big Cr.
Donahue Cr.
Big Sky Canyon Village
Porcupine Cr.
Beaver Cr.
Rock Cr.
Porcupine Wildlife Management Area
Miner
89
Red Cliff CG and access
Tom Miner Cr.
GALLATIN NATIONAL FOREST
Gallatin R.
Indian Creek
Taylor Creek
Taylor Creek
Kootenai
Glacier N.P.
Shelby
Milk
Kalispell
Marias
Havre
Missouri
Flathead Lake
Glasgow
Clark Fk.
Sidney
Polson
Missouri
Great Falls
Fort Peck Lake
Glendive
Missoula
MONTANA
Helena
Yellowstone
Deer Lodge
Hamilton
Butte
Musselshell
Miles City
Bozeman
Billings
Hardin
Yellowstone N.P.
Bighorn
Powder
Dillon
Madison
Gallatin
Map location
MONTANA
WYOMING
Yellowstone National Park

CHAPTER 3

Gallatin River

With the possible exception of Rock Creek, I can't think of another river in the state with as much access as the Gallatin. In fact, there are so many marked and unmarked pull-offs and parking areas along its banks that listing them all on a map is futile.

The Gallatin is the smallest of the three tributaries that combine near Three Forks and create the Missouri River (the other two are the Madison and Jefferson rivers), and as such, most of the trout average in the 10- to 16-inch range (though larger fish are frequently caught). Since it is illegal to fish from watercraft upstream of the East Fork of the Gallatin near Bozeman, the river is a gift for the do-it-yourself wading angler.

What the fishery lacks in fish proportions, it makes up for in scenery. In fact, though the core of the story takes place on the Blackfoot River, the rugged canyons and fast-water chutes of the Gallatin were better suited for filming Robert Redford's classic. "Most people have already seen the river in *A River Runs Through It,* and that's definitely a tie-in for a lot of folks that fish the river. They feel like they've seen it and know something about it," says TroutChasers owner and outfitter Jason Fleury.

The Gallatin is a freestone river formed in the northwest corner of Yellowstone National Park. The upper third is mostly braided, intimate water that snakes through a series of short, tight, high-elevation meadows. Most of this water is easily fishable from I-191, just park your car in a pull-off and trek across the meadow. Remember this is Yellowstone country, so keep your eyes peeled for wildlife.

The upper river is small water, so take a 2- or 3-weight for the small but abundant trout, and a Yellowstone Park fishing permit. If you find this part of the Gallatin suits you, you may want to consider hiking farther upstream along the Bighorn Pass Trail. It follows the river through a narrow meadow that eventually ends at Gallatin Lake.

The closer the river gets to the park boundary, the more it grows in volume. It's still a small piece of water by Montana standards, but little channels, islands, shallow riffles, and other structure make it an interesting place to fish. It maintains this character for a few more twists and turns even after crossing the park border. It's not until the river gets close to one of its tributaries, Tay-

The upper Gallatin River, just outside Yellowstone, winds through large meadows and is full of braids and islands. Because most of it flows through national forest land, anglers can explore at their leisure. JAY NICHOLS PHOTO

lor Creek, a little over two miles north of the park border, that it begins to pick up speed and a few more tumbling runs and riffle pools are thrown to the mix.

Taylor Creek (sometimes called Taylor Fork) is a major tributary that meets the main stem a few miles north of the Yellowstone National Park boundary. This creek can hurt the river as much as it can help. Silt deposits surround the headwaters of the Taylor and turn the creek, and the Gallatin, into a muddy mess with every passing rain shower.

"A flush from the Taylor can turn the Gallatin into a milk shake," Fleury says. "But one thing I've found is the river can still fish, depending on the severity of the flush. It definitely makes it more difficult, and you're better switching to a nymphing game. It's just a plug of mud coming through, so watch for better conditions as soon as the storm clears up."

If the passing storm is brief, the main stem can still fish, even with a few inches of visibility. "While it's smart to jump above the Taylor if the water is dirty and there is zero visibility, I see a lot of people moving when the lower river is fine with 18 inches or so of visibility," Alvin says. "As a result, the upper river gets a lot more pressure. But you can do well with only a few inches of clarity. On average, a good day above the Taylor is six fish or so, and it drives me crazy when guys can do twice as well down lower."

If the muddy conditions simply prove to be too much, however, there is no other choice than to move above the Taylor. There are only a handful of pull-off points between the Taylor and the park border (including a grassy parking area neighboring the Taylor's junction with the Gallatin), but the chances of finding clear water are substantially better. Some of my favorite stretches are just downstream of the park line. There are some nice pools, small gravel riffles, springs, boulders, and strings of islands that make it a structure-fisherman's dream.

From Taylor Creek to Big Sky, much of the land between the road and the river is private, but there are still plenty of roadside pull-offs and access points to park and fish like the Red Cliff Campground near the Buck Creek tributary. Use the high-water line to your advantage here and work up- and downstream. With low summer flows you can work these areas somewhat aggressively. Drop a few casts in the most likely holding areas, and rock-hop from pocket to pocket.

There are plenty of fishing points between Taylor Creek and Big Sky, so if you see someone working a few hundred yards of water, move on to another site. With so much to choose from in terms of water character, there's a good chance you'll find something even more to your liking.

"I tell people that if they want to have success and catch fish, visit the Porcupine Creek and Gallatin State Wildlife Management Area. If you start going upriver in the meadows and into the park, and you're a novice, you

When runoff muddies the lower Gallatin, look to the few miles between Taylor Creek and Yellowstone National Park. In most situations, you'll be able to find clearer water upstream of Taylor Creek. NICK ROMANS PHOTO

won't do well. I love fishing up there and there are bigger fish, but it's a different game better suited for folks that have handled a rod for a while," East Slope Outdoors owner/outfitter Dave Alvin says. "The lower river from Big Sky into the canyon has a higher fish-per-mile count and they'll just have better success down there."

The meat of the Gallatin River begins near Big Sky and is contained within the canyon downstream. From Big Sky to Squaw Creek Bridge is the fastest and toughest water to fish. Ironically, for anglers, it's also some of the most attractive water. Full of tumbling pools, gravel-bars and riffles, and other fish-holding structure, it's hard to drive along the middle river and keep both eyes on the road.

"The biggest thing on the Gallatin is just finding good holding water. You're fishing for rainbows predominately so any riffle-pool area is gold.

The Gallatin's abundant access is one of its attributes. U.S. Highway 191 parallels the river for much of its length, and aside from the public rest areas and campgrounds, dozens of roadside pull-offs offer wading anglers access to miles of fishable water.

There are some bigger fish in there, but all the fish are fun. They're feisty, and they're willing. Any good presentation should catch fish," Angler's West owner and outfitter Matson Rogers says.

The number of access points increases from town as you work north (downriver), and with the exception of a few private tracts, the river borders the road with more consistency. Look for unimproved pull-offs after the Jack Smith Bridge north of Big Sky as well as managed sites like Moose Creek and Greek Creek campgrounds.

The canyon stretch of the Gallatin is rich with access, but it sometimes comes with a sacrifice. US 191 neighbors the river for nearly its entire length and produces more than a fair share of traffic and road noise. There are some twist, turns, and bends that veer away from road, so if you're keen on getting as far away as possible, keep a sharp eye out as you drive for those stretches that break away from the shoulder and then find the closest pull-off or access and work your way up- or downstream. You may still have summer homes and resort cabins between you and the mountain backdrop, but it's certainly better than roaring eighteen-wheelers.

If you like to cover a lot of water when wading, look to the canyon area. From Big Sky to Squaw Creek the river has plenty of pocketwater, small eddies, and cascading pools to work through. Fish in this part of the river won't stretch your tape, but they are aggressive and a small box of attractors and terrestrials can be all you need for an afternoon.

"Access on the Gallatin gets better the farther south you go from Big Sky to the mouth of the canyon. Every corner has a pullout, and there's usually a good fishing spot within striking distance of many of them," Rogers says. "But it's difficult to get away from the road. It's great because it grants the access, but don't go over expecting some surreal wilderness experience. It's a blessing and a curse."

On the other hand, the steep rocky canyon walls make it a cool place to fish in the summer—temperature-wise. While some other "exposed" waters like the Bighorn and Madison sit under the blazing summer sun all day, the long shadows covering the Gallatin make the air substantially cooler when the mercury approaches triple digits.

Some fast-water, eddy-laden pockets after the Squaw Creek Bridge to the Williams Bridge access offer great fishing, but be wary of this water when it's running high. The rocks are slippery and water is powerful. There is another access point downriver near Spanish Creek Road and some roadside pull-offs as you head north where the river bumps up against the road—especially near the intersection of the river and US 191. A mile farther north is the turnoff (turn west) for the Williams Bridge access.

"Most of the Gallatin is tough to wade. It has those treacherous bowling ball–size rocks that are just round, slick, and no fun at all. But the farther down the valley the easier it gets," Fleury says. "If they have cleated wading boots, great, but I always tell guys to bring a wading staff, which provides an added bit of safety and assurance."

After Williams Bridge the river slows down, widens, works through a series of channels, and makes its way to Bozeman. Unfortunately, open terrain, housing developments, and agricultural tracts replace the rough-and-tumble nature of the river and the scenery within the national forest boundaries, and the number of access points upriver pale in comparison. Gallatin Gateway (Mill Street) and Axtell bridges are two good marks if you want to work some of the lower river's braids. If it weren't for the strict rule of no fishing from watercraft, the river from here to the formation of the Missouri would probably see more anglers, but as it stands, most opt to fish between the canyon and headwaters.

"The lower Gallatin can be hit-or-miss. You go one day, and you're skunked. Go again and you can catch every fish in the river. Go a third day and you'll catch two fish. There's no pattern. There is a lot of fish down there, and where they go and hide is beyond me. I've been down there in the spring when four hatches are going on at once and not caught a fish," River's Edge Fly Shop co-owner and outfitter Steve Summerhill says.

Shed's Bridge (MT 84) west of Bozeman is the next river-road intersection, and there is a pull-off area on the southwest side (River Road). There is also a place to park across the street from the Cottonwood Hills Golf Course, approximately 1,000 feet north of the River Road and MT 84 intersection. The slow, warm, braided water continues past Cameron Bridge, Erwin (Amsterdam Road), the I-90 intersection, and Four Corners access (East Manhattan Road).

"We concentrate a lot on the area around Gallatin Gateway. It's close to the lodge and I consider it a transitional area because in the upper canyon, you'll see tons of 12- to 16-inch fish. But down here you'll probably mix in an 18- to 20-inch fish," Fleury says.

The introduction of the East Fork of the Gallatin at the Gallatin Forks access (intersection of Dixon Creek Road Bridge and the river) is the lower river's saving grace. The East Fork is an undersized but fertile trout fishery, and its lack of good access and small size keep it off many radar screens.

"The East Gallatin is more of a local spot. We personally fish it on a few places on some ranches in the valley that allow access to it once in a while, but we don't do guide trips on it. It's small water. Most places it's barely ten feet across. It's close, there is easy access to it, and it gets fished hard at the public access points. It's a good spot for a few hours of fishing. I don't know many people that go out and pound it all day. No one is booking vacations to fish the East Gallatin, but if you are in town and have a few hours, it's a nice spot," Summerhill says.

The state permits fishing from a boat between the junction with the East Fork and the Missouri, but from Four Corners downstream, there are only two remaining points with boat ramps: the Logan Trident Bridge and the Missouri Headwaters State Park access a few miles farther.

"It's a beautiful float down there, but if you see two boats on the river, you're probably better floating somewhere else. It's small enough down there that if you get a few people ahead of you working the water, it's harder to catch fish," Summerhill says.

The Gallatin is loaded with structure that attracts fish, but don't linger in one area for too long. Make only a few casts to the best water and then move on. You'll cover more water and increase the odds of catching more fish. NICK ROMANS PHOTO

Lastly, whichever stretch or section of river you decide to fish, try to get away from the access points for better fishing, but be mindful of private property. While public lands surround much of the river, private holdings dot the landscape. As is the case with many other Montana waterways, the first few hundred yards up- and downstream of any access point are traditionally the hardest hit. If you want better fishing, hoof it.

Hatches and Flies

The Gallatin River has more than a handful of hatches through the season worth noting, but for the most part, you can get things done with only a few patterns, which lends itself to better-than-average dry-fly fishing with attractors and terrestrials. The river's trout aren't huge by any means, and their numbers spread out through the system, so when a meaty meal passes over them, they're not bashful about bellying up to the food trough.

"Don't get caught up on fly pattern selection. Last summer all I did was throw a Rogue Golden Stone, Spruce Moth, Green Drake, and a Blue-Winged Olive. You can mix it up with a Trude or something, but there's no need to go crazy," Alvin says.

Stimulators, small Club Sandwiches, Chernobyl Ants, Royal Wulffs, and the like are the mainstay in many parts of this river. Given the size of the fish though, #8 or smaller patterns are best. "During the winter, we'll fish #10

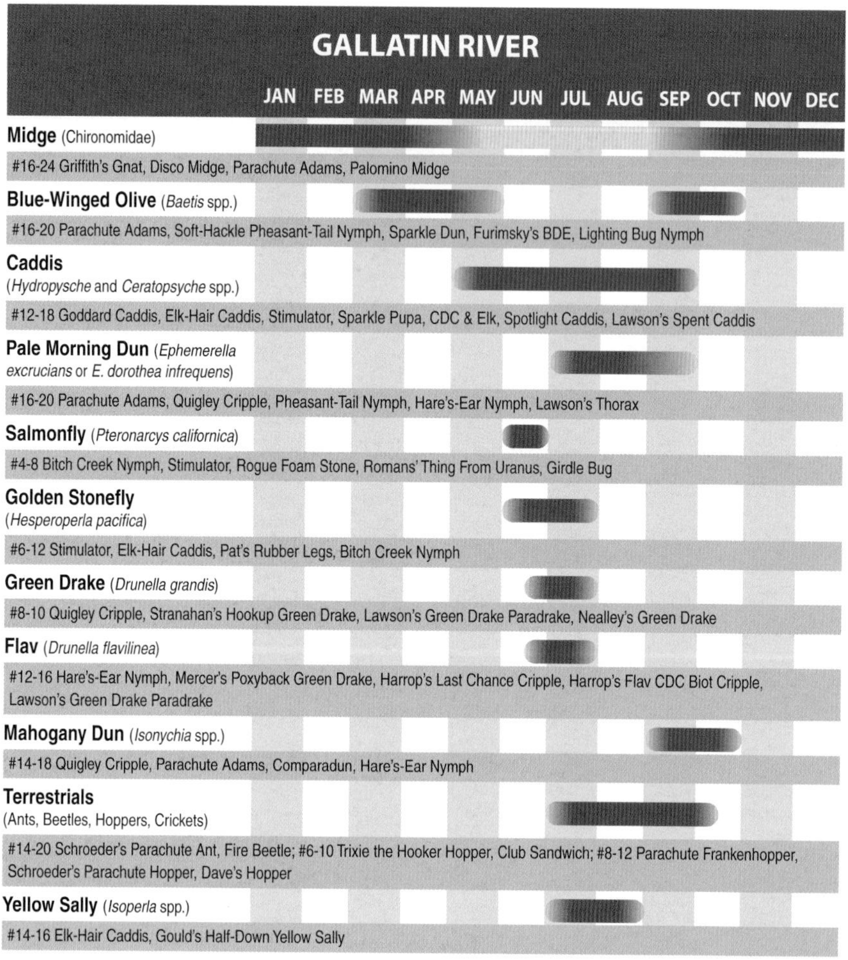

stonefly nymphs whether they're Girdle Bugs or something similar. I think it's a comfortable size that doesn't intimidate the fish," Alvin says.

Early season *Baetis* kick things off on the middle river near Big Sky and downstream while the upper river typically remains under ice. Natural features help keep the lower river slightly warmer and ice-free, even in subzero temperatures. "March 15 through April 15, before high water, you can find Blue-Winged Olives in the afternoon, and it's some of the river's better dry-fly fishing. We basically fish them in the canyon section and throw thorax and parachute patterns. Natural springs in Big Sky contribute about 20 percent to the river's flow and keep the water open. From town up to the Taylor, it typically freezes," Alvin says. "Winter fishing is great, though it's mostly a nymphing game, but I have seen fish rise when the air was 10 below zero."

While runoff and weather have a heavy hand in the appearance and number of Grannom Caddis in May, they signal the beginning of the fishing season and offer some terrific first dry-fly opportunities as long as the weather doesn't warm enough to start runoff. After May, various species of caddis continue to hatch throughout the season and offer dependable fishing.

As runoff subsides, Salmonflies and Golden Stones buzz about (there are typically more Goldens). While Salmonfly patterns work, be mindful of the size of the fish and its relation to the fly you have selected. A 14-inch bow will have a much easier time wrapping its mouth around a #8 or #10 Golden Stone pattern than a bushy #4 Salmonfly.

Stonefly imitations, especially nymphs like Bitch Creeks, are the winning ticket nearly year-round. Salmonflies typically appear in June, but other stoneflies like *Skwalas* (small hatches before runoff) and Yellow Sallies round things out. You do not have to carry a bunch of patterns for these insects. On one trip, my realistic stonefly nymph imitations were proving to repel more fish than they attracted. I returned to camp and swapped reports with a neighboring camper who then handed me a few flies that served him well that day. They were nothing more than chenille and rubber legs tied to a hook, but they outperformed anything else I used.

Green Drakes often make an appearance, and though I have never encountered what I consider an epic hatch, there doesn't need to be clouds of bugs to trigger the fish, and a simple #10 Lawson's Green Drake Paradrake is a great ace in the hole. It's easy to see in the tumbling waters of the Gallatin, and it floats like a champ, even after several fish get the best of it.

In the summer, terrestrials such as beetles, ants, and especially hoppers make up the menu. Use buoyant patterns like Dave's Hoppers or foam-bodied variations as part of a hopper-dropper system with either another terrestrial or general nymph like a Beadhead Prince or Beadhead Pheasant-Tail Nymph bringing up the rear.

Around the same time, summer caddis can come off in droves—especially in the evening. This fluttering activity brings many snouts to the surface, and if you're camping on the river and can fish until well past dark, you'll most likely have terrific fishing with patterns

There is an abundance of stonefly nymphs throughout the Gallatin system, so it shouldn't come as a surprise that it's a favorite food item for the river's trout. Whatever imitation you select, size it accordingly, since the average fish is around 14 inches long and has a much easier time wrapping it's mouth around a size 8 nymph rather than a size 4. JAMES ANDERSON PHOTO such as Elk-Hair Caddis, Spotlight Caddis, and Lawson's Spent Caddis. Caddis patterns also imitate Spruce Moths that descend from the pines and fall on the water.

PMDs and Tricos are other mayfly hatches worth noting, but *Baetis* rule the river in the fall when temperatures drop and cloudy, chilly days replace the warm winds of summer. Summer tourism is winding down and the river has half the crowds. In September and into October *Baetis* decorate the water, but the strength of the hatch and the time they appear rests at the mercy of Mother Nature.

"In late August there is still some good hopper fishing in the upper river, but it chills off quickly. By September or early October, it's much cooler than the lower river. You'll see more *Baetis* and smaller bugs than what you'll see downstream," Rogers says.

The Gallatin's cold water takes a toll on the fish—just one reason they're so aggressive when food is available. The fall *Baetis* hatches mark one of the last times they'll be able to feed with gusto, so seeing small pods of feeding fish in the calmest stretches is common. Don't look for fish around the fast-water pools at this time of year. Tailouts and soft-water seams will give up more action. "Small soft-hackle Lightning Bugs and soft-hackle Pheasant-Tail Nymphs cover everything in the river, and the fish just crush them in the riffles," Alvin says.

Streamer fishing is generally best in the lower river between Four Corners and the state park where you can lob lead and leather from a boat. "Streamer fishing is good on the river, but you have to cover some territory. You'll move them and see some fish pushing 20. But mostly, it's 18- and 19-inch fish. We do better early in the season for fish like that," Alvin says. Zonkers, Bunny Leeches, Slumpbusters, and Zoo Cougars work well. Floating lines with short sinking heads, short leaders, and an occasional pinch of additional weight above the fly will help drive patterns in front of fish.

A 3- to 5-weight rod is ideally suited for dry flies on the Gallatin. I've found that short leaders no lighter than 3X or 4X are perfect for the pocketwater. In addition to the right rod and reel, it's not a bad idea to bring studded boots. The current, slippery rocks, and Murphy's Law combine on the Gallatin and there's a solid chance of slipping and falling. To that degree, a wading staff is useful as well. But by far the best tool is common sense. No trout is worth a life, so wade with caution and be wary of any situation that could toss you into a deep pool or down a fast-water chute, bouncing off boulders like you're inside a giant pinball machine.

Directions

US 191 (Huffine Lane) begins making its way west out of Bozeman, but when it collides with MT 85 and MT 84 near Bozeman Hot Springs, it takes a turn south and leads to the small town of Gallatin Gateway, the upper Gallatin River, and the resort town of Big Sky.

Eventually US 191 (Gallatin Road) clips the northwest corner of Yellowstone National Park and deposits travelers and commercial trucks at Hebgen Lake. From here, you can either continue southward to West Yellowstone and reenter the park or go westward to Quake Lake and the Madison River valley.

To make the Gallatin River a DIY dream, there is a string of public campgrounds off US 191. Camp hosts do an excellent job maintaining these sites. They are equipped with public restrooms, and if you're lucky you can find a vacancy with riverfront access. Unfortunately, many of the other campsites feel like they're just off the shoulder of the road, so if you're a light sleeper, bring earplugs. The highway is a popular route for big rigs, and there's nothing worse than jumping awake to the thunderous rumble of a braking convoy. Road noise aside, these campgrounds are great low-cost resources if you're looking to make the most of your time on the water.

While there are a handful of designated fishing access sites, there are equally as many (if not more) simple roadside pull-offs where anyone can park and jump in the river. Some are only recognized by the large gravel swath carved out along the shoulder, but most are clearly marked with blue signs.

Rollin' Stone (Golden)

Hook:	#8-12 Tiemco 2302
Thread:	Yellow 6/0 Uni-Thread
Tail:	Small black rubber (round)
Body:	Yellow floss over yellow foam
Rib:	Ginger hackle
Legs:	Tan barred rubber (round)
Thorax:	Ginger hackle
Wing:	Elk hair
Back:	Tan foam
Indicator:	Yellow foam

Brook's Sprout (*Baetis*)

Hook:	#16-26 Daiichi 1130
Thread:	Olive 6/0 Uni-Thread
Shuck:	Rusty brown Antron
Body:	BWO goose biot
Thorax:	BWO Superfine
Post:	White foam
Hackle:	Medium dun

Madison River (Upper)

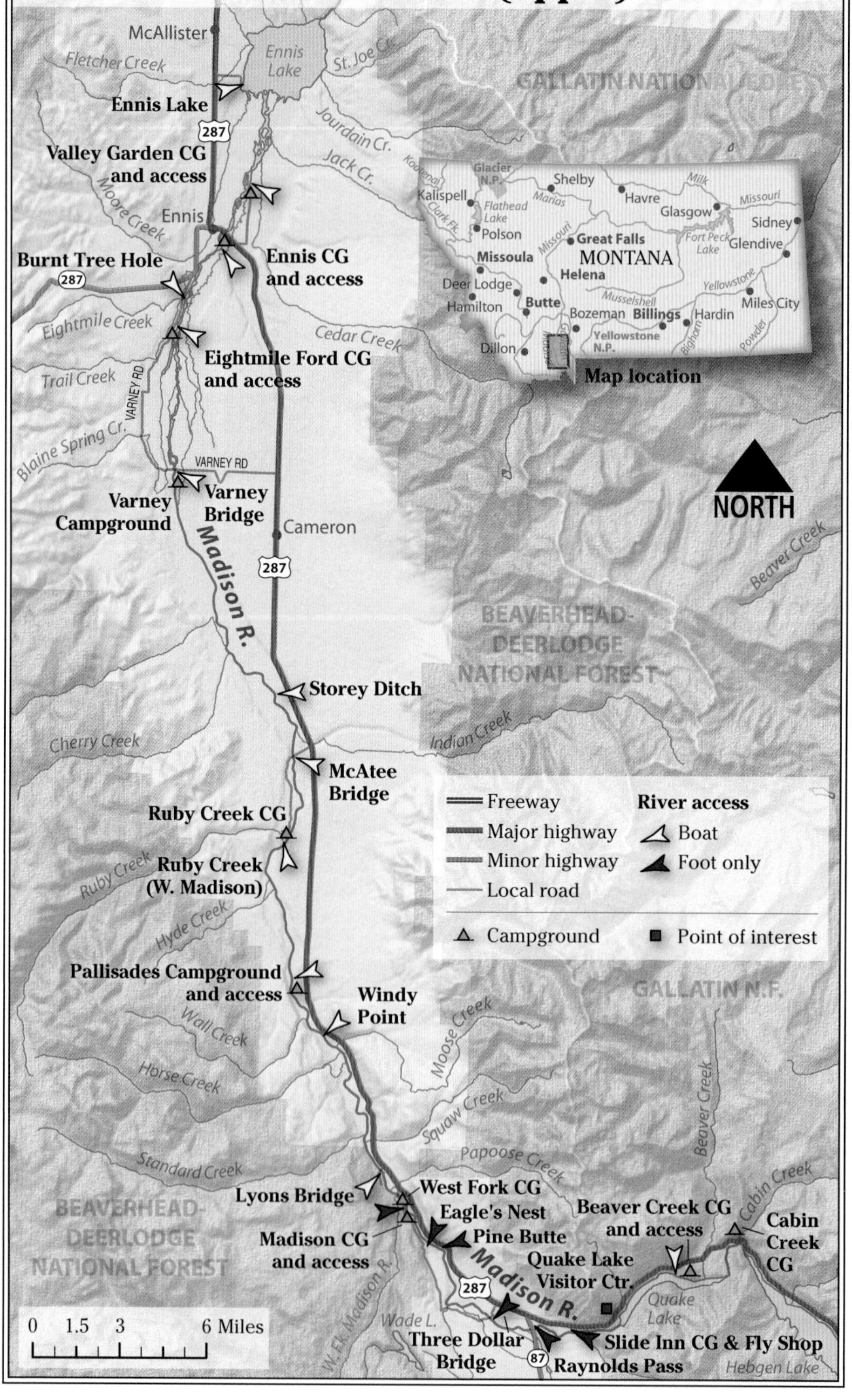

CHAPTER 4

Madison River

Without question, the Madison River is one of the most popular and heavily fished pieces of water in the state of Montana—a far cry from the mid-1990s when the shadow of whirling disease kept many out-of-state anglers at bay. But as the old saying goes, time heals all, and despite the still-present threat of the whirling disease parasite, the doomsday prophecy that spelled the end of this fishery fell short. Now, in the new millennium, this river continues to be one of the best.

What attracts so many anglers to the Madison? In a nutshell it provides anglers with what I think is best described as the real Western fly-fishing experience. It's an active river—not a flat, mirrorlike piece of water like the Missouri or Bighorn—with a respectable population of large trout willing to feed on the surface as much as they are to chase streamers. And despite its somewhat barren and treeless valley, towering mountains loom to the east providing the mountain backdrop most visualize when they think of Montana.

But anyone that visits the river quickly realizes the Madison has much more to offer. There are plenty of access points for the wading and floating angler alike, as well as public camping areas for do-it-yourself fishermen. Hatches like Salmonflies, caddis, and a variety of mayflies sometimes border on the insane. And lastly, its location makes it great for vacation plans with easy access from Bozeman and a stone's throw away from Yellowstone National Park.

Where and When

The Madison forms at the junction of the famed Gibbon and Firehole rivers inside the borders of Yellowstone National Park. From Madison Junction to Hebgen Lake, the moderately sized river is somewhat flat and boring compared with the rest of the river, and since the fish-per-mile count is substantially lower than portions downstream, it doesn't receive the same attention from anglers. I like this area, but I prefer water that is a little more alive with boulders, logs, and large riffles.

Hebgen Lake is not only loaded with massive rainbow trout, but it produces such rich aquatic insect hatches. The most famous is the *Callibaetis*

Madison River (Lower)

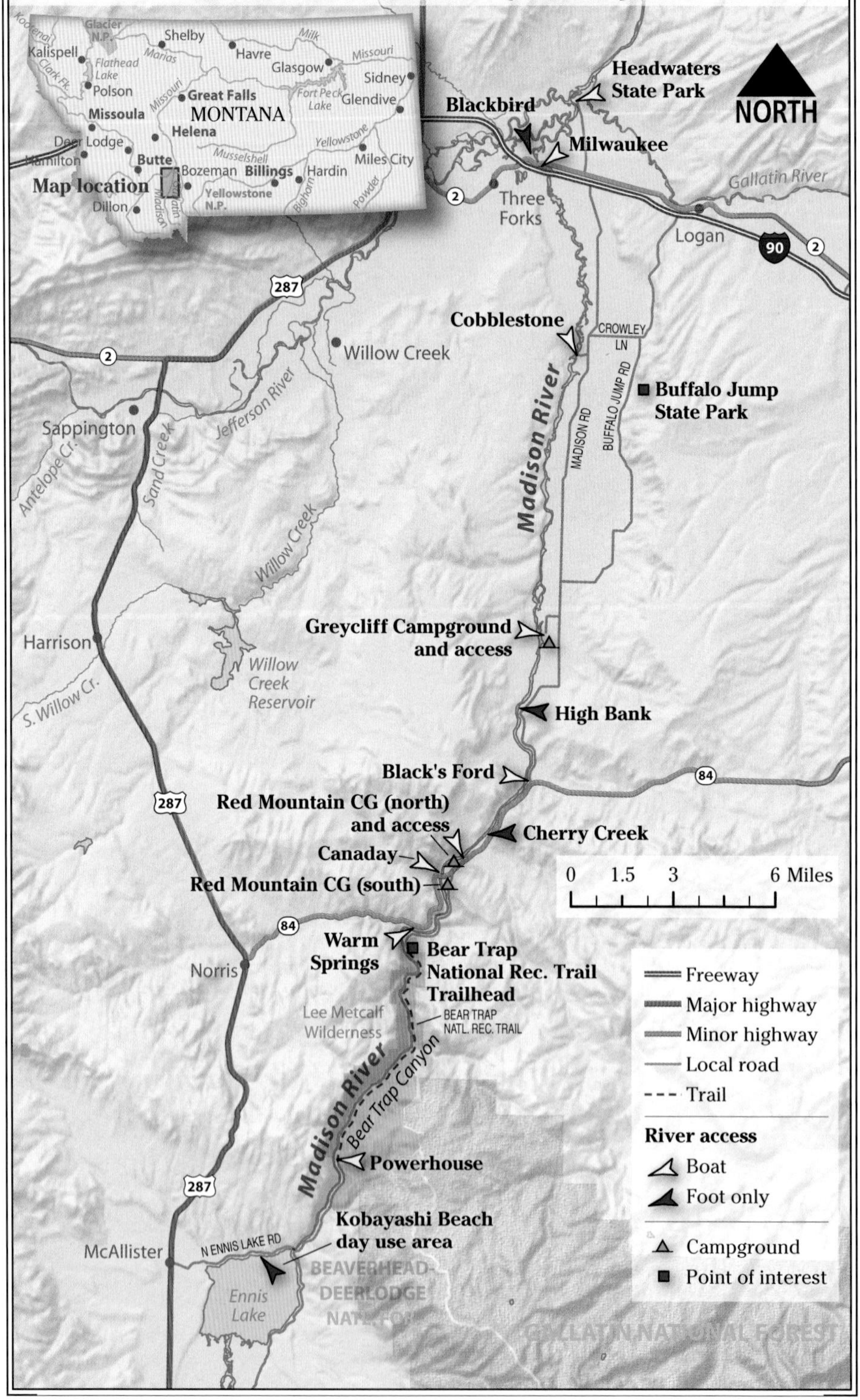

hatch, but damselfly nymphs, streamers, and a smattering of chironomid imitations will take fish as well. "*Callibaetis* are fun to fish on Hebgen, but there is a midge hatch from ice-out through June that would blow your mind," Slide Inn owner and outfitter Kelly Galloup says. "It's a big bug too, around a size 16, and when they come off it's like driving through fog. There are just these huge clouds of them all around the lake."

The Madison re-forms, albeit briefly, at the outflow of Hebgen and offers up some incredible fishing for the next mile and a half until it empties into Quake Lake. This natural reservoir formed in 1959 when a 7.3-magnitude earthquake instigated a landslide that formed a natural dam and flooded the river corridor.

The water between these two reservoirs closely resembles the rest of the river downstream—full of pockets, large boulders, riffles, and other structure. It's known to hold large fish that make their way upstream from Quake Lake in the spring and fall, so you can expect to share the water with many other anglers. When the lower river is otherwise unfishable, the water between Quake and Hebgen is often a solid alternative.

As fun as it is to take fish on dry flies, nymphing is one of the most effective techniques on the Madison River. For something different, try sinking a dry fly (like a hopper) and fishing it as part of a two-fly nymph rig with a weighted nymph on the bottom. JAY NICHOLS PHOTO

The Salmonfly hatch on the Madison is a famous event and generally the most crowded time of the year. Big foam patterns that ride low in the water are good choices as the hatch lingers on. As more anglers educate fish with every fly in their boxes, fish generally refuse patterns that are too bushy or float too high. JAY NICHOLS PHOTO

At the end of the 2008 season, the upper Madison saw a flush of irregularly high water from an inoperable spillway gate. Thankfully, workers eventually closed the gate, and the fishery below is back on track, but it's only a temporary answer until a permanent solution is in place.

With such a massive source, the Madison fared better than most rivers in the state during the drought years. It had its share of trials, but in the big picture, some people feel it should have no trouble bouncing back. "It usually takes about three years for a drought to really impact a fishery. The first year you have some reduced fish numbers. The second year you have more reduced numbers. But the third year you get the big impact of a drought. With less water you have less insects, less habitat, and the fish populations are going to shrink," Beartooth Fly Fishing owner and outfitter Dan Delekta says. "It's basically the rhythm of the West. I've been through a lot of these cycles and that third year just punishes the populations. The opposite can happen from several years of good water. Around the third year in that kind of cycle, the population is going to be just about as robust as it can be."

The most popular miles of the Madison River begin with the water spewing from a tight channel at the western corner of Quake Lake. This stretch (sometimes referred to as The Gorge) tumbles, crashes, and splashes over boulders and rocks and looks better suited for kayakers than anglers, but there are fish here. If you decide to fish it, approach and wade it carefully. The water is powerful and one careless move could flush you downstream.

At the end of the white water is the Slide Inn, a campground and fly shop. Owner Galloup, renowned fly-fishing author and fly-pattern innovator—given his proximity—has learned to fish the gorge section and fishes it well. "The trick is finding the little pockets along the shoreline or behind rocks—depending on the flow levels and where you see fish feeding. It's the only soft water in this part of the river, and if you're not an accurate caster, forget about it. A fish may be feeding in a window that's 6 inches square and ignoring everything else," Galloup says.

The river between Quake Lake and Ennis earned the nickname the "50-mile riffle" because of the upper portions, seemingly endless parade of tumbling water and fairly consistent depths. To catch fish, look for any breaks in

The river beneath Quake Lake is a turbulent mess of rocks and white water, but it holds fish. Approach with caution and look for rising trout along the banks or in the slow water behind large rocks. You must make accurate casts, and it's sometimes tough to pull a running fish from the current, but these challenges are half the fun.

the riffle pattern—structure along the banks or in the middle of the river, dropoffs in the streambed (no matter how slight they may seem), tributary mouths, and anywhere else you can drop a fly on a seam where the fast water collides with the slow.

Downstream from the Slide Inn is the heart of the Madison for wading anglers. Floating is permitted between here and Lyons Bridge, but anglers are not allowed to fish from a boat. That means a boat is only good to shuttle from one wading area to another, and since most spots are reachable on foot anyhow, most opt to leave the area to wading anglers. This includes approximately seven miles of water from the outflow of Quake Lake down to the Lyons Bridge access and is loaded with pockets, eddies, and seams to probe.

Raynolds Pass Bridge and Three Dollar Bridge just downstream are two of the most popular accesses to jump in the upper river. Wading anglers can work along the banks up- or downstream from these points and find a variety of water to fish. "When I fish, I'm usually hunkered down, wading on my knees, or scooching along on my butt," Craig Mathews says, "That's why I like the area around Three Dollar Bridge. But the water between Raynolds Pass down to the West Fork is my favorite."

The parking lots at these places can get full, especially when the fishing is good or a celebrated hatch like the Salmonflies are bouncing off the bushes. If you want to beat the crowds, hit the water at first light, take a break during the heat of the day, and return in the late afternoon/evening and fish until dark. You will increase your opportunities, see more bug activity, and surely encounter fewer anglers.

Downstream of Three Dollar Bridge the river twists and turns, and eventually intersects with other wade-access points like West Fork and Madison campgrounds or Eagle's Nest on the west side of the river. This area is incredibly popular with anglers camping out of their car as they tour the state. Many fish within eyesight of their cars. If you want to distance yourself from the community, hike upstream or downstream for a quarter mile or so.

Lyons Bridge marks the end of the float-fishing-regulated stretch and the first entry point for the Madison's wild bumper-boat ride. Arguably, the most popular boat launch site on the river, it's not uncommon to see 50 to 100 boats launch from Lyons' two ramps in June and July when the Salmonflies are out. Some days it's simply a madhouse. But don't be discouraged, just plan accordingly and you will catch fish. On the Madison, the fishing can be great around every bend no matter how many boats are ahead of you.

The water downstream of Lyons has plenty of shoreside structure like rocks and overhanging vegetation to fish around as well as small islands and brief side channels. The only downside to this float is it doesn't offer the magnificent views of the Madison Range to the east, but if you're like me and concentrate on the square foot of water around a fly all day long, you won't mind their absence. You can cut the float short at the Windy Point access, but it's difficult to get a boat in and out. It's on the east side of the river a little over a mile upstream from Pallisades. If you like to put down

While the Madison gives up big brown trout, the average fish is a healthy 12 to 18 inches long. Look for these fish in the soft-water breaks in the river's seemingly endless parade of riffles.

the rod now and again and soak in the scenery, consider the water from Pallisades downstream.

Pallisades (South Madison Recreation Area) is the next access downstream and is a good place to take out if you're coming from Lyons, or launch for a float to McAtee Bridge. There is plenty to see and fish around downstream of Pallisades, but because it's still considered the upper river and reportedly contains higher populations of fish than say near the town of Ennis, this is also a popular access point. Good manners and proper parking go a long way to avoid conflicts.

If you put in late, or want a shorter float, consider Ruby Creek on the west side of the river a few miles upstream from McAtee Bridge. From US 287, turn southwest as if you're heading to McAtee. After crossing the river, turn left and travel approximately three miles on a Bureau of Land Management road. Ruby Creek Campground and boat access is on the left.

McAtee Bridge to Varney Bridge is probably my favorite section of river. It's a large chunk of river to bite off, so I don't recommend it for an evening float. But if you want an all-day trip where you can combine great scenery with a mix of float- and wade-fishing and a nice lunch in between, consider this float. If you want to cut out some time, take out at Storey Ditch. Drive north on US 287 past the turnoff for McAtee Bridge for approximately two miles, and then turn left (southwest) on a dirt road leading to a ramp at the head of the ditch.

I like this water because in most places, you can fish both banks. Plus there are a few small riffles, a lot of midriver rocks and eddies, and an occasional feeder creek joining the party. The fish on average may be slightly smaller than what you will find upstream, but in my opinion they are less pressured than the fish from Lyons to Pallisades and not as persnickety when it comes to striking a fly. Look to the lower river when the upper river is crazy with anglers bent on following the Salmonflies. Hatches like caddis, Golden Stones, and PMDs shine and are somewhat overlooked until the big bugs disappear for another year.

In the late winter/early spring, the river from McAtee Bridge upstream is closed to all angling between the end of February until the third Saturday in May to protect spawning fish. You can work the water downstream but plan accordingly. The slow, low flows of winter combined with the short (and often cold) days of the early season make the Mac to Varney stretch a tough one to float in a day (even more so if the weather changes and you're faced

The Madison River valley is home to a variety of wildlife, not just trout, and valuable winter range for antelope, elk, and deer. Take the time to look up from the water to enjoy the mountain peaks, forests, and all the other incredible scenic attributes this watershed has to offer.

with a cold, steady wind). It usually requires putting in early when the water and air are too cold to inspire any fish to move far. You may have to float a few miles before the sun warms things up enough for any decent action.

There are a few ways to approach the river between Varney Bridge and Ennis—both for boaters and wading fishermen. Varney Bridge is a good starting point (especially in the off-season) with three take-out options downstream—Eightmile Ford, Burnt Tree Hole, and Ennis respectively. Choose one depending on how much time you want to spend on the water. If you plan to float below these points, check conditions with a local fly shop before settling your plans. In the summer, the water can be skinny for a boat from Burnt Tree downstream, and in the winter and early spring, Ennis access is typically inaccessible because of snow and ice.

If you're floating, there are some great nymphing runs in this stretch. Dozens of small islands, side channels, and some of the deepest pools in the river are located here. It's also one of the best places to find fish rising to Blue-Winged Olives and midges through the shoulders of the fishing season. Many of these areas are accessible on foot if you work up- and downstream from the access points—just remember to stay below the high-water mark to avoid trespassing.

Downstream of the Ennis access is Valley Garden, the last public-access point before the river washes into Ennis Lake on the north side of town. This stretch also doesn't open until the third Saturday in May, but it is a good spot for wade fishing (fishing from boats is not permitted downstream of Ennis access to the lake) and some nice fish make their way upstream. If you're interested in fishing Ennis Lake, Ennis Lake and Meadow Lake accesses are on the western shore off US 287.

The outflow of Ennis Lake marks the beginning of Bear Trap Canyon, a 7-mile wilderness section of the Madison that shoots through a tight mountain corridor. Some anglers prefer to tackle this section on foot since there is limited access, chiefly a hiking trail easily reached at the north end of the canyon off MT 84 (watch out for rattlesnakes). Take the gravel road across the street from the Red Mountain Campground for 3 miles to find the trailhead. The trail is fairly easygoing for the first few miles, but gains elevation over the river. Contact the Bureau of Land Management (BLM) for maps and camping information.

"There's a high population of nice big brown trout in the lower Madison," River's Edge Fly Shop owner and outfitter Steve Summerhill says. "There also seems to be a rising population of 12- to 16-inch rainbows in there as well."

Only experienced oarsmen should float the canyon, which is home to a few significant white-water chutes—the most famous is the Kitchen Sink Rapids—and an abundance of big boulders that make it tough to negotiate. "I do not recommend this area of the river to those with hard-sided drift boats. I don't even recommend it to a lot of people with rafts," Galloup says. "You can still see chunks of fiberglass from the last guy that tried to do it

THE MADISON RIVER FOUNDATION

Ennis is the self-proclaimed fly-fishing capital of the state, and it shows. You cannot walk through town without seeing some symbol, sign, or talisman connected with the sport. The town's annual late-summer fly-fishing celebration, the Ennis Fly Fishing Festival, has been going strong since 2003, attracting all ages with fly-tying demonstrations, art displays, a barbeque, raffles, casting clinics, and other events.

The proceeds from the event benefit the Madison River Foundation—a nonprofit organization based in Ennis dedicated to preserving the river and valley for the mutual benefit of wildlife and people. In years past, this group has been involved with community planning projects, population growth issues, and restoration projects like the planting of willows and cottonwoods on O'Dell Creek, an important tributary to the Madison River.

"Our mission focuses on the Madison with the goal of protecting and preserving the resource," Madison River Foundation Executive Director Richard Lessner says. "We're a relatively new foundation—we formed in 2003—and we have two main functions. The first is advocacy—to be an advocate of the river in the public-policy arena. The second is our 'boots-in-the-water' conservation efforts. We are trying to grow that aspect of what we do as a foundation and are mainly focusing our efforts on the tributaries." For more information on the Madison River Foundation, or to learn about the annual Ennis Fly Fishing Festival, visit madisonriverfoundation.org. ■

with a hard drift boat, and rafts flip over all the time—even the big ones made for white water."

If you decide to float it, use the launch site near the old Madison Power Plant. Take US 287 to the north shore of Ennis Lake, then turn east at McAllister on North Ennis Lake Road. Turn left (northeast) after crossing the bridge across the northeast corner of the lake. This is a boat access only and off-limits to hikers. The trail that follows the river from the north entrance is inaccessible. Also, to maximize the experience for everyone, floaters are not allowed to camp overnight in the canyon. The closest boat-accessible public campground is Red Mountain Campground outside the canyon's northern border. Since some of the river runs through BLM land, shuttle services must be licensed by the agency. At the time of writing, there are only two shuttle services available for the lower river: Rivergal Shuttle (406-685-3500) and Bob's Hook Line & Sinker (406-595-0587).

For the most part, angling interest in the river after the canyon tapers off dramatically. This is largely due in part to the slow, warm nature of the water during the summer and its shallow, weedy character. But there are big fish in the lower river from Norris Bridge to Three Forks. Populations aren't what you'll find upstream of Ennis Lake, but it's a trade-off since boat traffic is substantially lower.

"The temperature of water can reach upward of 70 degrees. Ennis Lake is shallow, and so it's a big solar panel up there. In fact, PPL (the electric company) has an agreement with the fisheries to pump water out of Hebgen and pulse water during the summertime to try to keep the water cooler in the lake and downstream, which they do on a fairly regular basis if the lower river gets warm. Unfortunately it can screw up the water on the upper river, or it can for a few days, but that's helped keep the lower fishery going," Summerhill says.

In the spring and fall, however, the lower Madison is a viable option all the way to the Jefferson. The water temperatures are acceptable, and hatches that go hand in hand with long, flat water are abundant. Bursts of Blue-Winged Olives and caddis (especially the Mother's Day Caddis of early spring) are the main draw, but bring streamers. Its big-fish water, and the moderate flows make it easier to pitch and swing a meaty fly in front of a fish's nose.

"Crayfish are a huge deal on the lower river. We struggle because the crayfish patterns that are out there are tied for bass fishermen. We look for really light patterns that aren't going to get caught in the weeds. We break the lead eyes and stuff out of commercial patterns," Summerhill says. "Fishing them in between the weed pockets, or over the top of them, is very produc-

The Madison River is renowned for its diverse aquatic insect life, and sometimes fish can key on the lesser species when two or more hatches occur in the same window. Take the time to study the water and watch what the fish eat before settling on a pattern. JAY NICHOLS PHOTO tive. We've got a few good crayfish patterns we tie for the shop, but we fish the Clouser Crayfish and Haddon's Dead Drift Crayfish a lot. They're nice and light."

Warm Springs, Red Mountain Campground, Black's Ford, Greycliff, and Cobblestone access points are strung out along the lower river between Bear Trap and Three Forks. MT 84 (Norris Road) runs along the southeastern side of the river and connects with the first three points. At the Black's Ford access head north on Madison Road to reach Greycliff and Cobblestone. It eventually meets a highway frontage road just east of Three Forks.

Hatches and Flies

Aside from the fishing and the scenery, many anglers flock to the Madison for the diversity of hatches. Almost any month of the year there's something stirring in the water that fly fishermen can imitate. Even in the dead of winter, die-hard anglers can catch fish rising to the surface for midges. Winter and early spring is a fun time to fish because you don't have to be on the water at the crack of dawn or stay out until midnight—bankers' hours are the rule.

Adult Salmonflies are prone to taking a swim when the wind blows or they haphazardly try to fly over the water. To attract trout, add a twitch or skitter a Salmonfly pattern to mimic the natural struggling on the surface. JAY NICHOLS PHOTO

You won't catch hordes of fish. But if you're lucky, there's enough action above and below the surface to relieve cabin fever. Use Griffith's Gnats, midge cluster patterns, and Delektable Twinkle Midges in the #18-24 range.

"So often the rising fish on the Madison are taking midges—even if caddis are on the water. The average guy gets to the river, jumps in waist deep, and doesn't spend time studying what's going on. The Madison reads like an open book. If you sit there and study, just invest 10 minutes and let the river tell you what to do," Mathews says. "The Madison throws curves. Up until a few years ago, you could throw a Royal Wulff and catch every fish in the river, but the river has matured and the fish don't let you do that anymore, and each fish can be feeding on something different."

Baetis hatch in late March when the valley begins to shake winter's grip. Misery loves company, and I can't think of another hatch where this is truer. I've stood in the middle of the river, covered with falling snow, trying to force-feed a #20 parachute to pods of fish feeding on *Baetis*. They'll also come out when it's pleasant, but these bugs simply love the nasty weather. Carry small (#16-20) mayfly imitations like Parachute Adams, CDC Baetis Spinner, or an ICU Baetis.

"Early in the season we get some *Baetis* before high water," Mathews says. "We had really strong fall *Baetis* in late August and September, but they quit fairly early. It's just a guess, but I think that the huge flows we had from the dam malfunction washed a lot of *Baetis* right down to Ennis."

If there don't seem to be any bugs coming off, which is sometimes the case in the early spring, nymph rigs are by far the most effective way to tackle the Madison. Big stonefly nymphs, caddis larvae, and San Juan Worms should be at least one fly in the setup if you're using multiple flies. Other times small ties that mimic *Baetis* nymphs, eggs, or some of the river's smaller caddis work better. "My favorite time to fish the Madison is March, April, and May," Delekta says. "The fish haven't been harassed, the water is at its lowest level, the weather is getting warmer every day, and we have some nice mayfly hatches with the Mother's Day Caddis and *Skwalas* mixed in."

Mother's Day Caddis sometimes appear riverwide just before high water, but anglers sometimes find higher concentrations in the lower river. "The Mother's Day Caddis hatch can be unbelievable in some years. Whenever you get into one of those great hatches, you realize how many fish, and how many nice fish, are in this river. The lower river is one of my favorite places for this hatch, particularly in the evenings." Summerhill says. "The hatch always moves up the river for a week or so before spring runoff kicks into high gear, so the water can be clean for a day or two and then get dirty and kill the hatch. But if you have good weather and good conditions, you'll have good fishing."

Runoff typically rears its ugly head sometime between the middle of May and June, but the river can come back into fishable form in a hurry. In fact, some parts of the river, like above the junction of the West Fork of the Madison, may remain clear enough to fish (albeit high).

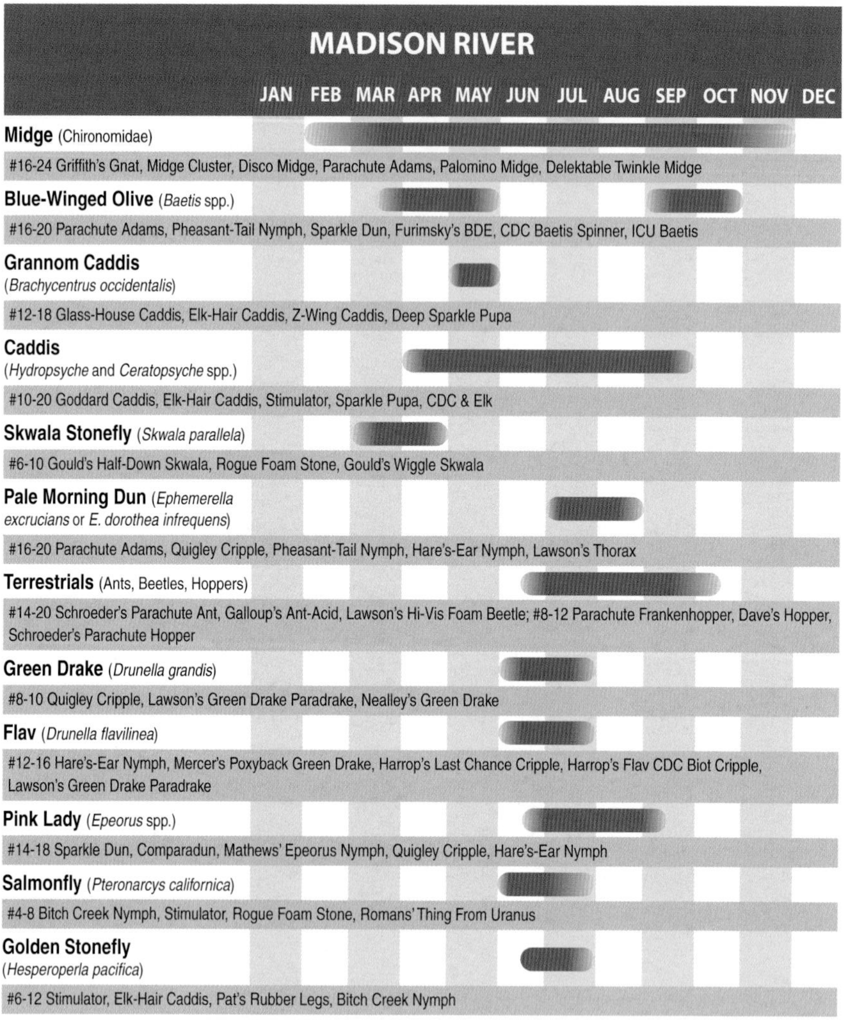

The big bugs of summer and the summer crowds collide as runoff ends. The Madison's Salmonfly and Golden Stonefly hatches attract anglers from all over the world. Typically, these hatches begin on the lower river near Bear Trap Canyon and progress upstream a few miles a day depending on weather conditions. If it's especially windy, or a cold front moves over the valley, expect the hatch's progression to stall a little until summerlike conditions return. It typically takes the stones anywhere from two to four weeks to move from the lower river to Hebgen Lake. Big (#4-8) Rubber-Legged Stimulators, Rogue Stones, and just about any other foam or bullethead stonefly pattern will work. Experiment with low-riding dry flies and those with rubber legs that seemingly kick on their own.

If you want to escape some of the hordes of boats and anglers, look for where the other summer hatches are popping. Yellow Sallies, Quill Gordons (*Epeorus*), and caddis debut on the middle and lower river as the stoneflies reach the upper river. "*Epeorus* have become the major mayfly hatch on the river over the years," Mathews says. "Some people find it a little disturbing because it is generally a warm, prairie-water mayfly, but it's also a fast-water mayfly. Because they're running more water from the lakes at critical times to keep it cool below Ennis, we're seeing that population explode. We have them from the end of June almost through August."

Craig Mathews and the late Gary LaFontaine described the Madison as a "caddisfly river" in their book *Fly Fishing the Madison,* and it's hard to argue with that. On just about any day of the fishing season there's a solid chance you'll encounter caddis is some size or color. From the #10 Great Gray Spotted Sedge to the #14 Spotted Sedges, bring a box of your best caddis ties if you plan on fishing any evening on the Madison.

"We get good concentrations of *Hydropsyche,* which is the main caddis on the Madison, but it sometimes comes off a little bit later, about July 10, and lasts

The short section of river below Hebgen Lake is an alternative when the lower river is too high or too muddy to fish or when some of the large trout make their way upstream from Quake Lake.

about three weeks," Mathews says. "Last year I had the best caddis fishing in the morning. Tremendous *Hydropsyche* egg-laying activity and I looked around and there was no one on the river. I'd fish from 7:30 until about 10:30 AM when folks started showing up, and then I'd pack in and go to work. I had mornings that were embarrassingly good and caught more fish than a guy should."

I like to be on the water as early as possible, partly to avoid the boats but mostly because I like getting a jump on the action. So for the most part, that makes PMDs my best friend. I don't often encounter huge masses of these bugs, but there is certainly more than enough above and below the surface to keep fish interested. If you want to really tag-team the fish, tie on a two-fly rig with a Parachute PMD in the lead and caddis trailing behind. Aside from PMDs, other mayflies like March Browns, Green Drakes, Tricos, and more *Baetis* take to the air throughout the season.

Terrestrials make up the last of the great summer bugs. Beetles and grasshoppers are two popular choices given the abundance of overhanging brush and grassy banks along the river, but ants are an often overlooked food item. Give Galloup's Ant-Acid a try as a dropper off the back of a hopper or cricket pattern.

"A lot of people don't think about sinking a dry fly, but that's something I've done for a long time here with good results at times," Delekta says. "We sink hoppers with split shot. It's an old technique in the guide community here.

Fishing streamers is a good strategy to hook up with some of the river's larger brown trout. When water temperatures are cold, however, slow down your retrieve. With so much food to choose from, fish sometimes won't chase a fleeing streamer as much as they would when the water is warmer.

In the 1990s, the effects of whirling disease threatened the future of the rainbow trout fishery on the Madison. Today, rainbow trout populations are strong and anglers are once again catching some large fish.

If you get fish that are coming up and looking at the hopper but not eating it, well, try sinking it. Real ones do drown and sink, and of course the fish aren't as concerned about getting hooked when they're eating something that sunk."

As the summer winds down and fall begins, continue to fish terrestrials, especially on warm days, and since it's the time of year when the river's fish are strapping on the feed bag, it never hurts to put a hefty meal in front of their face. *Baetis* will return as well and bring fish up, as will caddis hatches wherever you can find them. The lower river below Bear Trap is a good place to start looking.

Kelly Galloup says you can fish streamers on the Madison nearly year-round with good results, but during the fall, the big fish are on the prowl. Most of the time you can get hookups imitating an injured fish trying to fight the current by casting upstream and bringing the fly across or slightly downstream to your position. But one of my favorite techniques is to pound the banks from the boat. I cast as close as I can to any structure, vary my retrieve speed and strip lengths, and if I don't get any strikes or chases, I yank it out and hit the next pocket.

"The Dungeon is one of our best-selling streamers. After that its Delekta's Double Screamer, the Butt Monkey, and Galloup's Nut, which is an easier-to-cast variation of Russ Madden's Circus Peanut," Galloup says.

Directions

For those traveling to or through Montana on vacation, there's a good chance you'll be near the Madison River. It begins in one of the country's most popular national parks, and when it's finished is a stone's throw away from Bozeman.

Beginning at Madison Junction in Yellowstone, the river basically follows the West Entrance Road and then heads north to Hebgen Lake just before the park's western boundary. If you're interested in fishing Hebgen Lake, Quake

Lake, or the short portion of river in between, head north on Gallatin River Road (US 191 and US 287) at West Yellowstone and then turn west on Quake Lake Road (US 287). If you want to head straight to the heart of the Madison, take US 20 west from West Yellowstone and then head northwest (right) on MT 87 just before you reach Henry's Lake. This will deposit you at the Raynolds Pass access just before the road intersects with US 287.

US 287 is the main thoroughfare for reaching the river's access points between Hebgen Lake and Ennis. Nearly every bridge, boat ramp, and parking area on the upper river is accessible from this road. The exception is Eightmile Ford and Burnt Tree Hole. These are on the western shoreline, just south of Ennis, off Varney Road (CR 249). If you're coming from Ennis, take MT 287 toward Virginia City, but continue south at the intersection of Varney Road. The other option is to head north from Varney Bridge upstream, but since the dirt road is a rough ride, most circle around through town.

While MT 287 heads toward the old mining town of Virginia City, US 287 continues north around Ennis Lake to Norris. If you're looking to float Bear Trap Canyon, turn east on North Ennis Lake Road and drive around the north shore to the dam. To fish the river below the canyon, turn east on MT 84 in Norris. This road intersects a few access points like Red Mountain, the road to the Bear Trap Canyon trailhead, and Black's Ford. At Black's Ford, MT 84 continues east and Madison Road heads north along the river to Greycliff and Cobblestone access points. If you stay on MT 84 east, it becomes US 191 about 7 miles from Bozeman.

Delektable Lil' Spanker

Hook:	#14-18 Tiemco 5262
Thread:	Brown 6/0 Danville
Bead:	Gold
Tail:	Eight fibers of mallard dyed wood-duck gold
Body:	Six fibers of brown pheasant tail covered with Super Glue (do not get glue on tail)
Rib:	Counterwrapped gold wire
Thorax:	Peacock Ice Dub
Wing Case and Legs:	Light blue dun Midge Flash
Hackle:	Natural gray CDC
Collar:	Dark Hare's Ear Plus dubbing

Note: Wing case and legs are formed from 8 strands of Midge Flash pulled over thorax, then split equally.

Galloup's Ant-Acid

Hook: #14-18 Tiemco 100
Thread: Tan 8/0 Uni-Thread
Body: Brown and tan Wapsi Ultrafine dubbing
Underwing: Gold Flashabou
Wing: Natural elk hair
Legs: Small white barred rubber legs (round)

Galloup's Smokewagon

Hook: #6 Daiichi 1750
Underbody: Lead wire
Thread: Light olive 6/0 Uni-Thread
Tail: Yellow dyed grizzly saddle hackles
Body: White Crystal Chenille
Fins: Bar-dyed olive chickabou and white marabou
Collar: Yellow dyed grizzly saddle hackles

CDC Egg Laying Caddis

Hook: #16 Tiemco 100
Thread: Tan 8/0 Uni-Thread
Egg Sac: Highlander green Z-lon
Body: Dark brown CDC dubbing spool
Wing: Natural brown CDC feathers
Thorax: Natural brown CDC dubbing

Epeorus Nymph

Hook: #16 Tiemco 200R
Thread: Camel 8/0 Uni-Thread
Tail: Natural brown Hungarian partridge fibers
Body: Pheasant-tail fibers
Rib: Brown Ultra Wire (small)
Wing Case: Black Flashback
Thorax: Brown-olive (#8) Nature's Spirit Emergence dubbing
Legs: Hungarian partridge

Jefferson River

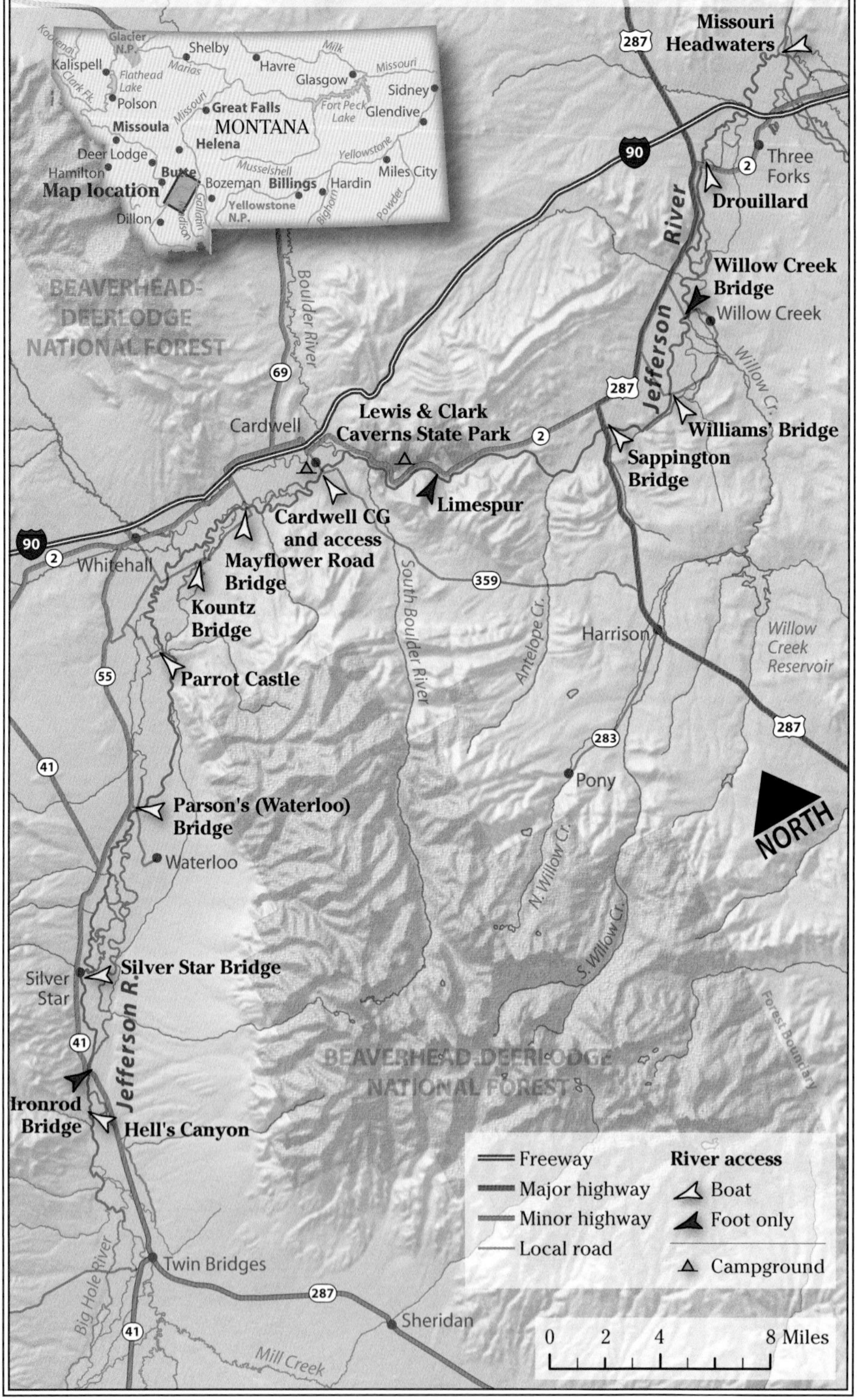

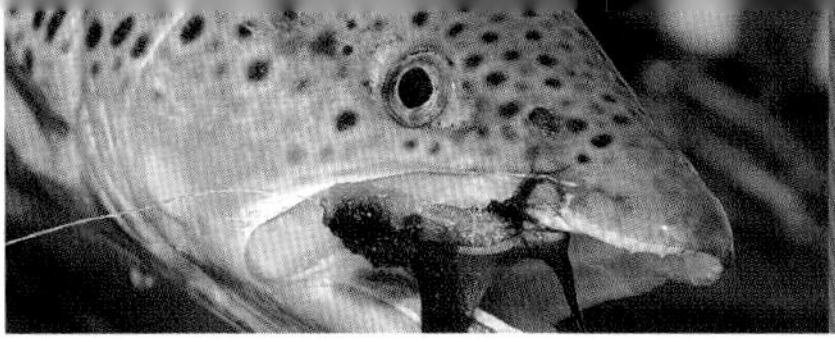

CHAPTER 5

Jefferson River

Without question, the Jefferson is the red-headed stepchild of all Montana's trout rivers. Finicky and temperamental, it can be hot one day and cold the next. It is typically too slow and cold in the winter; muddy and high in the early season; warm and low in the summer; and by the end of the year, so forgotten and overshadowed by other waters that few make the effort to fish it.

It's a beautiful river—full of bends, riffles, and structure that make anglers salivate. But historically, at the height of the summer fishing season, when most anglers visit the state, drought and dewatering reduce the Jefferson to a warm trickle. In some seasons, the corridor between Whitehall and Three Forks lost all but a few cubic feet per second to the hayfields of neighboring farms and ranches.

But, above-average snowfall in the winter and local efforts to conserve water have breathed life into the river and once again made it a three-season fishery, though the shoulders of the summer season and early fall are still my favorite windows. The water is staying cool enough to spur the river's brown trout (and increasing rainbow trout population) into feeding even in the height of summer. Most visiting anglers aren't aware of this, and for those consistently making the effort to fish the Jeff over the years, they'd just assume it stay that way.

In my opinion, the Jefferson is one of Montana's best-kept secrets—if not for the fishing than for the light angling pressure. On a midsummer day last season, my brother and I floated from sunrise to sunset and never saw another angler or boat. The action is better than most people realize, and when the river is in the right mood, it gives up some terrific days.

"The Jefferson gets very little press, and the press it does get is typically negative," Four Rivers Fishing Company owner and outfitter Greg Smith says. "Some of it is pretty dismal. But the highlight is I've been able to enjoy the river almost exclusively for the past five years since the fishing has been coming back gangbusters. I know we won't keep it quiet forever, but there's still enough people that go down there, get beat, and don't come back that I don't see the place becoming as crowded as other neighboring rivers like the Big Hole or Madison."

While nymphing and dry-fly fishing bring more fish to the boat, many anglers venture to the Jefferson to cast streamers, hoping the next tug on the end of the line will be one of the river's monster trout. Yellow- and brown-colored streamers are some of the most effective.
NICK ROMANS PHOTO

Formed by the Beaverhead and the Big Hole, the Jefferson begins behind the eight ball so to speak, basically picking up where the other rivers leave off—unlike a typical freestone river that begins with cold springs, alpine lake runoff, or snowmelt from high peaks. This also means it's one of the last to clear from runoff and the first to close when summer water temperatures skyrocket. High water temperatures, low visibility, and plummeting summertime flows (because of drought and irrigation draws) are three common problems on the Jefferson.

But ranchers and neighbors of the river are curtailing water usage in years of low flows, and with conscientious anglers keeping away during periods of dangerously high water temperatures, the fish are able to sit relatively unstressed in the deep pools until conditions are optimal. The water is doing so well that although the river was once known as primarily a brown-trout fishery, rainbows are now locking on to the end of anglers' lines with some regularity. "Trout Unlimited and some Jefferson biologists are doing some work and planting fingerlings," says StoneFly Fly Shop co-owner Mike Marcum. "So now people are catching as many rainbows as brown trout."

That said, most of the action is subsurface whether your weapon of choice is a pair of nymphs or tandem-rigged streamers. At times, fish do come up to feed, but don't expect to see pods of them just because bugs are in the air. In fact, one of the most incredible hatches I've ever witnessed was late in the day near Cardwell. Millions of mayflies, caddis, and stoneflies were in the air—more than I've ever seen in my life—and not a single fish broke the surface.

The fish are also spread out. You can go miles without seeing or feeling a fish on the end of your line and then suddenly stumble on a pool full of gorgeous browns. "Some days, you'll find fish in the riffles; other times you'll find them on the soft, gooey, almost stagnant inside water. There are days when you'll find them on inside seam edges. The flow really changes the fish's habits and where they lay. That river is wicked hard to pinpoint fish, and you just have to spend time on it. It's a big river with only 700 or 800 fish per mile, and when they disappear, they're sometimes tough to find. But that's the lure of the Jefferson to me," Smith says.

Though there aren't that many fish in the system, those that call it home are sizable, including trout that reach out to the 22- and 24-inch mark on the tape. A sincere shot at a true trophy trout is probably the biggest draw that keeps the diehards coming back. "The river isn't back to its grandeur of the 1950s and 1960s, but it is getting really good. If you want to go after a trophy trout, or the trout of a lifetime, it's the only place you want to be around here," Smith says.

The Jefferson is loaded with side channels, islands, sloughs, and undercut banks that hold fish. Break up a long float by anchoring the boat and exploring these areas on foot.

NICK ROMANS PHOTO

Where and When

Given the Jefferson's size, length, and distance between access points, it is best fished from a boat as long as you watch where you're floating. Some braids and side channels can cause you to lose your direction or send you down a canal that leads into neighboring fields. Also, remember that summer flows on the lower river are low in some spots, making for skinny water in a boat. There are hundreds of ranches and farms stretched along its length, and with Montana's hot, dry summers, the water is a priceless commodity.

"Irrigation demands really hurt that river," Stonefly Inn and Outfitters owner and outfitter Dan "Rooster" Leavens says. "But the state, Trout Unlimited, and the Jefferson River Watershed Council set up minimum flow requirements for the river and that has helped over the years."

The Jefferson isn't one of those rivers you should simply decide to try on a whim. Talk with local fly shops and guides about conditions given the time of your visit. Then watch the water temperatures, flows, and conditions for the best shot at the huge fish buried in the river's deep pools. Flows change so much in a given year the pockets, seams, and structure you remember from the spring look completely different come fall.

"You won't be productive if you fish everywhere," Leavens says. "There might be a mile of water that we don't even cast over, we just row through it. The fish just aren't there. Think about it like this, when it's really hot out,

During the summer, the Jefferson gets warm. Look for cold-water sources like springs, tributaries, or even the inflow from ditch returns, and you may find water that's a few degrees cooler than the rest of the river.

where do people like to sit? They like to sit next to the air conditioner. If it's cold out, they want to be by the woodstove. If you apply that kind of theory to the fishing down there, you'll begin to figure out where they are."

The upper portion from Twin Bridges to Whitehall is an unhurried, meandering piece of water that makes its way through a sizable valley. The water is wide, full of attractive pockets, structure, side channels, islands, and with the exception of the diversion dam near Parson's Bridge, it's perfect water for even novice rowers and one of those places where you can see a rising fish in smooth water 100 yards away before reaching it. The proximity to Twin Bridges and the Big Hole and Beaverhead watersheds make it one of the most popular Jefferson stretches to float, but even on a busy day this means seeing less than a handful of boats.

A popular Jefferson float actually begins on the Big Hole. The High Road fishing access is just west of Twin Bridges. In years past you could drop in a boat and float into the Jefferson junction and take out downstream at either Hell's Canyon or the Silver Star Bridge. However, high water ruined the High Road site forcing the Montana Department of Fish, Wildlife, and Parks (MDFWP) to close it, and at the time of this writing, there were no plans to reopen it.

If this site is reopened in the near future, there are plenty of islands and channels in the water below, and it's not far from the Beaverhead and Big Hole watersheds if that's where your base camp is located. On the south side of Twin Bridges, Melrose Bench Road merges with MT 41. Follow the highway west. The access site is on the northwest side of the bridge crossing the Big Hole.

Hell's Canyon access and boat launch is just north of Twin Bridges. Follow MT 41 north from town. Turn left on Allen Cutoff Road immediately after crossing the river. Follow the dirt road for close to .5 mile until you see the access area on the left. Silver Star access is only a few miles farther (north) along MT 41. Just south of town, turn east on Primrose Lane. The boat ramp and parking area are on the northwest side of the bridge.

Whether you enter the water at Hell's Canyon or Silver Star, the water downstream flows mainly through private land, and given the nature of the river, foot access is difficult and the river is best tackled from a boat. Parson's Bridge on Waterloo Road (sometimes called Waterloo Bridge) is a tough access for waders because the water up- and downstream is wide and deep. Even some floating anglers stay away from it because of the boat ramp's steep grade and loose gravel. I recommend four-wheel drive if you plan to back a trailer down to the water.

Once you're on the water, the next task is navigating the diversion dam just downstream—one of two big hazards on the river. If the conditions allow, try maneuvering the boat along the shoreline to the downstream side of the dam before shoving off. If you're feeling brave, however, you can work your way through the rocks and pick up your companions downstream of the dam on the west shoreline, but I'd vote for option number one first. Study the water before launching your boat and find a channel that looks navigable.

Though the Jefferson River doesn't have high fish-per-mile counts like neighboring rivers, local ranchers and neighbors are curtailing their water usage to help the trout. DOMINIC VALPIANI PHOTO

MT 41 intersects with MT 55 a few miles north of Silver Star. Waterloo Road connects with MT 55 a few miles north of this intersection. The bridge is only a few hundred yards after the turn, and the boat ramp and small parking area are on the northeast side.

After Parson's, the Jefferson moves a little closer to the northern finger of the Tobacco Root Mountains. There aren't as many twists and turns as the upper river, but the many banks, small riffles, and overhanging vegetation make this one of my favorite stretches to fish terrestrials.

Parrot Castle access downstream is mainly a walk-in point. You can drop in a boat, but the primitive launch is situated down a drainage canal approximately 50 yards from the river (in the heart of mosquito country). Once you launch, you have to row upstream to the main stem and then work through the second of the Jefferson's two diversion dams.

If you are taking out at Parrot, watch for the Parrot Ditch water return just upstream. It's a sizable waterfall on the side of a sandstone cliff and a good landmark. Downstream of the waterfall, an island divides the river. Take the river left channel, and the irrigation canal is a few hundred yards downstream on river left. A path to back down a trailer is on the west side once you're in the canal. Getting a trailer to the boat ramp requires driving through a shallow portion of the canal system, which I don't advise during high water or in anything without four-wheel drive. Turn east from MT 55 onto Parrot Castle Road, and then turn right (south) at the third intersection (Daly Road). The dirt road will head south and then jog to the southeast. The access lot is at the end of the road.

Parrot Ditch siphons a lot of the Jefferson's water, so the water downstream is slightly skinnier than it is upriver. However, Parrot's close proximity to Kountz Bridge makes it a good option to put in for a short float if you are willing to negotiate the canal and dam at Parrot. This stretch's close range to Whitehall make it easy to get to, and the water downstream is full of channels, islands, and sloughs. To get to Kountz, take South Division Street south from the heart of Whitehall. It quickly changes to Kountz Road, and after a few miles, turns east instead of south. The access is on the southeast side of the bridge.

Downstream of Whitehall the river flows into an aesthetically pleasing though slightly different landscape compared with the typical Montana mountain setting. It doesn't border high-mountain peaks or steep-walled canyons. Instead there are a few dry foothills, grassy fields, and dense pockets of trees suited more for whitetail deer and pheasants than elk and antelope. It is beautiful country, and the floats between Whitehall and Cardwell are some of my favorite.

Kountz to Mayflower is another option if you're short on time or you're in nearby Bozeman and want a float that's close to I-90. The bridge on Mayflower Road (Tebay Lane) has a great parking area and boat ramp on the northwest side. Whether you're taking out or putting in, the road is barely over a mile from MT 2, which connects to Whitehall (west) or Cardwell (east). Both towns have ramps to I-90.

Mayflower to Cardwell Bridge is the last stretch of river that flows through the ranches, fields, and trees before entering the London Hills and Lewis and Clark Caverns State Park. The fishing is good and at any given time, but I favor the late season when hoppers are falling off the grass and into the water. Cardwell Bridge is approximately 2 miles from the intersection with I-90 on MT 359. The primitive access is on the southwest side of the bridge.

Now that the river has worked through the gauntlet of diversion canals and irrigation draws, the portion along MT 2 that runs through the Lewis and Clark Caverns State Park can be skinny come summer, so if you're considering fishing it, check to make sure it's open. MDFWP enforces closures or restrictions to protect the fisheries on some rivers depending on water levels and water temperatures.

While the drought took its toll on the Jefferson, just as it did on many

Brown trout are the predominant species in the Jefferson River, though rainbow trout populations are booming thanks to the help from neighboring landowners and several conservation organizations. Be mindful of rehabilitation efforts and regulations as you explore the river.

THE RUBY RIVER

At the tail end of the Beaverhead River near Twin Bridges, the Ruby River brings a much-needed cold-water infusion to the system. While it's too small for it to compete with the other "big name" rivers in the state, it does provide a great reprieve for anglers visiting the area who want a change of pace from larger rivers like the Big Hole or Jefferson.

For years, the Ruby was known less for its fishing, and more for its pivotal role in the scene playing out between wealthy absentee landowner James Cox Kennedy, access advocates, and the county commissioners. The issue was whether the public could access the water where Kennedy's land intersected public bridges. In October 2008, a federal judge ruled that in fact yes they could, and in one swoop strengthened the state's unyielding stream-access law.

The river starts high in the Gravelly Mountains, and because it's surrounded by national forest lands, access abounds. Up here, you'll find mostly rainbows and cutthroat, and an occasional grayling, but treat these fish gently—the state is trying to establish their populations in the upper river.

It makes its way into Ruby Reservoir and flows out the other side into the valley where it twists and turns through ranches, farms, and trophy properties. The Kennedy case aside, the lower Ruby has few access points. "It's not a place you're going to plan your summer vacation around, but if you're in the area, it's worth stopping by for an afternoon or evening of fishing," Leavens says.

Wading anglers will find better fishing the farther they can move from access points, though the brushy banks make casting difficult at times. Floating anglers can also make a go of it, but if you think the narrow braids of the Beaverhead are tough to navigate, you won't like floating the Ruby.

"The Ruby is a place that I send guests that are here for a four- or five-day trip and they want to take a day for some nonguided fishing," Leavens says. "It's pretty small water, and while some people like to have the confidence of a guide next to them, a lot of people don't need one up there. Just throwing a Stimulator and a Prince dropper will land you a couple trout." ■

other rivers in the state, the Jefferson's saving grace has been the past few seasons' precipitation and snowfall accumulation. It's helped drive the river through some of the best seasons many have seen in some time. "In 2008, our water stayed up, and the water temps stayed fairly cool, and the river fished well from April through November. We're seeing some good two- and three-year age classes of rainbows, but I think we need a couple more years of good water," Leavens says. "Trout Unlimited has been doing some great work on Hell's Canyon Creek and Willow Springs Creek, and you can't fish around the mouths in April and May when the fish are running up there to spawn. It has done wonders for our trout populations."

The lower Jefferson is big water and flows through a landscape strikingly different from many of the state's other rivers. Floating the river allows you to cover more area, and you may find fish where few anglers venture.

Limespur fishing access site (best suited for anglers without boats) off MT 2 is next in line and a state-managed campground is downstream and open year-round (with showers, RV dump facilities, and rental cabins), perfect for the angler passing through.

Sappington Bridge and Williams' Bridge are two small sites downstream of the state park. It may seem like these two points are relatively close to one another, but at this point, the slow, wide nature of the river makes it tough to cover as much ground in a boat as you would in the upper river. In the summer, this is the low, warm, froggy water most fly anglers stay away from. In the fall, when water temperatures drop, these stretches and the foot access at Willow Creek Bridge can be worth revisiting. When it's fishing well, hoppers and large attractors work on the surface, but like the stretches of water before it, don't neglect streamers.

Drouillard is on the southeast side of Three Forks Road Bridge (MT 2). Three Forks Road connects with US 287 a few miles west of Three Forks. From here, you can float into and take out at the Missouri (River) Headwaters State Park (marked Missouri Headwaters on the map in this book).

Hatches and Flies

Timing is everything on the Jefferson, and there are small windows of opportunity in the spring before runoff, and again just as runoff subsides. Late March, April, and early May can offer some good fishing with nymphs and

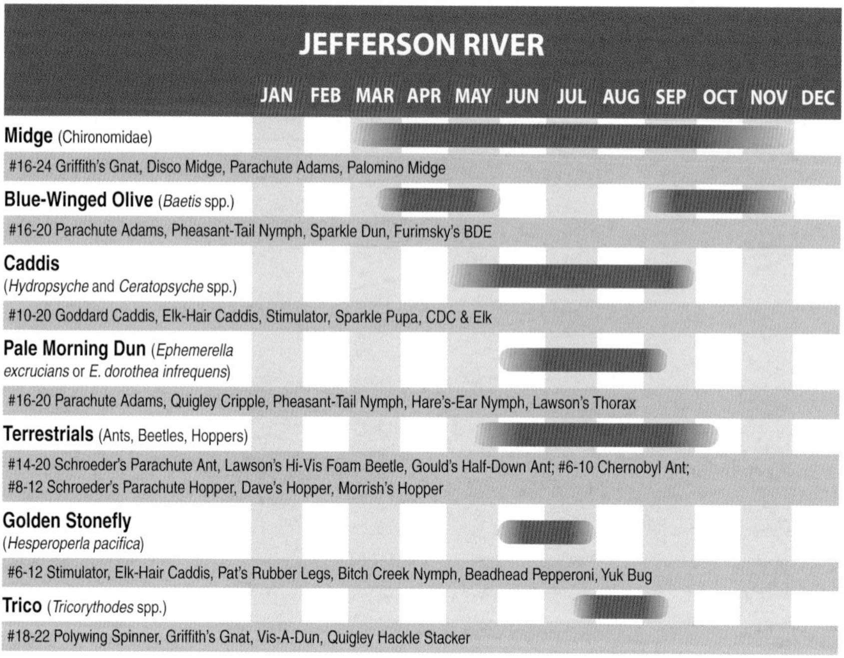

the occasional dry fly, but this early in the year, it's simply a matter of catching the river as it balances between its winter slumber and the sometimes sudden onslaught of runoff.

I've been lucky enough to be on the water when it's warm enough to bring out some spring stoneflies, *Baetis,* and caddis as well as a handful of fish willing to eat them off the surface. This is a rarity, and most fish won't be the 20-inch plus fish you'll find on streamers, but it's a welcome sight all the same.

"Generally, I'll fish starting around the Mother's Day Caddis. After runoff, we'll fish it till it freezes," Smith says. "Standard caddis patterns work well, but most times I will fish an emerger behind dry flies, like a LaFontaine Caddis Emerger."

Runoff hits hard sometime around mid to late May and can extend into July. The Jefferson is high, brown, and off-limits until you see levels beginning to drop. That's the good thing about early-season fishing on the Jefferson—it can still fish well with a foot or two of visibility. Like the Big Hole and Blackfoot, some anglers prefer tea-colored water over perfectly clear conditions. It allows you to get away with thicker tippets and shorter leaders.

The other abnormality on the Jefferson can occur after a heavy summer thunderstorm. Large amounts of rain muddy the water quickly and shake loose some of the moss and grass from the tributaries and stream bottom. This not only makes water clarity an issue, but the need to constantly clean moss from flies is annoying. If a thunderstorm has passed through the area, call a local fly shop for conditions before making the drive—you may want to fish other waters and give the Jeff a day or two to clean up.

If it's better-than-average year, and there is enough water to fish the river after runoff and through the tough months of July and August, you can encounter Yellow Sallies, a few PMDs, and more caddis than you can shake a stick at—especially in the evenings. Hoppers also have their place. "I think the Jefferson is one of the better hopper rivers because of all the hayfields and farming going on over there. There's a lot of terrestrial action in general—beetles, ants, hoppers," Marcum says. "It's one of the best terrestrial rivers."

With all the overhanging brush and grassy banks, it doesn't take a rocket scientist to figure out terrestrials fill the gap during the heat of the day when other hatches are stifled. But don't stop there. "I like to fish Chernobyl Ants for hoppers, and actually move them. Skate them, pop them, and put any kind of movement on them—especially if you're in dirty water. You've got to throw some motion on them or the fish aren't going to come up," Smith says.

"Most people come here and fish the river as an early-season and late-season streamer river. But it's also a midsummer river when we can keep it open. There is good hopper fishing, Brown Drakes, PMDs, and caddis."

This river truly shines in the fall. The landscape begins changing colors, water temperatures drop, irrigation demands diminish leaving more water in the system, and the brown trout are preparing to spawn. This is the time to pound the water with streamers; however, I have seen a few hefty caddis hatches that made me trade the sinking-tip line for a weight-forward floater.

Big flies equal big fish. I like experimenting with a variety of patterns and colors until I can find something that works with a reasonable degree of consistency. But if you ask a local, you can't go wrong with anything yellow.

"If you're fishing streamers, yellow and brown are the go-to colors. You can't beat a JJ Special. I get mine tied by a local, and he ties an immense amount of grizzly hackle into them. Then, depending on water conditions and clarity, we trim hackle from the middle of them," Smith says.

When it comes to streamer selection, guides and outfitters in the know say you can't go wrong with anything yellow. However, if you need some backups, try patterns with muted earth tones like black, brown, rust, olive, or tan.

Aside from the abundance of big, aggressive brown trout, another factor that makes the Jefferson such a great streamer river is the amount of natural foods that anglers can imitate with rabbit, marabou, and a few hints of flash such as leeches, small baitfish, and another food not often considered on Montana streams—crayfish. "Pepperonis are a good pattern to imitate the crayfish in that river. You can catch fish on those about every day of the year down there. Sometimes you strip them, sometimes you dead-drift them," Leavens says.

Directions

On the Jefferson many of the access points are near or next to bridges, making it somewhat easy to find the points and access the main roads after exiting the water. From Twin Bridges follow MT 41 north along the upper river for points like Hell's Canyon and Silver Star. A few miles after Silver Star, the road splits so follow MT 55 to reach Parson's Bridge (look for the signs pointing toward Waterloo a few miles north of Silver Star) and MT 2 in Whitehall.

Wherever you're driving in the Jefferson Valley, drive with caution in the early morning and evening. The whitetail deer population in this area has exploded, and they bounce back and forth across the road between fields.

MT 2 runs close to the middle portion of the river near Cardwell (with routes to Mayflower Bridge, Cardwell Bridge, and Limespur), joins US 287, and then emerges to run near the completion of the river's journey in Three Forks. This route will also take you through the Lewis and Clark Caverns State Park where there are a few roadside pull-offs and public campsites. I-90 also intersects the towns of Whitehall, Cardwell, and Three Forks (from which you can access MT 2, MT 55, or US 287) if you're traveling from elsewhere in the state.

Delektable Double Screamer

Hook:	#8 Tiemco 5262
Head:	Gold cone
Weight:	.025-inch-diameter tin wire
Thread:	Yellow 6/0 Uni-Thread
Body:	Gold Lite Brite dubbing
Rear Tail:	One yellow marabou with 4 yellow saddle hackles (splayed evenly)
Rear Wing:	Yellow grizzly chickabou
Connection:	Fifteen-pound fluorocarbon with 1/2" gap between hooks
Front Tail:	Yellow marabou with 4 yellow saddle hackles (splayed evenly)
Front Wing:	Yellow grizzly chickabou
Collar:	Yellow saddle hackle

Conehead JJ Special

Hook:	#2-10 Tiemco 5263
Thread:	Black 3/0 Uni-Thread
Head:	Copper cone
Tail:	Brown marabou feather topped with yellow marabou feather topped with copper Krystal Flash
Body:	Brown chenille
Hackle:	Grizzly saddle
Legs:	Yellow rubber (medium or large)

Beadhead Pepperoni Yuk Bug

Hook:	#4-10 MFC 7027
Bead:	Gold
Thread:	Rusty brown 6/0 Uni-Thread
Weight:	.6 mm lead wire
Tail:	Natural red fox squirrel tail
Rib:	Copper wire
Abdomen:	Black chenille
Thorax:	Burnt orange chenille
Legs:	White Centipede Legs (#2)
Hackle:	Furnace rooster saddle

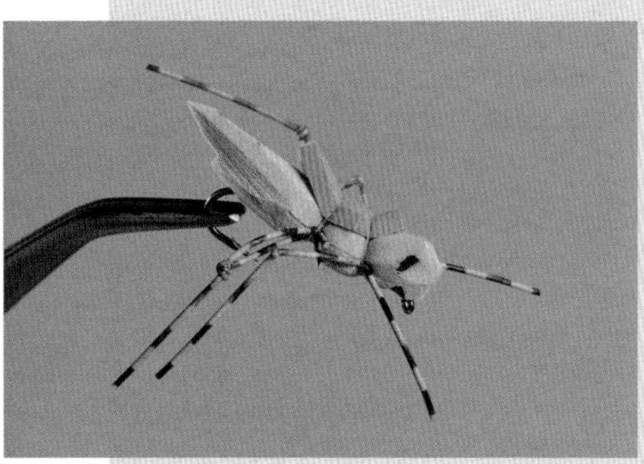

Morrish Hopper (Tan)

Hook:	#6-8 Tiemco 5263, #10 Tiemco 3761
Thread:	Beige 6/0 Danville
Eyes:	Burnt umber Chartpak marker
Body:	Cocoa 2 mm foam (2 layers) and tan 2 mm foam (1 layer), glued together
Legs:	Tan round rubber (medium) with brown barring
Indicator:	Orange 2 mm foam

Beaverhead River

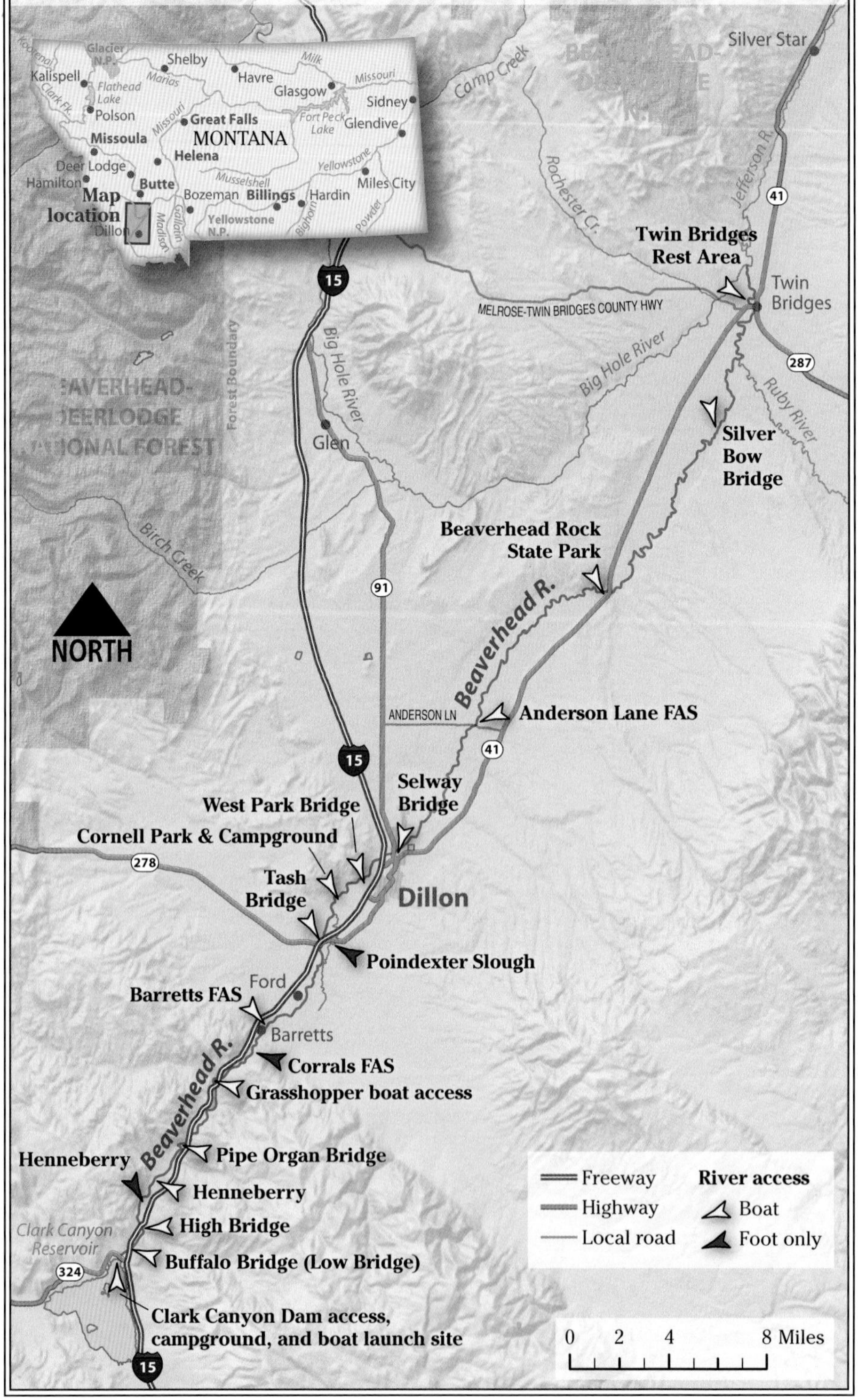

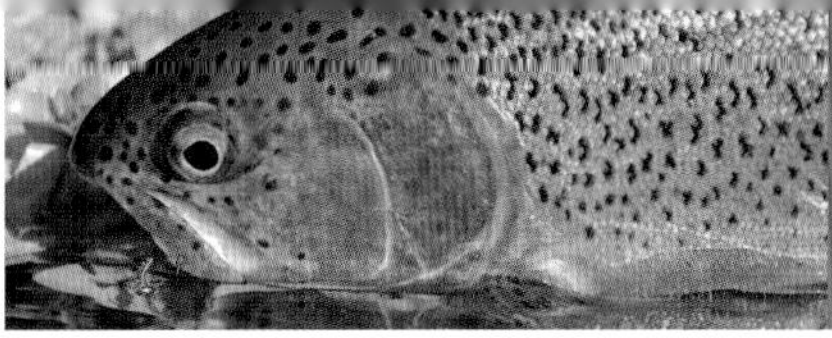

CHAPTER 6

Beaverhead River

Cold, clear water releases from Clark Canyon Reservoir, a healthy streambed that bolsters terrific aquatic insect hatches, and strict angling regulations are the three biggest reasons Beaverhead trout are able to pack on the pounds. But with so much going for them, fooling fish becomes significantly more difficult. They see a lot of food, a lot of flies, and just like the fish on many other tailwaters, these trout have perfected "the snub"—the moment when a particularly cruel fish approaches like it's going to strike, nearly touches the fly, and then turns away at the last moment). Dwelling in such tight quarters and dealing with the constant bombardment of flies nearly every day of the year, they've come to see a thing or two and the old-reliable patterns you dig out on the state's freestone waters don't fool "Beav" fish like they used to.

Since 2000, summers have been brutal in southwestern Montana. Fires, drought, and record high temperatures have forced full and partial closures on many of the state's waterways. The Beaverhead's blessing is that it flows through an arid landscape and there's little danger of forest wildfires flanking its banks. What's more, the bottom-flow releases from the reservoir maintain a comfortable water temperature for trout on days when freestone water temperatures approach 70 degrees. This makes the first 10 miles or so of the Beaverhead a solid alternative if you're forced to change travel plans because Mother Nature deals an unlucky hand elsewhere. From Dillon downstream, however, diversion dams and irrigation demands take their toll and the number of fish per mile declines substantially.

When flows are high (800 to 1,200 cfs) float fishing is the best method for tackling this river, though use caution in the deceivingly swift water. Powerful currents, willow-choked banks, and a slippery stream bottom make it tough to get a decent presentation otherwise. Boats are also a great tool for reaching side channels and backwater sloughs—favorite haunts for some of the river's largest trout and the ultimate challenge for anyone looking to test their spot-and-stalk fishing skills.

Unfortunately, there is no easy way to float the Beaverhead. I often joke there isn't a straight line on this river, and when you combine a series of twists and turns, high flows, and an armada of drift boats and rafts, it pays to have a skilled set of hands on the sticks.

The water between Clark Canyon Dam and Buffalo Bridge (aka Low Bridge) is the most popular on the river because it often produces the largest fish. To avoid crowds, plan your trip for the early morning or early evening when pressure is lighter.

Outside of the public-access points, private land boundaries and natural structure such as bankside willows make it tough for wading anglers to reach some areas of the river. So in my opinion, if you want to get the most out of a boat on the river, use it as a shuttle from hole to hole. In doing so, remember that sometimes the best fishing isn't along the banks or near structure; it's in the middle of the river, and the only way to reach it is to shore the boat, jump out, and run a few casts in slicks you would normally drift over.

Unfortunately, crowds and fly fishing don't mix, so courtesy and polite boat handling are a must. In areas where boats are anchored and fishing a particular run, it's sometimes impossible to float anywhere but over the pool they're targeting—but do it as quickly and quietly as possible. Don't slow the boat or cast over a fish someone else is pursuing.

"On the water, we strive to smile, say 'Hi,' and be polite, because everyone is out there for the same reason, and that is to enjoy themselves," Tim Tollett, owner of Frontier Anglers says. "Come late July things change and settle a bit. After the big bugs go away, the number of boats is a fraction of what it was and the fishing is just as good." Water levels usually drop later in the summer and hover between 300 and 500 cfs, making it easier to reach certain areas both on foot and from a boat. Rocks, short riffles, undercut banks, and overhanging branches are good places to look for fish, as are incoming springs and tributaries. At times, I've seen dozens of fish jockey for position below tributaries, some with their backs sticking out of the water, feeding on any appetizing morsel within reach.

"You have to fish this river a little differently than you would fish others," guide Leon Sagaloff says. "Look before you start flinging away. Most of the fish are caught really close to you. They'll be right at your feet. I'd rather have a guy that can cast 15 feet and get a good drift than a guy that can throw 40 feet and not get a good drift. The presentation is everything."

Coincidentally, as the water level drops, the amount of underwater vegetation often increases, providing fish with ample cover. They can hang out in the middle of the river inside the eddy of the largest chunks of swaying grass, or wedge themselves between a moss bed and undercut bank. "The moss comes in August, and it's hard to get a longer drift because your fly is going to get caught on something. But if you can find the little channels between the moss beds, you will find some fish," Sagaloff says. Granted, you have to clean the moss off your flies from time to time, but for the most part they slide through patches of underwater grass without a problem. Whenever I visit the Beaverhead it takes me a moment to get used to seeing the always changing swirls and eddies. Sometimes a haphazard swirl spinning from the tips of waving grass ruins the perfect drift.

When water levels drop to 300 cfs or lower (usually during the late summer when the growing season winds down) the fish become concentrated, and you will see many more fish than you will catch. It's also the best time to wade-fish since shallow areas make it tough to float. The river's large browns and rainbows can hold in only a few inches of water along the banks, near

As water levels drop on the Beaverhead, navigating by boat becomes more difficult. Instead, float to good areas, anchor the boat along the shoreline, and approach on foot. This tactic spooks fewer fish and leaves the main channel open to boat traffic.

tributaries, or next to undercut banks. They're accustomed to high angling traffic, and large fish will feed without abandon a few feet from you. One day I spotted an 18-inch rainbow in ankle-deep water feasting on spent Tricos almost directly behind my friend. Unbeknownst to him, I made a slack-line cast downstream, fed line into the drift, and fooled the fish into rising. Unfortunately, the hook pulled free, but the moment gave us a good laugh on an otherwise frustrating morning.

Where and When

The most popular area is below Clark Canyon Dam to Grasshopper access. In the 1990s, this area was subject to so much angling pressure the state enacted special regulations that dictate when outfitters and nonresident anglers can fish different sections, depending on the day of the week. Though this helped alleviate some crowding issues, the Beaverhead's width still makes it feel like one of the most crowded waters I've ever fished.

The campground and access just below Clark Canyon Dam on the western shoreline is the uppermost access. The boat ramp is unimproved, but since it's the highest point anyone can launch on the river, it's popular. The whirling pools on the left and right of the dam's outflow have plenty of fish to target, though catching them is another issue altogether.

The outflow of Clark Canyon Dam attracts hordes of trout, and in the early morning and late afternoon, it's tough to continue downstream when dozens of noses are rising behind you. Try a few casts if you must, but make them count—the fish are wise to the game and won't fool easily.

Below Henneberry, Beaverhead trout seem easier to catch. Blind-cast along the banks as you float downstream, but keep a careful eye open around every corner for any rising fish.

It's a short float from the dam to Buffalo Bridge (Low Bridge). This public access is nearly invisible from the road, and a gravel pathway along the southern edge of Armstead Campground makes it appear as a private launch. From here, the river follows a frontage road and eventually intersects the High Bridge access—so named because of the elevated highway bridge (I-15) that looms overhead. The unimproved boat ramp and small parking area make this access a popular one for short floats. It's also a good spot for wading anglers to jump in and work downstream when water levels are 300 cfs or lower.

There are two Henneberry access points on the Beaverhead River downstream from High Bridge. The southern access is for foot traffic only; the northern (nearly two miles downstream) sits next to a small bridge and affords a place to load or unload a boat. From the Henneberry boat ramp floating anglers can cover a healthy portion of the Beaverhead and take out at Grasshopper. If you put in late, however, look to Pipe Organ Bridge just a couple of miles downstream. One of my favorite summertime schemes is to

POINDEXTER SLOUGH

Poindexter Slough is sometimes crowded in the summer, but this slow, spring creek–like neighbor of the Beaverhead has great hatches (midges, small mayflies, Tricos, and caddis) and large, smart fish. Long, light leaders and small flies will be your best bet, but on rare occasions the fish prowl the bankside willows for beetles, ants, and hoppers.

"There are more big fish in the slough now than there ever have been. Some are rainbows, but 98 percent of the fish are browns. I caught more fish over 20 inches there last season than I have in the past 30 years put together," Tollett says. There is a public access site approximately 3 miles south of Dillon off MT 41 near the Tash Bridge. ■

float the upper river early, relax through the heat of the day, and float again from Henneberry to Pipe Organ during the waning evening hours. Not only do I rarely see anyone else fishing, but the fish are seemingly more willing to rise when evening caddis are popping.

The river twists, turns, and forks a few times below Pipe Organ Bridge. This makes for some tight quarters if you're in a boat, but keep an eye out for good wade-fishing areas and use the boat more as a shuttle, at least until channels rejoin on the downstream side of islands and it's easier to maneuver.

"We all love the upper river, but I like Hennebery down to Grasshopper or Barretts as much as anything. It's quieter, less boats, and has plenty of fish—though maybe there are not as many big ones. To me it's like a different river," Sagaloff says. "One thing I like to do is go from Henneberry to Pipe Organ, which is a really short float. But with good water conditions and patient clients you can make that a whole day. Same with the dam to Buffalo Bridge or High Bridge."

The river straightens and the flow picks up in the last mile just upstream of Grasshopper. I almost always switch to streamers or large terrestrial patterns and pound the banks from a boat since there's nowhere to run but the middle of the river. It's one last opportunity to pick up a fish or two before reaching the Grasshopper boat ramp. During runoff, Grasshopper Creek pushes a decent amount of muddy water into the system, so if you're looking to begin your float here, check the conditions first so you're sure to have clear water downstream.

From Grasshopper to Dillon the fish are less concentrated but also less finicky. Given that, it doesn't receive as much pressure from anglers. Before you decide to drift it, remember Barretts diversion dam cuts the flow substantially (and requires a portage) greatly affecting its navigability, and what's left flows mainly through private land with limited access.

Fishing prospects decline from Dillon to the junction of the Ruby River outside Twin Bridges. In the summer, irrigation demands, water temperature, and limited access make for tough fishing. When water temperatures drop in the early fall, conditions improve, but plan your put-ins and take-outs carefully to avoid unnecessarily long days on the water. In some cases, drought or other issues may force trout from the Big Hole or Jefferson up into the lower Beaverhead.

Hatches and Flies

By and large, nymphing is the most effective technique on the Beaverhead, especially in the upper river between the dam and Henneberry. Dry flies have their place, but I keep them stashed unless I'm targeting a specific rising fish. It doesn't matter if you're casting from the bank or a boat, it's hard to beat a two-fly nymph rig and indicator—though some go without "a bobber" under the theory that Beaverhead fish are so smart, they've learned to recognize what they mean. My exception to the rule is downstream of Hennebery or Pipe Organ Bridge where I've had some success blind-casting terrestrial and caddis patterns while floating in the evening and early morning.

Common tippet sizes range in the neighborhood of 3X through 6X. That said there's a price to pay for going light, and finding a balance between hooking fish and not breaking the line is sometimes tough. There is also the issue of overplaying fish. While the last thing you want is your 6X tippet to snap while fighting a 22-inch brown that just sipped your spent Trico, a 20-minute battle isn't healthy for the fish.

"I like to use long leaders that go 12 or 15 feet, but they're not light. Guys that have never been here before come into the shop and buy 6X and 7X. They may hook a lot of fish, but they won't hold them," Sagaloff says. "Last spring I had some guy that said 'screw this 4X, I want some 2X' and we were fishing size 16 and 18 flies. I figured I'd humor the guy, and we were whacking one after another with 2X. And he didn't lose any fish either."

When it comes to hatches on the Beaverhead, one noteworthy improve-

Beaverhead trout often congregate around tributary mouths as levels drop, and in many cases, you can sight-cast to fish.

ment over the last few years is the abundance of mayflies. "We're seeing extended hatches over longer periods of time—as well as mayflies we've never seen on the river before," Tollett says. "The dry-fly fishing was great this past year. This fall there were so many mayflies on the water—Pseudos, Tricos, Blue-Winged Olives—all mixed together in different forms, all at once. It was some of the best, most challenging dry-fly fishing I've ever had."

Baetis hatches seemingly begin and end the fishing season on the Beaverhead. In March through May and again in early fall they're one of the most sought-after food items both above and below the surface. Size 16-20 Pheasant-Tail Nymphs imitate the river's tiny *Baetis* nymphs and are by far one of the most popular patterns on the river, but in recent years some other imitations like the Split-Case BWO have come to the forefront.

Summer caddis hatches on the Beaverhead are incredible, but you have to be willing to fish until dark to get the best action. Skitter a sparse pattern across the surface if dead-drift presentations aren't working.

Caddis are another prevalent species up and down the river. In the summer they can hatch by the thousands in the evening after many anglers head back to their lodges; so if you want to make the most out of your trip, eat dinner early and return to the river until dark (but bring mosquito repellent) for some good dry-fly fishing. It shouldn't be a problem seeing rising fish, but enticing them to strike is sometimes tricky. Beaverhead guide Joel Silverman recommends throwing a little action into the fly to make it stand out.

"In the evening, there are huge caddis hatches and Pale Evening Dun spinners and there's nobody around," Silverman says. "When I'm fishing caddis hatches, I like patterns that are sparsely dressed and sit low on the surface, or even slightly under the water. After the cast, I mend upstream and present the fly on a dead-drift; but toward the end of the drift, I'll keep a tight line, slowly raise my rod tip, and add a twitch now and then to make it look like a fluttering bug trying to get off the water. If you can get the fly to make the slightest wake on the water, you're doing it right. The fish chase it and you can get some hard strikes."

Stoneflies, while not considered a signature hatch on the river, squirm out of the rocks in July. Nymph patterns take most of the trout, but if you pitch some low-riding dry patterns among the willows and banks while the early season water levels are at their highest, you can turn heads. Look to the lower river from Pipe Organ to Dillon for some of the best action.

"Not a lot of people talk about the Beaverhead's Golden Stone hatch. Once you start seeing the little Yellow Sallies on the upper river, Golden Stones will pop on the lower river, typically around July. They're not as consistent as they are on other rivers, but when it's there, it can be a lot of fun, and it's not fished heavily," Silverman says.

Midges, PMDs, and terrestrials round out the peak-season selection. If you bring an array of attractor and specific nymphs like Copper Johns, Barr Emergers, Hare's-Ear Nymphs, and of course, the San Juan Worm (and variations like Silverman's Sparkle Worm) you can cover most bases. I like to fish two flies separated by 16 to 20 inches of tippet and a small indicator set at 1½ to 2 times the depth of the water I'm dredging. Reaching the bottom is crucial, so if my bugs aren't bouncing off the rocks, I'll add a small piece of weight above the point fly, but this usually only occurs when I'm running through the deepest, fastest water.

Next to caddis, Tricos are my favorite hatch on the Beaverhead. Appearing sometime around the middle or end of July, they offer somewhat consistent morning action well into September. If you want to hit the meat of the hatch, get on the water as early as possible. As the sun rises you'll start to see bugs dancing and have some areas of the river all to yourself. This will also help you beat the wind—a sometimes nasty element of the valley that can shut down the best Trico action in a matter of minutes.

"Tricos are underrated below Hennebery. Some days they'll go until noon, especially if it's a cloudy, cool morning. It's not fishing to big pods of fish. You'll mostly see singles or small groups of three or four. You're head-

BEAVERHEAD RIVER

Hatch	JAN	FEB	MAR	APR	MAY	JUN	JUL	AUG	SEP	OCT	NOV	DEC
Midge (Chironomidae)		■	■	■	■	■	■	■	■	■	■	
#16-24 Griffith's Gnat, Disco Midge, Parachute Adams, Palomino Midge												
Blue-Winged Olive (*Baetis* spp.)			■	■	■				■	■		
#16-22 Parachute Adams, Pheasant-Tail Nymph, Sparkle Dun, Rusty Spinner, Tollet's PT Cruzer, Tim's Smidget, Split-Case BWO												
Grannom Caddis (*Brachycentrus occidentalis*)				■	■							
#12-16 Glass-House Caddis, Elk-Hair Caddis, Z-Wing Caddis, Deep Sparkle Pupa												
Caddis (*Hydropsyche* and *Ceratopsyche* spp.)					■	■	■	■	■			
#10-20 Goddard Caddis, Elk-Hair Caddis, Stimulator, Sparkle Pupa, CDC & Elk												
Pale Morning Dun (*Ephemerella excrucians* or *E. dorothea infrequens*)							■	■	■			
#16-20 Parachute Adams, Quigley Cripple, Pheasant-Tail Nymph, Hare's-Ear Nymph, Harrop's PMD Cripple, Lawson's Thorax, Copper John, Barr Emerger												
Terrestrials (Ants, Beetles, Hoppers, Crickets)					■	■	■	■	■	■		
#14-20 Fur Ant, Gould's Half-Down Ant, Fire Beetle; #8-12 Lawson's Henry's Fork Hopper, Parachute Frankenhopper, Schroeder's Parachute Hopper												
Yellow Sally (*Isoperla* spp.)							■	■				
#14-16 Elk-Hair Caddis, Gould's Half-Down Yellow Sally												
Trico (*Tricorythodes* spp.)							■	■	■			
#18-22 Polywing Spinner, Griffith's Gnat, Vis-A-Dun, Quigley Hackle Stacker, Gould's Chernobyl Gnat												
Crane Fly (*Tipulidae* spp.)								■	■			
#8-18 Barr's Crane Fly Larva, Mackay Special, Beadhead Prince Nymph												
Spruce Moth (*Choristoneura occidentalis*)								■				
#8-10 Elk-Hair Caddis, Stimulator, MFC Spruce Moth												

hunting. They love the backwater—swirly pools around the corners of the river—and that type of water makes it tough to present a fly, so you have to pick a fish and work it from the pocket. When the fish are in backwaters like this, I like to use cluster patterns like Griffith's Gnats and Gould's Chernobyl Gnats," Silverman says.

Even though the Beaverhead is a tailwater, you won't always be fishing flies size 18 and smaller. In the late summer, crane flies also start darting across the surface. Resembling mosquitoes on steroids, these leggy bugs skate across the surface of the water and provoke some violent surface strikes from the river's browns. "Use a long rod when you're fishing crane-fly dry flies and skate them across the surface. You can dead-drift them and get a fish to hit, but if you skate them you get some really good action. To me it's more exciting than Salmonfly fishing," Sagaloff says. Nymphs like Barr's Crane Fly Larva work well under the surface. Above the waterline, some say you can get away with an assortment of patterns, including locally tied custom flies available at the fly shops, as long as they're actively fished.

"There are all sorts of crane-fly patterns out there, but sometimes I get away with just using a big Dave's Hopper and a size 8 or 10 Beadhead Prince Nymph. You need the big hopper not just to hold up that heavy nymph, but you want it riding high enough that you can still skitter it," Silverman says. "It's really killing two birds with one stone since the crane flies show up in August when the hoppers are still out. Cast toward the bank, keep your rod tip high, and slowly dance the fly across the surface with a jumpy motion. This is best in the early morning and late evening unless it's a cloudy, overcast day."

Like on other rivers in the southwest portion of the state, August's Spruce Moths are coming on in stronger numbers over recent years. A simple #12-14 Elk-Hair Caddis tied with a light body does the trick. If the fish are eating the spent naturals, splay the elk-hair wings for a more realistic profile. "We'll go through the slick just fishing dry flies and outfish the nymph guys," Sagaloff says. "It can be some fabulous fishing that's overlooked."

Streamers have their place on portions of the river. Don't expect to bounce them behind boulders and near logjams like you would on the Blackfoot or Big Hole. Instead, look for undercut banks and soft water between the middle of the river and shore. "Streamer fishing is good everywhere. On really cloudy, nasty, classic streamer days you're just getting hit

While it's fun to cast dry flies to Beaverhead trout, nymphing is the most effective technique on the river. If possible, use a two-fly rig with enough weight to fight the river's swirling currents and keep your flies in front of fish.

after hit," Sagaloff says. "I've thrown them on sunny days for a change of pace, especially if I'm with guys that want to learn how to do it, and we'll still pick up fish."

Because it is a tailwater, the cold water from the reservoir makes it different from most other rivers in the state—freestone rivers susceptible to warming and closures. Even on 100-degree days, the Beaverhead fishes. "It's never too hot to fish the Beaverhead. This tailwater delivers insect action throughout pretty much any day of the year." I've been on the Beaverhead when the summer days are so hot I can't even find relief in the shade, so why torture myself? When it's burning into the high 90s and the sun is high, I like to limit my time on the water to the early morning and evening hours. I don't have to fight the crowds through the meat of the day, and I don't become burned out from sunrise to sunset marathon sessions. Instead, I fish until sometime between lunch and midafternoon and then grab a stool at the Buffalo Jump Saloon on the hill overlooking the dam. It's a great place to enjoy the air conditioning, get a drink, a bite to eat, and recharge my batteries. Once the sun starts to set, I head back to the water and finish off the day.

Directions

I-15 connects the town of Dillon with both Clark Canyon Reservoir and the Beaverhead River. To reach access points, look for the frontage road (also called High Bridge Road) just east of exit 44 off I-15. This road drops down into the valley and leads you to High Bridge, Henneberry, Pipe Organ, and Grasshopper, but you can get into the river wherever it bumps into the road, like "the slick" between Buffalo Bridge and High Bridge (just make sure you pull completely off the shoulder first). To reach the access below the dam, head northwest across the dam from exit 44, and take the first right. The dirt road winds down to a camping/recreation area at the base of the dam.

The middle river access points include Corrals (no boat ramp), Barretts, Tash Bridge near Poindexter Slough, Cornell Park and Campground southwest of Dillon, West Park Bridge in Dillon, and Selway Bridge near Clark's Lookout State Park.

Many of the access points for the lower river branch off MT 41 between Dillon and Twin Bridges. Heading north from Dillon you can reach Anderson Lane, Beaverhead Rock, Silver Bow Bridge, and the town bridge on the south side of Twin Bridges. The current is slow down here, so put in early or plan to stay late to complete such long floats.

No mention of the Beaverhead River would be complete without noting its important place in history. The Lewis and Clark expedition visited the area several times and recorded their observations in journals. The handful of parks, markers, and interpretive signs along the river valley signify each place's importance as it relates to those historical events—including the Beaverhead Rock landmark recognized by Sacajawea in their search for her tribe.

Tollet's PT Cruzer

Hook:	#12-18 Tiemco 2488H
Bead:	Tungsten
Thread:	Dark brown 8/0 Uni-Thread
Tail:	Olive pheasant tail
Body:	Olive pheasant tail
Rib:	Amber Ultra Wire (small)
Thorax:	Bronze peacock Arizona Synthetic and olive Ice Dub blended together
Wing Case:	Brown Scud Back
Wing:	Pearl Krystal Flash

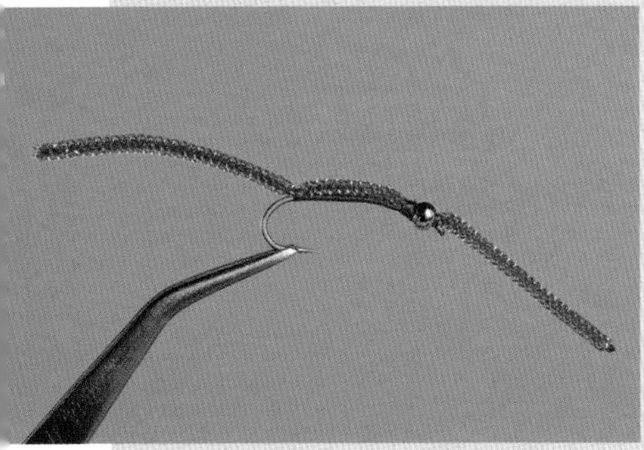

Silverman's Sparkle Worm

Hook:	#8-10 MFC 7045
Thread:	Pink 6/0 Uni-Thread
Bead:	Gold
Body:	Pink pearl Core Braid

Split-Case BWO

Hook:	#18-22 Tiemco 3761
Thread:	Olive 6/0 Uni-Thread
Underwing:	.5 mm olive foam
Wing Case:	Brown goose biot
Tail:	Mallard flank dyed wood duck
Legs:	Mallard flank dyed wood duck
Body:	BWO Superfine
Rib:	Monofilament

Barr's Cranefly Larva

Hook:	#8 Tiemco 200R
Thread:	Olive or tan 70-denier Ultra Thread
Weight:	Lead wire
Body:	Arizona Simi Seal dubbing
Tail:	Marabou
Rib:	Monofilament
Shellback:	Tan Thin Skin

Big Hole River

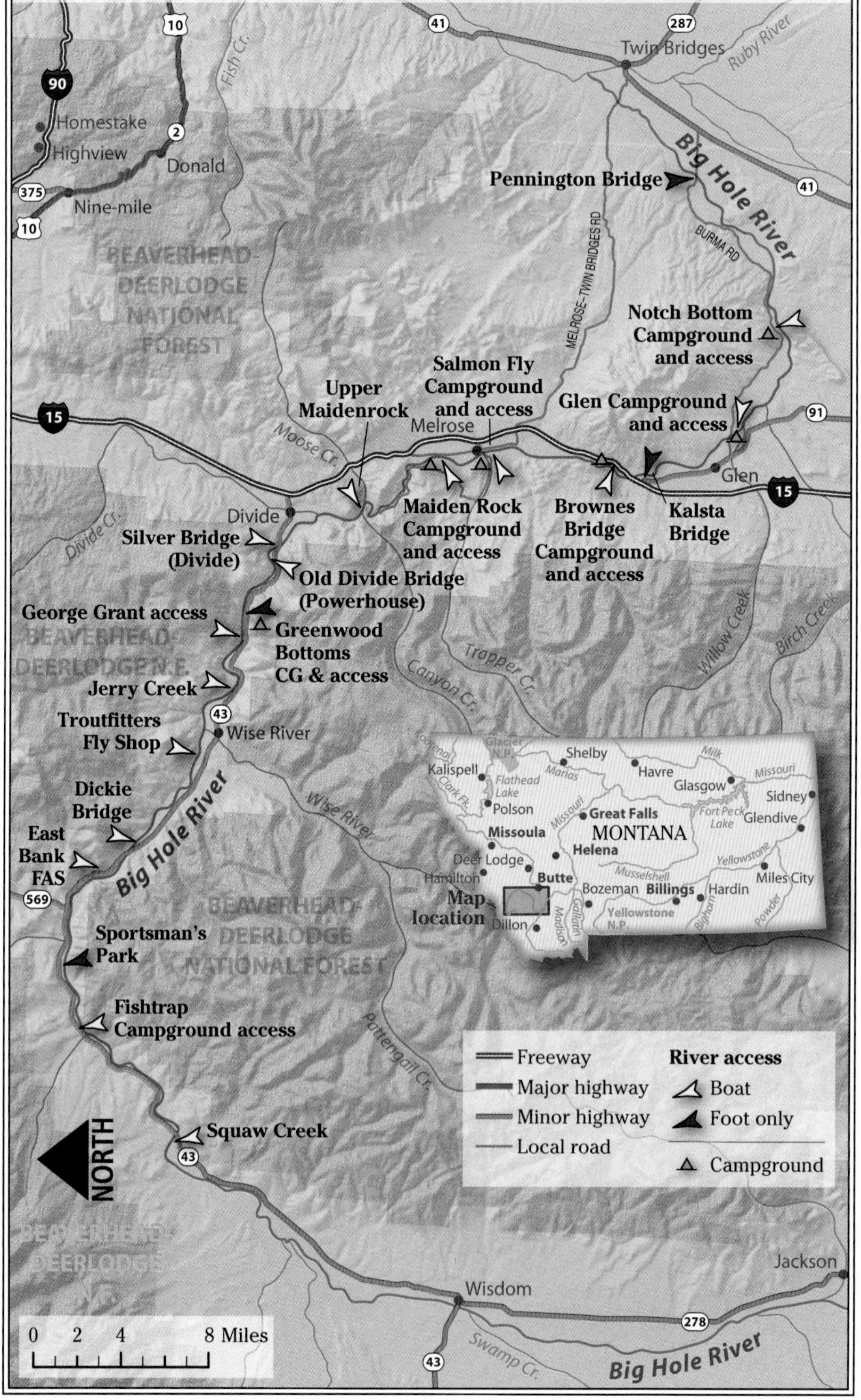

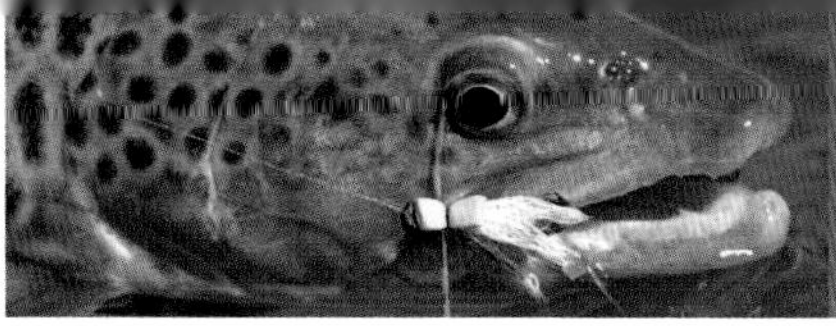

CHAPTER 7

Big Hole River

The Yellowstone and Madison river valleys set the standard by which many anglers judge the beauty of Montana's other waters. Open basins, towering mountain peaks, and an abundance of wildlife make these areas popular among those looking for breathtaking scenery and great fishing. However, for my money, I'll trade the Yellowstone or Madison for the Big Hole River any day of the week. There isn't a stretch on this system that doesn't make me sit back and gaze in complete awe. From the upper half's long meandering meadow stretches, to the lower river's dry, desertlike canyons, the Big Hole is a magical place to fish.

Where and When

Created from the outflow of Skinner Lake just inside Beaverhead-Deerlodge National Forest, the Big Hole begins as a high-mountain stream that snakes through private ranches, gaining volume on its way toward Wisdom. Relatively few anglers travel to this portion of the river, though there are a handful of access points along Skinner Meadows Road. It isn't until the junction of the North Fork of the Big Hole that the river takes the shape most fishermen are familiar with. This upper river between Wisdom and Wise River is by far my favorite. Forested slopes, rolling hillsides, and the distant snowcapped peaks of the Beaverhead and Pintler mountains make each turn look like something from a postcard.

"The upper Big Hole is a unique area. You can go in there and catch what I call a Big Hole grand slam, which includes a cuttie, whitefish, cuttbow, rainbow, brown, grayling, and brookie. And it's one of the only places in the United States that you can do it," Four Rivers Fishing Company owner Greg Smith says. "The chance to catch a nice brookie is always there. They typically shut down the upper river above Dickie Bridge by mid-July to protect the grayling during low flows."

Fish populations in the upper river are not as strong as the lower sections, but the quality remains somewhat consistent until the warm water temperatures of late summer push them downstream. You will find a fair number of brown trout and an occasional rainbow, but it's the brook trout that keep me

The canyon portions of the Big Hole are incredibly popular, and they're one reason the state enforces specific boating policies depending on the day of the week. Make sure you comply with regulations before launching a boat.

coming back. Some of the finest brookies I've landed (many over 16 inches long) were between the Squaw Creek, Fishtrap, Sportsman's Park, East Bank, and Dickie Bridge accesses—all of which are off the shoulder of MT 43 between Wisdom and Wise River. Try pitching small black or olive streamers that represent leeches or sculpins below any cold, clear inflow from tributaries or irrigation runoff.

"The upper river is good for big fish in the early season. You won't catch as many, but I've found the bigger browns hang out in that area. It warms up fairly quickly, so after runoff it's the pits," StoneFly Fly Shop co-owner Mike Marcum says.

Drought and insufficient winter snowfall has hurt the entire Big Hole in years past, but it's the fish of the upper Big Hole that get the worst of both extremes—an unbelievably cold, sterile, ice-covered canopy in the winter and

As water levels drop, look for side channels, sloughs, and other water passages branching off the main stem. In some cases, these waters go untouched and can offer some challenging dry-fly fishing. JAY NICHOLS PHOTO

low, warm flows in the height of summer. Keep an eye on water levels and temperatures, and if conditions are stressful to fish limit your time on the water to early morning and evening hours or relocate to another stretch of water. The Montana Department of Fish, Wildlife and Parks often closes the water or enforces strict angling restrictions to protect what populations remain in the upper river through the summer, so be alert for any notices posted at public access points.

Travel north from Wise River on MT 43 a few miles toward Divide and Melrose and you'll acquire a uniquely different experience as you enter what locals call the canyon stretch. The smooth, spring creeklike nature of the upper river becomes intermittently interrupted by riffles, fast-water runs, side channels, boulders, and other structure. A tight mountain corridor suddenly cuts off the views of the sweeping hillsides, and before you know it the terrain is an experienced oarsman's game from Jerry Creek to Powerhouse (sometimes called Old Divide Bridge), especially during high flows. If you're not intimidated, some of the best the Big Hole has to offer anglers is within the canyon stretch.

If you're short on time, consider the Dewey site (sometimes called the George Grant Memorial site) on the north side of MT 43 to Powerhouse float. For the wading angler, there is Greenwood Bottoms about 1.5 miles downstream (east) from Dewey. This area has plenty of fish—including some that push the tape over 20 inches—but with that sort of notoriety comes the angling traffic, so remember your manners.

Most floaters use the Powerhouse (Old Divide Bridge) access and primitive boat ramp almost exclusively for a take-out. A large, dangerous diversion dam just downstream of the bridge makes the area between Powerhouse and Divide Bridge (Silver Bridge) downstream nearly impossible to float, but the state is discussing plans for a possible portage route in the future. If you're fishing on foot, there are some solid wade-fishing opportunities here, especially upstream of the bridge. The riffles, pockets, and eddies behind the rocks are great for bouncing off a wicked-looking foam attractor. Some nice fish live in this stretch, and once the craziness of Salmonfly season winds down, it's worth revisiting on foot. Turn northeast on Powerhouse Road from MT 43. The road is short and drops down onto the bridge. Parking and the boat ramp are on the north side.

Downstream of the diversion dam is the Divide Bridge (Silver Bridge) site on the southwest side of MT 43. Much of the water between here and the upper Maiden Rock area is wide and open like the meadow stretches of the upper river. It is popular during stonefly season though because the brush-

The upper Big Hole's soft, meandering meadow stretches are a stark contrast with the lower river's rocky canyons. However, warm water temperatures can endanger fish in the summer, so restrict your fishing to times that don't stress trout. NICK ROMANS PHOTO lined banks are a haven for stoneflies, and as high-water tapers off it's a great time to float and pitch big patterns around and under the vegetation. Some say the highest fish-per-mile counts are from Silver Bridge downstream.

Upper Maiden Rock (there are two Maiden Rock access points that locals typically differentiate by calling them Upper and Lower Maiden Rock) marks the beginning of the famous Maiden Rock canyon stretch. Popular because of its scenic qualities and fish populations, this area sees the most traffic when Salmonflies appear. A frontage road intersects with MT 43 near Divide. Maiden Rock Road connects with the frontage road a few miles south of Divide. It's a dusty, bumpy dirt road that drops down into the canyon and connects with the river. There is a large parking area on the east side of the river, but the boat ramp is on the west side, slightly upstream from the bridge.

Lower Maiden Rock is a little tougher to reach. From the town of Melrose, take Trapper Creek Road (CR 40) west. It crosses the river (where you'll see the Salmon Fly access) and works up into the hills. Maiden Rock Road branches off to the north and works back toward the river's western shore. After passing Meriwether Ranch Estates, the road passes several pull-offs and small camping areas where you can jump out and walk to the river. There is a sign and campground at the Maiden Rock site. If you have trouble finding either Upper or Lower Maiden Rock, ask for directions at any of the local fly shops and they'll put you on the right path.

When stoneflies are hatching in June and July, dozens of boats put in at Divide Bridge, Upper Maiden Rock, or Lower Maiden Rock, float the canyon, and take out at Salmon Fly (stay river left—the river forks and the access is in the left channel near a bridge neighboring the town of Melrose). The seclusion of the canyon, fast-water runs, and big bugs draw people from all over the world, but once the flows drop and the fishing pressure spreads out more evenly across the state, this stretch remains a terrific place to fish. In years when drought conditions and river closures aren't such an issue, the areas up and downstream of Divide and Melrose are some of my favorite places to fish Tricos.

After Melrose, the valley opens up, and there are a handful of other access points like Brownes Bridge, Kalsta Bridge, Glen, Notch Bottom, Pennington Bridge, and High Road before the river merges with the Beaverhead near Twin Bridges and forms the Jefferson. Look for some of the river's largest browns near fallen timber, inside seams bordering sharp banks, side channels (of which there are many), and any other structure that creates "ambush" pockets.

Brownes and Kalsta bridges are close to one another and easy to reach from the frontage road between Melrose and Glen. After the town of Glen, turn east on Burma Road to reach the Glen access. It's on the southwest side of the bridge before crossing the river. Continue on Burma Road, winding along the bottom of the hills, and you'll eventually work back to the river and Notch Bottom. To reach Pennington Bridge, you can stay on Burma Road or drive around on MT 43 toward Twin Bridges and turn west on Pennington Bridge Road. The last access on the river is High Road, though high water recently destroyed this site, and at the time of this writing, the MDFWP has no plans to reconstruct it. In the event they do rebuild the access, from MT 43, turn west on Melrose Bench Road approximately one mile south from Twin Bridges.

This area is also a good choice if you're looking for some early- or late-season action. In most years the upper river remains under a blanket of snow and ice well into spring (Wisdom is one of the coldest towns in the state), and since the river doesn't receive much sunlight in some canyon segments, it takes time for the river to warm up enough that fish are motivated to feed. Nymph rigs (with stonefly patterns) are the weapons of choice, but if you're lucky enough to hit the water during a warming trend, slow-stripped streamer patterns fished deep can also yield results.

"The streamer game from Melrose down is different than what it is upriver. Up by Wise River the river is wide and shallow. From Divide and Melrose on down you get more pocketwater and deeper pools, especially down to the end of the river. But there's still some rocks and good structure to fish around," Montana Fly Company fly-shop owner George Goody says.

In the fall, the browns are packing on the pounds before winter and can hit streamers with ferocity. If you're a big-fly enthusiast, revisit the lower river at this time. The climate makes for a pleasant day on the water, and you can find solitude as the tourism season winds down.

Hatches and Flies

Fishing on the Big Hole can kick off as early as March depending on weather patterns and water temperatures and extend into mid-May. Diehards looking for that early-season fix can find smatterings of *Baetis,* midges, March Browns, and *Skwalas,* but it is mostly a nymphing affair. Being the case, why would anyone hit the Big Hole this early in the season? Simple. It's one of the few times you can seemingly fish an entire day and see only a handful of anglers. Postrunoff crowds on the Big Hole are legendary, so while you may catch fewer fish than you would in the peak of the season, you can travel downstream without playing bumper boats.

"Early season is day-to-day. If you get a little warm weather and runoff, and river is on the rise, it's not going to fish well. But typically, as spring approaches and we get a mix of cold and warm weather fronts, the river goes through this up-and-down trend. When it's on the drop, it fishes very well. In April and May, I typically tell people to spend at least five days here. You will have good fishing, you just have to work with what Mother Nature is giving you. Those can be some of the best days of the year," Sunrise Fly Shop co-owner Ryan Barba says. "We have *Skwalas* on the lower river, especially from Maiden Rock downstream toward Pennington Bridge. Though it can be tough to hit, you get those days where it's really good."

If the Salmonfly hatch is the number one event on the Big Hole, then the Mother's Day Caddis hatch has to be a close second. It typically starts and ends

While many anglers visit the Big Hole when the big Salmonflies are present, mayfly hatches, like PMDs and Tricos, keep fish looking up through the rest of the season. JAY NICHOLS PHOTO

a week or two before Mother's Day, but the holiday acts as a good reminder to watch the weather patterns, water temperatures, and streamflow gauges. At its peak, this hatch looks like an explosion of fluttering tan wings dancing and darting above the water, near brushy banks, and eventually into the mouths of surface-feeding fish. Size 12-14 Goddard Caddis, Elk-Hair Caddis, Stimulators, and tan Spotlight Caddis are good patterns.

"The Mother's Day Caddis is off the charts. It's as good as it gets anywhere," Smith says. "During blanket hatches, you want to fish something different than an exact imitation. Fish have so much to choose from, you sometimes can't convince them to eat your bug. Wait for the hatch to wind down; then you can pluck them one at a time."

Although spectacular, the Mother's Day Caddis hatch is typically short-lived and flirts with the beginning of runoff. Sometimes you hit epic fishing; other times the hatches are sporadic or the fish never key in on them. Finding fishable hatches is a tough balance between water temperatures and weather patterns. A mounting trend of warm weather slowly brings the water temperature up without flushing the system with snowmelt. But a sudden and drastic rise in daytime temperatures, though it may put some bugs in the air, will bring on the muddy water. Given these temperamental thresholds, the Mother's Day Caddis is typically the last hatch worth targeting before runoff rears its ugly head.

Runoff typically begins near the middle of May and lasts several weeks depending on snowfall amounts and daytime temperatures. The fishing, however, can kick-start again with only a foot or two of visibility (perfect for streamers) and the flows begin to diminish. If you're trying to coordinate a trip, keep in touch with the local fly shops as they see the water daily, can somewhat predict streamflows, and let you know what is working.

Without question the marquee hatch on the Big Hole are the Salmonflies. In years past there have been so many anglers converging on the lower river, the boat ramps and access sites have populations that rival neighboring towns. The key is patience and courtesy. Don't block the ramps while you load or unload your gear, and remember that wading anglers need space too.

The tea-colored Big Hole is a great river to fish streamer patterns, especially as runoff subsides. Use patterns with earth tones such as brown, olive, black, and yellow.

The Salmonfly hatch typically begins on the lower river and migrates upstream a few miles a day. While some local guides and outfitters claim you'll catch the biggest fish if you stick with nymphs like a brown Pat's Rubber Legs, it's hard to resist the temptation of throwing #4 dry flies on short, stout tippets.

Salmonflies are haphazard fliers that crash to the water, so do not be afraid to slam large dry patterns onto the water near bushes or any structure hanging over the water. Then add an occasional twitch or two for the illusion of a struggling bug. I've found this makes my fly stand out from any naturals and shows the fish something different when many others are simply dead-drifting their flies.

Once the madness of the Salmonfly season ceases, expect hatches of Green Drakes, PMDs, Yellow Sallies, Tricos, hoppers, and caddis to give you pockets of opportunity through the heat of the season. When it comes to dry-fly selection on the Big Hole, however, don't get pigeonholed into thinking specific imitations are the only way to go. You may be on the water witnessing the biggest hatch of *Baetis* you've ever seen in your life, but for some reason, the fish are willing to eat a #8 Stimi Chew Toy with just as much enthusiasm. I don't have the same experience anywhere else—but attractor patterns, for whatever reason, appeal to these fish. If you aren't seeing fish rise to specific naturals, or they aren't interested in the imitation you're offering, go with the buggiest attractor in your box.

The Spruce Moth hatch in late July and August is another headline, though the intensity of the hatches can vary from year to year. "The Spruce Moth hatch is crazy, though it won't always be a thick hatch," Marcum says. "A biologist from California told me it's not really natural for Spruce Moths to come off in droves. When there are huge emergences, it's just part of a cycle with peaks and valleys depending on the year. They [biologists] really don't know a whole lot about it so if you have a year or two where the bug numbers aren't strong, look to the following years for activity to be a little better."

These light tan, slightly mottled soft-winged bugs look strikingly similar to caddis, so nearly any light-bodied caddis pattern like a simple Elk-Hair

Caddis, small Stimulator, or spent pattern like Lawson's Spent Partridge Caddis works. Whatever pattern you choose, splay the wings as you dress the fly with floatant to imitate the way the naturals fan their wings when they struggle to escape the water.

"There are a lot of people that fish Salmonflies and the Trico hatch because they like the abundance of bugs in the air and seeing reckless fish on the surface," Barba says. "But few pay any attention to the Spruce Moths, and in the past few years it's been one of our best hatches. The bugs hatch in pine trees, move around and mate over the water in the mornings, and since they're such clumsy fliers, they come crashing into the river. Fish love them. And because it's midsummer when water is lower, you're able to fish #12-14 patterns to fish holding in a few feet of clear water. It's exciting stuff."

In midsummer to late summer, hoppers line the banks and a twitched parachute or foam pattern near any type of vegetation or structure is aces. Guide Joel Silverman says one of his favorite patterns from July to September is a #12 Black Magic, which is a cricket and grasshopper imitation. There are also plenty of beetles and ants to warrant a change-up now and again. "People don't fish ants and beetles enough," Marcum says. "I've been out on days when flying ants were everywhere and you could fish ants and beetles on two-fly rigs all day long. Sometimes the Tricos come out as well and we fish a #10-12 beetle or ant with a Trico or Purple Haze behind it."

While the Trico hatch on the Big Hole is one of my favorites, their intensity has waned in recent seasons. While the fish are up on them, myself and other area outfitters haven't seen the massive clouds of bugs on the lower river that were common in the late 1990s. Some blame the drought and the

In the height of summer, imitations for terrestrials such as beetles, hoppers, crickets, and ants are some of the most effective dry-fly patterns.

BIG HOLE RIVER

Hatch	Patterns	JAN	FEB	MAR	APR	MAY	JUN	JUL	AUG	SEP	OCT	NOV	DEC
Midge (Chironomidae)	#16-24 Griffith's Gnat, Disco Midge, Parachute Adams, Palomino Midge, Zebra Midge			X	X	X			X	X	X	X	
Blue-Winged Olive (*Baetis* spp.)	#16-20 Parachute Adams, Pheasant-Tail Nymph, Sparkle Dun, Purple Haze, Furimsky's BDE				X	X				X	X		
Skwala Stonefly (*Skwala parallela*)	#6-10 Gould's Half-Down Skwala, Schlotter's Rogue Foam Stone, Gould's Wiggle Skwala			X	X	X							
March Brown (*Rhithrogena* spp.)	#12-14 Comparadun, Parachute Adams, Gray Wulff, Flashback Pheasant-Tail Nymph				X	X							
Grannom Caddis (*Brachycentrus occidentalis*)	#12-16 Glass-House Caddis, Elk-Hair Caddis, Z-Wing Caddis, Deep Sparkle Pupa, Goddard Caddis, Spotlight Caddis, Stimulator					X							
Caddis (*Hydropsyche* and *Ceratopsyche* spp.)	#10-20 Goddard Caddis, Elk-Hair Caddis, Stimulator, Sparkle Pupa, CDC & Elk, Peeking Caddis						X	X	X				
Pale Morning Dun (*Ephemerella excrucians* or *E. dorothea infrequens*)	#16-20 Parachute Adams, Quigley Cripple, Pheasant-Tail Nymph, Hare's-Ear Nymph, Harrop's PMD Cripple, Lawson's Thorax						X	X	X				
Terrestrials (Ants, Beetles, Hoppers)	#14-20 Schroeder's Parachute Ant, Lawson's Hi-Vis Foam Beetle; #6-10 Trixie the Hooker Hopper, Black Magic; #8-12 Dave's Hopper, Schroeder's Parachute Hopper						X	X	X	X			
Salmonfly (*Pteronarcys californica*)	#4-8 Bitch Creek Nymph, Pat's Rubber Legs, Stimulator, Rogue Foam Stone, Romans' Thing From Uranus					X	X						
Golden Stonefly (*Hesperoperla pacifica*)	#6-12 Stimulator, Elk-Hair Caddis, Pat's Rubber Legs, Bitch Creek Nymph, Stimi Chew Toy						X	X					
Yellow Sally (*Isoperla* spp.)	#12-16 Elk-Hair Caddis, Gould's Half-Down Yellow Sally							X	X				
Mahogany Dun (*Isonychia* spp.)	#14-18 Pheasant-Tail Nymph, Quigley Cripple, Rusty Spinner, Comparadun						X	X	X				
Brown Drake (*Ephemera simulans*)	#10-12 Parachute Adams, Lawson's Brown Drake Paradrake, Olive Hare's-Ear Nymph						X	X					
Green Drake (*Drunella grandis*)	#8-10 Quigley Cripple, Lawson's Green Drake Paradrake, Nealley's Green Drake						X	X					
Gray Drake (*Siphlonurus occidentalis*)	#10-14 Gray Wulff, Parachute Adams, Quigley Cripple							X	X	X			
Trico (*Tricorythodes* spp.)	#18-22 Polywing Spinner, Griffith's Gnat, Vis-A-Dun, Quigley Hackle Stacker, Purple Haze								X	X			
Spruce Moth (*Choristoneura occidentalis*)	#8-10 Elk-Hair Caddis, Stimulator, MFC Spruce Moth, Lawson's Spent Partridge Caddis								X	X			

The upper Big Hole is one of the last remaining refuges for fluvial grayling, but it's also home to some large brook trout. Look for fish along soft-water breaks or close to tributaries.

increased sedimentation, but others say it's cyclical. "The good Trico fishing is mainly from Maiden Rock down to Notch Bottom. Hit the river early in the morning and you can have as much fun as you want," Smith says.

While Salmonflies, caddis, and a host of terrestrials have no trouble bringing the big boys to the surface throughout the season, I am a firm believer in going deep and going big in search of those fish over 20 inches. The Big Hole is a terrific river for streamer fishing. When flows are up, I like to use weighted patterns and a sinking-tip line. Later in the season I'll switch to a floating line and smaller, lighter ties. I'm addicted to the rush that comes from seeing big fish ambush a streamer. So when the water is clear and slow, I retrieve my pattern just beneath the surface where I can see it. Occasionally I'll let it dip a few feet, but I never lose sight of the silhouette.

"In May, when the upper river thaws, there is great streamer fishing above Jerry Creek. The water isn't as high above where the Wise River enters it," Barba says. "The streamer fishing is prime when the river gets that good tea color in the spring with only two feet or so of visibility." Most local guides and fly shops agree that yellow streamers are the winning ticket. A few favorites are appropriately a Yellow Yummy and a yellow JJ Special, as well as Kelly Galloup's Dungeons.

Directions

The most popular (and easiest to access) portions of the Big Hole are an easy reach from MT 43. If you're in the Bitterroot Valley, a simple jump across Chief Joseph Pass from US 93 puts you in Wisdom (stop by Fetty's for breakfast and the Antler Saloon in the evening for drinks and pizza). If you're near Dillon or coming from Butte, take I-15 south and exit at Divide, Melrose, or the interchange with MT 278 to reach the river.

Between Divide and Glen a highway frontage road (MT 91) will help you connect with both Maiden Rock access points, as well as Salmon Fly, Brownes Bridge, and Glen.

Later in the season, when Tricos arrive, get on the water early because the activity tapers off as the sun rises. Look for rising fish at the head and tailout of pools below riffles, but expect to encounter a few whitefish as well.

To reach Pennington Bridge and Notch Bottom take Burma Road via either the frontage road south of Glen or from MT 43 a few miles southwest of Twin Bridges. The High Road access is just west of Twin Bridges near the mouth of Rochester Creek.

Conehead Yellow Yummy

Hook:	#2-10 MFC 7008
Cone:	Gold 6 mm
Thread:	Yellow Nymo thread
Weight:	.8 mm lead wire
Tail:	Yellow marabou blood quill and pearl Flashabou Accent
Rib:	Copper wire
Hackle:	Yellow rooster saddle
Body:	Yellow chenille
Legs:	Yellow Centipede Legs (#2)

Black Magic

Hook:	#6-12 MFC 7022
Thread:	Black Nymo thread
Body:	Black foam
Underwing:	Pearl Flashabou Accent
Wing:	White calf tail
Legs:	Orange Barbed Wire Scaled Sili Legs
Indicator:	Orange foam

Sculpzilla

Hook:	#4-8 Gamakatsu Octopus #2408
Shank:	Mustad 34007 cut short
Thread:	White 6/0 Uni-Thread
Cone:	Black nickel Cross Eye
Eyes:	Red stick-on eyes
Tail:	Olive-variant rabbit strip
Body:	Pearl Ice Dub
Gills:	Red dyed guinea
Collar:	Olive marabou
Thorax:	Golden olive grizzly chickabou
Connection:	50-pound Spectra

MFC Spruce Moth

Hook:	#10-14 MFC 7000
Thread:	Tan 6/0 Uni-Thread
Rib:	Tan Nymo thread
Hackle:	Cream saddle hackle
Body:	White Antron dubbing
Wing:	Bleached cow elk

Pat's Rubber Legs

Hook:	#4-10 Daiichi 2220
Thread:	Brown 6/0 Uni-Thread
Weight:	Lead wire
Body:	Brown chenille
Legs:	Olive-brown Super Floss

Rock Creek

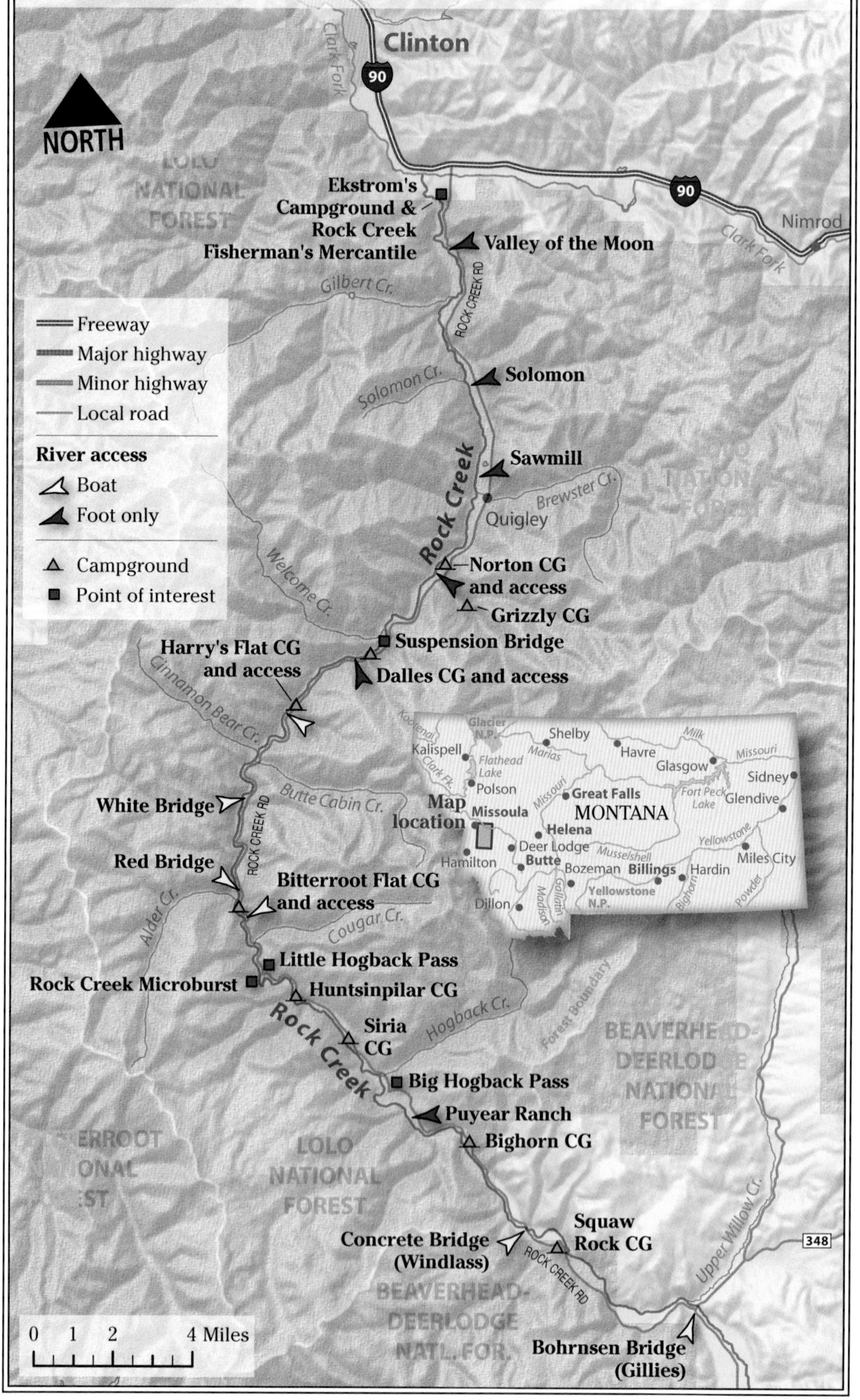

Clinton
90
Clark Fork
NORTH
LOLO NATIONAL FOREST
Ekstrom's Campground & Rock Creek Fisherman's Mercantile
Valley of the Moon
Nimrod
Clark Fork
ROCK CREEK RD
Gilbert Cr.
Freeway
Major highway
Minor highway
Local road
River access
Boat
Foot only
Campground
Point of interest
Solomon
Solomon Cr.
Sawmill
Rock Creek
Brewster Cr.
Quigley
Welcome Cr.
Norton CG and access
Grizzly CG
Suspension Bridge
Harry's Flat CG and access
Dalles CG and access
Cinnamon Bear Cr.
Butte Cabin Cr.
White Bridge
Red Bridge
Bitterroot Flat CG and access
Alder Cr.
Cougar Cr.
Map location
Kalispell
Shelby
Havre
Glasgow
Sidney
Polson
Great Falls
Glendive
Missoula
MONTANA
Helena
Deer Lodge
Butte
Hamilton
Bozeman
Billings
Hardin
Miles City
Dillon
Yellowstone N.P.
Little Hogback Pass
Rock Creek Microburst
Huntsinpilar CG
Siria CG
Hogback Cr.
Forest Boundary
BEAVERHEAD-DEERLODGE NATIONAL FOREST
Big Hogback Pass
Puyear Ranch
Bighorn CG
LOLO NATIONAL FOREST
Concrete Bridge (Windlass)
Squaw Rock CG
348
Upper Willow Cr.
BEAVERHEAD-DEERLODGE NATL. FOR.
Bohrnsen Bridge (Gillies)
0 1 2 4 Miles

CHAPTER 8

Rock Creek

Rock Creek is the first river I ever fished in Montana. I was so enthralled with the scenery, the fish, and my experience, it became the river I measure all others against. For anyone who's cast into its tumbling pools or driven along the water on its neighboring pothole-laden road, it's easy to see why the angling community reveres this river. "If you are a wade fisherman, Rock Creek is pretty much where it's at. It's not a big river like the Clark Fork, it's easy to read, and there is plenty of access," Flint Creek Outdoors manager Matthew Churchman says.

Nevertheless, its reputation for beautiful scenery and hard-fighting fish has turned Rock Creek from a secret into a worldwide destination. That's not to say you can't find solitude on the river, you just have to be smart about when you visit and where you fish. Some argue the best time to fish the creek is during the peak of the Salmonfly hatch, but the early and late edges of the fishing season also offer quality fishing and reliable hatches. Before runoff, March Brown and *Skwala* stonefly hatches get fish looking to the surface, but unpredictable spring weather patterns keep many anglers away. Most days start and end with freezing temperatures, but this is a great time to fish the creek.

The same holds true for the late season. In the early fall, hatches of caddis and occasional mayfly hatches provide decent action on the surface and consistent hookups underneath. While many sportsmen take to the hills in search of deer and elk, brown trout are migrating from the Clark Fork to spawn. On some days you can have entire stretches of water to yourself, which is uncommon through the rest of the season.

Like many other waters in western Montana, Rock Creek has had its share of struggles. Drought, whirling disease, and more recently wildfire plagued the river at one time or another. Despite these problems, it continues to be a first-class fishery; and in many seasons, while other river flows dipped below average, Rock Creek's flow rate remained above average nearly the entire season.

In 2007 a wildfire raged on the creek's west side, forced the evacuation of several homes, and effectively closed all access to the water for over a month. Rock Creek Fisherman's Mercantile owner Doug Persico reported that when

While Rock Creek has gone through tough times, including forest fires and the threat of whirling disease, it remains one of the healthiest rivers in the state. It's one of the few places where you have the chance to catch cutthroat, brown, and rainbow trout in a single day.

the smoke finally cleared and the road reopened, the fishery was vibrant and catch rates were up.

On the whirling-disease front, Persico's opinion is the creek is following the same path as the Madison River. A few rainbow-trout age classes were lost but quickly replaced by a growing population of brown trout. Furthermore, he said catch rates of juvenile rainbows are slightly rising, though he doesn't believe they'll eventually outnumber the browns.

Cutthroat, rainbow, and brown trout between 8 and 18 inches make up most of the fish in the river, but don't be surprised to catch a bull trout at some point. They are a threatened species but their populations are becoming stronger, and while accidentally catching one is a treat, it is illegal to intentionally pursue them. If you hook one, release it immediately. Montana game wardens are not shy about approaching anglers who appear to be purposely targeting these fish.

Camping sites are plentiful along the entire length of the river and make it easy to maximize your time on the water. Most are complete with picnic tables, fire rings, and outhouses while others are more primitive. Whichever site you choose, respect other campers. Too often, I've traveled to the water expecting a peaceful weekend only to have a neighboring camper blast music or party late. Have a good time, but not at the expense of someone else's experience.

The last thing that sets Rock Creek apart from other waters in the state is the road that follows its length. It's dusty and bumpy in the summer, icy and snowpacked in the winter, and you should always expect to face a speeding car around every turn. The nice thing is you're almost always within eyesight of the river, and there is access to nearly every portion. Respect other drivers, the creek's residents, and the wildlife by driving with caution. There's nothing more irritating (and dangerous) than coming around the top of Big Hogback and seeing a speeding SUV coming from the other direction. Go slow around blind corners and pull off to let others pass if there is space.

Where and When

Rock Creek actually begins as three separate streams. The West Fork of Rock Creek starts in the steep mountainous terrain of the Sapphire Mountains near Hamilton. Receiving much of its volume from snowmelt and natural springs, the West Fork weaves through the terrain and ultimately parallels Skalkaho Highway (MT 38), a seasonal dirt road between Rock Creek and the Bitterroot Valley.

The Middle Fork begins deep in the Anaconda-Pintler Wilderness. Much of this small stream is accessible by Forest Service roads but rarely fished. The East Fork forms from the outflow of the East Fork Reservoir and continues outside the Beaverhead-Deerlodge National Forest boundary before finally joining the Middle Fork.

Rock Creek has abundant access. Use the pullouts and parking areas, but don't be afraid to gain some distance from the road up- or downstream. You'll often find better opportunities and less-pressured waters. NICK ROMANS PHOTO

All three converge and form the main stem near the intersection of Skalkaho Highway and Rock Creek Road where it flows north through several private ranches before reaching Bohrnsen Bridge (formally Gillies Bridge). Fences and no-trespassing signs buffer the upper river, but there are one or two places where the absence of blockades allows you to jump into the water. This is good to know if you're looking to escape the more heavily fished portions downstream, but upper Rock Creek doesn't always fish as well as the lower half.

From Bohrnsen Bridge downstream to the next one, Concrete Bridge (called Windlass Bridge on a USGS topographical map), the river has good fishing for browns and cutthroat for those who are willing to walk. Access is plentiful but many anglers simply park, jump in the water, and rarely leave sight of their cars. This stretch winds through ranches, next to private property boundaries, and is sometimes shadowed by rock bluffs, but if you are mindful of the high-water mark, there shouldn't be any problems working anywhere on foot.

The water between Windlass Bridge and Big Hogback Pass (near mile marker 31) is some of my favorite. With the exception of runoff, it's swift but intimate water surrounded by what I believe to be the best scenery Rock Creek has to offer. Large red-rock cliffs, open meadows, and steep forested hillsides make it a magical place to fish.

The suspension bridge on the lower river is one of Rock Creek's most famous landmarks. The pools up- and downstream from this area are great for streamer fishing, but don't spend too much time in one spot. After making a few good presentations, move on to another pool.

The Puyear Ranch (also known as the Morgan-Case Homestead) is a popular public access point just upstream of Big Hogback and one of my favorite sections on the river. The Forest Service purchased the property, placed it on the national register of historic places, and recently completed renovations on a public cabin rental (check the Lolo National Forest website for reservation information). There are a few places to park around the ranch as well as trails leading to the water.

Downstream of Big Hogback the river is mostly riffles broken up by large rocks and small gravel islands, though there are occasional deep pools under the bridges, on the outside corners, and near logjams. Rock Creek Road follows the water closely so access isn't a problem, but this also means the water is fished often. The farther you can work from the road the better. Make a few casts in any fishy-looking pocket, seam, or eddy and head to the next spot. The fish in Rock Creek are aggressive enough that if I don't get a taker after a few casts I move on.

Little Hogback (another steep switchback between mile marker 26 and 27) and the Microburst area neighbor each other. In spring 1988 a microburst, a sudden downdraft of hurricane-force wind, plowed across the river and valley knocking over everything in its path, including a few automobiles. A swath of fallen trees remains.

Much of the space between the hogbacks remains unseen from the road, but this doesn't mean it isn't accessible. The few cabins and chunks of private property are clearly marked. The rest is public land, so feel free to park and hike through the trees until you reach the water. Unfortunately, many people never see this part of the river because they'd rather fish in sight of their cars. One of my favorite areas requires a short hike through the woods near an old Forest Service cabin around mile marker 29.

The water feels wide and fast in this stretch, and it may seem like much of it is flat or has little character. Look for fish in the small pockets formed by fallen logs, subtle riffles that drop off into pools, or undercut banks. Walk carefully on the slippery rocks (I recommend cleated soles) because it's easy to lose your footing.

The area immediately upstream and downstream of the microburst has more character and wonderful fishing, though it sees a fair share of anglers. This portion has the steepest elevation drop, so the water is faster, cooler, and more aerated than other stretches.

After the microburst, the river and road become close neighbors once again, and it's easy to spot likely pools and holding areas while driving. The area on both sides of Bitterroot Flat Campground has some terrific water, but make sure you pull completely off the road before getting your waders wet even if it means driving away from where you want to fish and backtracking on foot. The width of the road, the potholes, fallen rocks, and other debris make Rock Creek Road barely wide enough for one automobile, especially between Little Hogback and the Dalles access. Be courteous and make sure there's plenty of room to pass before you park.

FISHING THE SALMONFLY HATCH

Fishing the Salmonfly hatch on Rock Creek has become a circus. The popularity of the river, the bugs, and the fish draw people from all corners of the world, and the boat traffic gets downright nasty. If possible, fish during the middle of the week when traffic is sometimes lighter or float earlier or later in the day when traffic isn't at its peak.

If you really want to avoid the crowds, wait until the hatch is slowing down before heading for the water, or fish the lower portion of the river where the hatch has already passed by. You may not catch as many fish, and you won't see the hundreds of bugs flying through the air, but you won't be playing bumper boats either. Even though the bugs have moved upriver, the fish will still move on imitations. In fact, most of them will have digested their fair share of Salmonflies and will be looking for more, which can play in your favor.

Fishing the Salmonfly hatch is fast-paced action. The water is moving fast and you have to be on your game to hit the pockets and slow-water breaks before you float past them. If your arm isn't sore and tired at the end of the day, you didn't try hard enough. Cast and drift your patterns near any vegetation or structure both in the middle of the stream and off the bank. Salmonflies are clumsy fliers and always fall off leaves, branches, and grass, especially when the wind blows. Don't be afraid to lose flies. Placing patterns tight to logs, islands, and bushes is the key to catching fish during this hatch.

This bug's appearance usually coincides with spring runoff and the river is high, tea-colored, and littered with so many obstacles it feels more like a slalom course than a freestone river. By the end of the day, your arms are exhausted and hands full of blisters—but it's worth it. Fun aside, the water's turbid nature and the likelihood of running into logjams, rocks, or other debris make this float for experienced oarsmen only—the ability to quickly maneuver a boat and avoid trouble is crucial. Boats are punctured and lost every year, so let common sense be the rule. With that in mind, I recommend rafts over hard-sided drift boats because of the numerous obstructions and the occasional need to portage.

If you decide floating Rock Creek is in the cards, a ten- to twenty-mile trip is customary. It may seem like a lot of water to cover, but the current is swift and it doesn't take long to go far. The portion between Concrete Bridge (Windlass) and Harry's Flat is the most popular, though some launch below Bohrnsen Bridge and take out at Bitterroot Flat. For a shorter float, look to the Bitterroot Flat, White Bridge, or Red Bridge as possible launches and takeouts. For news on flows, logjam locations, and any other crucial information, call or stop by the Rock Creek Fisherman's Mercantile (406-825-6440) or Flint Creek Outdoors (406-859-9500). The river is closed to floating from July 1 through the end of November. ■

Between Bitterroot Flat and Harry's Flat campgrounds there are plenty of places to pull off and jump in the water. There are even some areas where the outside bends of the river are the deepest portions and best fished from the side of the road. Look for fish in riffles that drop into deep pools, slow-water channels (there are a few small islands in this stretch), and slack water behind logs and rocks.

Below Harry's Flat, the 5-mile section of the river known as the Dalles is some of the gnarliest yet gorgeous water on the river. It's a streamer fisherman's dream, littered with huge boulders, crystal clear water, bottomless pools, and eddy after eddy. Unfortunately, I have not found the Dalles to be as productive as the rest of the river. I have caught trout on nymph and streamer rigs, but not with the consistency as other locales. Despite this fact, I never pass without probing at least a few of the pools—you never know when it might be your lucky day. Apparently, it has that effect on others as well. Cars are parked in at least half the pullouts whenever I drive by.

If you're like me and can't resist stopping, by all means get out and fish it, but don't let the pools mesmerize you for too long. I give myself 15 to 30 minutes to fish through as many pools and pockets as I can. If it's not producing, I pack up and move on.

The swinging cable bridge near mile marker 11 is one of the most recognizable landmarks on Rock Creek. It's a popular place to stop for photos, use the outhouse, or swing a streamer even though you know you're the eighth person to fish the hole that day. From this point to the junction with the Clark Fork River, the creek has some great holes to nymph during the late season as well as some slow runs where you can target rising fish.

From here to the junction of the Clark Fork is where walking away from access points can really pay off. The last few miles of road are paved, and it's the easiest section to reach from Missoula, which means two things: it receives the most pressure and anglers pound any water within eyesight of the road all

Accessibility is one highlight of Rock Creek. However, the farther you walk up- or downstream from common parking areas, the more solitude and unpressured fish you'll find.

season long. This valley is also a residential area, making it tough to reach some holes unless you stay below the high-water mark and walk from a designated public access point. Do yourself a favor and walk up- or downstream along the banks and out of sight of the road or access before you start fishing, especially if you know the next access point is a distance away. You will see more water and more fish. Norton Campground and Sawmill access are two good examples of where walking can put you in better water.

In most years, the area between mile marker 4 and Valley of the Moon (mile marker 2) is a great place to find side channels and sloughs off the main river, especially as high water recedes. Though some channels are shallow, there are some good pools created by logjams or riffles. I've had some fantastic PMD fishing in these channels, and they're a good way to get away from the road.

Just downstream from Valley of the Moon, the river and road separate for the last time. You can park and work your way behind Ekstrom's Stage Station to the junction of the Clark Fork, but keep in mind you'll pass a campground and several other private access points where someone else may have the same idea as you. This water has some great pools, riffles, and pockets.

Lastly, for a few days at the end of summer, Rock Creek is a madhouse. The annual party known as the Testicle Festival (locally referred to as the "TestyFesty") sponsored by Rock Creek Lodge near the junction of I-90 and Rock Creek Road attracts hordes of people from all over the Northwest who want to eat deep-fried bull testicles and drink lots of alcohol. Naturally, festi-

Though you probably won't catch any record fish, Rock Creek trout average a solid 12 to 16 inches and are perfectly suited for a 3- and 4-weight rod.

valgoers fill up the campgrounds on the lower river. The festival dates change from year to year, but it's something to keep in mind if you want to avoid crowds. This is typically a rated-R event, so leave the kids at home if you decide to attend.

If you're not the camping type, there are several cabins available for rent throughout the corridor. Some are available for a quick weekend trip while others require a week stay. Many are located on the water and are great if you plan on fishing with a large group. Visit rockcreektroutbums.com for more information on rentals. Rock Creek Mercantile also has several nice motel rooms for rent. Call Doug Persico at (406) 825-6440 or visit rcmerc.com.

Hatches and Flies

Cold temperatures, snow, and ice don't make Rock Creek a viable option for anglers until early spring at best, and even then it's a gamble. Because it flows through such a tight, mountainous corridor, the middle river sees little sunlight or warmth until later in the season, so you're better off sticking to either the extreme upper or lower sections of river. Those areas receive much more sunlight, so the water warms enough to get the bugs moving much sooner in the season. One word of caution: the cold temperatures and Rock Creek's slippery bottom are nothing to laugh at. Bring a change of clothes (or two if you're clumsy like me) in case you go for a spill.

Midges, Blue-Winged Olives, and tiny black stoneflies will be the first to hatch, but such tiny meals do little in the way of getting the fish to feed in such cold water. In mid to late April, March Browns, *Skwalas,* and a few caddis usually start fluttering over the water and get the fish's attention. "We get a great March Brown hatch," Doug Persico says. "And we're getting more and more *Skwalas* up here all the time. Spring fishing is good overall, but we never seem to have as many fishermen in the early season as we should." This is a great time to fish nymph rigs with a Hare's-Ear or Pheasant-Tail Nymph as the lead fly and a heavily weighted stonefly as a dropper. If your weighted flies aren't getting down in swift Rock Creek, add some weight to the leader. If the weather is cooperative and the fish are feisty enough to feed on the surface, you can switch to #12-18 Parachute Adams or small Bullethead Skwala patterns.

When Rock Creek fish aren't chowing stoneflies on the surface, they're eating nymphs. They're large, full of protein, and an easy target for any fish even if they're streaking by in the current of a fast-water chute. Big Beadhead Prince Nymphs, Kaufmann's Stonefly, and rubber-leg patterns like Bitch Creeks or Pat's Rubber Legs are good for starters. Without a doubt, the most famous stonefly hatch on Rock Creek is the Salmonfly. Not only do these hummingbird-size bugs bring nearly every fish in the river to the surface, but they bring every angler that owns a boat to the water.

The appearance of Salmonflies typically coincides with receding spring runoff, and as the water levels drop and the water clears, the fishing can be epic. This is also the best time to float the river (the entire river is closed to

boats after June 30). You probably won't catch a trophy, but you will have plenty of opportunities at average-size fish. "I tell people to switch to a less outlandish and more realistic #6 pattern, especially later in the hatch. The smaller, more realistic flies that sit low in the water typically work better than the bushy, huge patterns," Churchman says.

Golden Stones appear after the height of the Salmonfly hatch and usually peak when Salmonflies are tapering off. Though they aren't as large, they are

If you're willing to endure the ever-changing weather patterns, early spring offers the chance to fish Rock Creek when angling pressure is light. Skwala *stoneflies,* Baetis, *and March Browns keep fish in the mood to eat, and on some of the warmest days, you may even be treated with some dry-fly fishing.*

more plentiful, equally attractive to the fish, and fuel the action until the river is either too low to float or closed to boats. If you're lucky, you may encounter Golden Stones and Green Drake hatches on the same days. In fact, Persico often recommends fishing Golden Stone patterns through the Salmonfly hatch and continuing as the Goldens slowly disappear. They're prolific enough that the fish stay on the prowl for them even when their numbers are few.

After the stonefly hatches die down, Rock Creek gets a little break from the traffic. You can still expect to encounter other anglers in some of the best stretches, but it won't be as crowded as the early season. Other rivers in the state are coming into shape and pulling away some of the angling pressure.

Summer hatches include a gamut of mayflies like Green Drakes, but the PMDs offer another great chance to target fish feeding on the surface. Comparadun-style patterns, parachute patterns, and lightly dressed CDC flies like René Harrop's CDC Biot Emerger or CDC Floating PMD Emerger are good choices.

The appearance of summer terrestrials like hoppers and ants is a welcome sight. At a time when water levels are dwindling and the summer heat pounds the water, the sight of a big hopper meal landing on the water can make trout giddy. Because hopper patterns are usually large and buoyant, tie a nymph dropper to appease those fish feeding under the surface. Or, if you don't want the extra weight, trail a small ant imitation off the back. If the hoppers aren't working, and no other naturals are in sight, switch to attractor patterns.

In recent years, the Spruce Moths have increased in numbers, especially on the lower river, and captured the attention of anglers. For the most part a #10-12 light-colored Elk-Hair Caddis works fine, but any similar splayed-wing pattern should work as well.

Stoneflies are like candy to Rock Creek trout, and fishing a two-fly nymph rig that includes a stonefly imitation is one of the most successful tactics anglers can employ.

Once autumn rolls around and the browns are in a mood to spawn, the cooler air and water temperatures make Rock Creek a great place to finish the season. This is a great time to throw small streamers as fish strap on the feed bag in preparation for winter. Fish small Woolly Buggers and rabbit-strip streamers through semideep holes and large eddies or soft-water breaks. Cast across stream and bring your pattern perpendicular to where you think fish are holding like a fleeing or injured baitfish. I almost never get strikes when the pattern is swimming directly upstream. A sinking-tip line is handy, but you can get by in the moderately deep holes with a floating line and some extra weight.

Directions

Two main routes reach Rock Creek at opposite ends of the system. From I-90 you can take exit 126 and travel south along the river on Rock Creek Road. The first 12 miles are paved (be mindful of the speed limit), but then it turns to dirt. To reach the upper portion, take MT 348 west from Philipsburg for approximately 8 miles. Bohrnsen Bridge crosses the river just before the road turns to dirt. Immediately after crossing, turn right and travel north along the river, or continue on the dirt road to reach the forks.

In the summer, you can cross Skalkaho Highway (MT 38) from Hamilton to reach the creek. Though scenic, the drive is long and dusty, and I only recommend it if you're camping and fishing on the creek for more than one day. It is a seasonal road and closed when sufficient snowfall makes travel impossible.

Doug Persico is a Rock Creek legend and owns the Rock Creek Mercantile near the junction of the river and the Clark Fork. He has an intimate knowledge of the water and is always willing to talk to those who ask politely or happen to buy a couple dozen flies. I highly recommend stopping by if you're unfamiliar with the conditions or are curious what's been working for other anglers. If you drive through Philipsburg, Matthew Churchman at Flint Creek Outdoors can point you in the right direction. In the summer, Churchman is typically fishing either Rock Creek or Flint Creek every day after work, so he's in tune with hatches and water conditions.

Strung-Out X2 Adult Stone (Salmonfly)

Rear Hook:	#6 Spear It #CS057
Front Hook:	#10 Spear It #CS057
Connection:	10-pound Spectron
Thread:	Brown 6/0 Uni-Thread
Body:	Body Stretch over foam
Underwing:	Two brown CDC feathers, brown poly yarn, and pearl Mirror Flash
Wing:	Natural deer hair
Thorax:	50/50 blend of chocolate-brown On-the-Take and root-beer Diamond Brite
Legs:	Brown Flex Floss
Eyes:	Burnt mono
Antennae:	Brown Flex Floss

CDC Floating PMD Emerger

Hook:	#16-20 Tiemco 100
Thread:	Light olive 6/0 Uni-Thread
Tail:	Yellow mallard flank
Rib:	Fine gold wire
Abdomen:	Yellow-olive Superfine
Wing:	Yellow Z-lon, dun CDC, and brown partridge
Thorax:	Yellow-olive Superfine

Barr's Web-Wing Caddis

Hook:	#14-20 Tiemco 101
Thread:	Tan 8/0 Uni-Thread
Body:	Tan Superfine
Wing:	Mottled Web Wing
Hackle:	Brown rooster

Blackfoot River

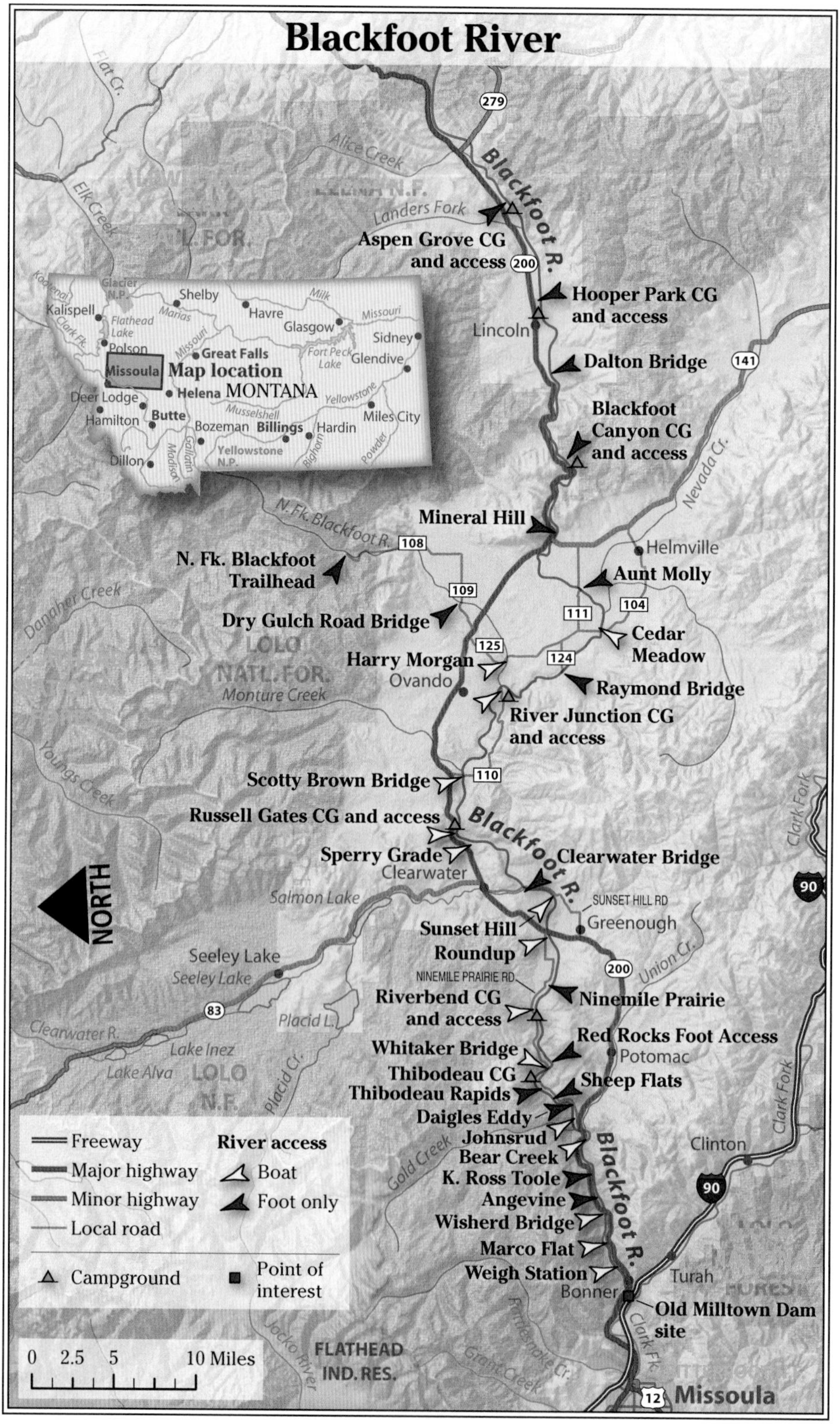

CHAPTER 9

Blackfoot River

From the fast-water chutes of the lower river to the crystalline cutthroat sanctuaries of its headwaters, the Blackfoot has something to offer everyone. Dense mountainside forests, rocky canyons, and a variety of wildlife like bighorn sheep, elk, and deer make the area feel much farther away from Missoula than the atlas shows.

The river has more than a fair share of opportunities for dry-fly anglers (hatches of big bugs like Salmonflies, Golden Stones, hoppers, and October Caddis keep fish active and well fed) or those looking to dredge up fish with double-nymph rigs and indicators. But the abundance of rocks, logs, underwater shelves, rapids, pools—and the trout that lurk within—make this river a streamer fisherman's dream. No matter where you are, even floating through tumbling white water, you can always find a soft edge along the bank or behind a rock to unload a cast. Big flies; the constant action of casting, mending, and stripping; and the simple pleasure of banging a rabbit and marabou concoction next to every structure I pass on the water is exciting business. That's why I like the Blackfoot River.

Made famous years ago by Robert Redford's movie *A River Runs Through It*, the beauty of the area, the cold water, and the brief white-water chutes have only added to its popularity as a recreation destination. Besides those chasing trout, kayakers, rafters, and tubers escaping the summer heat sometimes make the lane between the banks feel like a crowded place. This is mostly a concern on the lower half of the river, but that's not to say you won't feel the squeeze on the upper reaches as well.

Where and When

The North Fork of the Blackfoot hails from the southern fringe of the Bob Marshall Wilderness and the main stem deep in the Helena National Forest near Rogers Pass and the Continental Divide. Much of the upper Blackfoot, upstream from the junction of the North Fork extending well past the town of Lincoln, is somewhat isolated and relatively untouched compared with the main stem. It snakes through the hills of the Rocky Mountain Front, occasionally through swamp and marsh, looking more like moose territory than

From the fast-water chutes of the lower river to the crystalline cutthroat sanctuaries of its headwaters, the Blackfoot has something to offer everyone. The banks along much of the North Fork of the Blackfoot are steep and contain loose gravel. Access the river using safe routes either up- or downstream from where you plan to fish to avoid a possible accident.

trout country. I like this part of the river if I'm on foot and looking to get away from any boat traffic downstream. Stemple Pass Bridge in Lincoln, Dalton Bridge, Blackfoot Canyon, Mineral Hill, Aunt Molly, Cedar Meadow, and Raymond Bridge access sites are easily reachable by car.

The North Fork, on the other hand, is distinctly different. It cuts its way through a steep, tight mountain corridor creating a short series of white-water chutes, deep pockets, and fast-moving riffles. Despite the loss of trees from a

The North Fork of the Blackfoot is worth exploring on foot. Simple patterns like Elk-Hair Caddis, Royal Wulffs, Stimulators, and Parachute Adams should have no problem fooling the resident cutthroat.

1988 wildfire (that Kingfisher Fly Shop co-owner and outfitter Jim Cox says improved the fishing), many people comment it is the most beautiful trout water they've ever seen. The bottom of the stream is made up of rust-, pale-blue-, and amber-colored rocks that offer the perfect backdrop to the icy, turquoise water.

Leaving the Bob Marshall boundary, the upper North Fork continues through Lolo National Forest for a few more miles, offering those willing to walk the perfect option for escaping crowds. The banks and hillsides are steep in many places, so watch your footing. Once on the water, you'll find more than enough cutthroat willing to play on the surface with general patterns like Elk-Hair Caddis or Royal Wulffs.

The North Fork then winds through a small valley filled with farms and ranches and access is difficult. The Harry Morgan access near the town of Ovando is not only a good place for wading anglers to jump in the water and move upstream, but floating anglers can launch their boats, float the last 2 miles of the North Fork, and end the day fishing the main stem.

The North Fork gets skinny in the late season (making it tough for hard boats), so for those who still want to fish the upper Blackfoot, consider the River Junction access—a campground and boat-launch area on the south side of the river, directly across stream from the junction of the North Fork. The road to River Junction (accessible via Scotty Brown Road from MT 200) is bumpy and dusty, but it's a good choice if you want to concentrate your efforts on the larger water and forgo the North Fork.

VISITING OVANDO

There are some services in Ovando if you're in need of gas, water, or flies. The Blackfoot Angler (blackfootangler.com) is a small fly shop in the heart of town across the street from the Blackfoot Inn (blackfoot-inn.com). The inn has rooms for rent (all come with a complimentary breakfast) and features the Blackfoot Commercial Company, a general store where you can stock up on snacks and refreshments or arrange a shuttle.

Of course, no voyage to the North Fork is complete without a stop at Trixi's Antler Saloon and Family Diner on the eastern side of town. This landmark is the place to go for local flavor, a hearty burger, or a cold beer. It's just what the doctor ordered after a few nights of camping or an especially long day on the river. Just remember it's a long drive back to Missoula, so gauge your consumption accordingly. ■

The area between River Junction and Russell Gates (sometimes called County Line) is a scenic float and includes the popular canyon portion of the Blackfoot. It has its fair share of riffles, deep pools, and structure that make it especially fun to fish with streamers or large dry flies like hoppers. If you're launching late, or feel like taking the float at a slower pace, consider the access at Scotty Brown Bridge (just downstream of the mouth of Monture Creek). You won't get to fish the canyon, but this part of the river is incredibly scenic during a sunset.

Russell Gates is easily reachable via MT 200 and is a popular put-in and take-out for boaters as well as those making a pit stop in their RVs and campers. From this point floaters have the option of taking out at either Sperry Grade, Clearwater Bridge, Sunset Hill, Roundup, or Riverbend. These points are better suited for rafts as opposed to hard boats because they're easier to carry uphill, which is required at some points like Roundup.

Sunset Hill Road connects with MT 200 next to the Clearwater River. Turn south and follow this dirt road if you want to reach Clearwater Bridge or continue over the Blackfoot and along the river to reach the unimproved Sunset Hill site. Both are good for wading anglers, especially Clearwater Bridge later in the season when flows are low. There is plenty of structure to work around, and it's easy to walk along the banks.

Roundup is slightly more than two miles downriver. Unfortunately, for novice rowers, the water below Roundup is somewhat more technical than between River Junction and Russell Gates. There are several fast-water areas, the most substantial being the few miles from Roundup downstream to Riverbend. For those who are good on the sticks, it's a wild ride. There's nothing better than fishing this area as runoff subsides, getting hit with water on all sides, and trying to toss Salmonfly patterns in every pocket as you go.

Some people don't like barreling downriver through rocks and debris while water washes inside the boat. I find it exciting. If you're the same, then

Roundup (there are timbers to help slide your raft downhill to the water) is for you. During high water it's easier to float over many of the rocks in this section, but when it drops, it's like rowing through a slalom course. In either case, you can cast streamers out either side of the boat and always be within casting reach of some fishy-looking pocketwater.

If you want to avoid the rough water, or float through the heart of the Blackfoot River corridor, consider the foot access at Ninemile Prairie downstream or the float from Riverbend to Whitaker Bridge. There is still a good amount of fast water, but during high water you can complete these drifts in a few hours and have plenty of places to anchor and fish swirling foam pockets or jump out and fish on foot. You can also make a day of it later in the season as levels drop.

Whitaker Bridge is a convenient access if you're coming from Missoula. In the fall, Whitaker to Johnsrud Park is one of my favorite short floats. It's only a few miles, but plenty of structure, seams, and frothing pools make the hours fly by. This stretch does contain the famous Thibodeau Rapids (as well as some smaller chutes) so float with caution. If you'd rather fish this water on foot, try nearby foot accesses like Belmont Creek, Red Rocks, Thibodeau, Sheep Flats, and Daigles Eddy.

In the summer, Johnsrud Park is a popular local hangout for swimmers and float-tubers. If you're looking for any degree of solitude at the height of the season, don't expect to find it here or the few miles downstream. You can beat a majority of the crowds if you hit the water early, but if it's a scorcher, it won't be long before the black rubber donuts and bobbing coolers begin drifting by. Crowding is sometimes an issue on the Blackfoot, and in 2009 the

Cutthroat in the North Fork of the Blackfoot don't have discerning tastes. In fact, one of the most effective patterns can be a simple size 12 Royal Wulff, so don't overthink your pattern selection or presentation.

The Blackfoot is loaded with boulders and logjams that create soft-water breaks. Present flies along the seams where the currents collide and in the downstream eddy where fish often rest and feed. JAY NICHOLS PHOTO

MDFWP began exploring options, like those in place on the Beaverhead and Big Hole, to reduce conflicts and enhance the experience for everyone.

From Johnsrud you can fish the last few miles of the Blackfoot before it dumps into the Clark Fork River near Milltown. Bear Creek, Rainbow Bend, K. Ross Toole, Cable Crossing, Angevine Park, Wisherd Bridge, Marco Flat, and Weigh Station just upstream of Bonner (sometimes called the Game Check access because the MDFWP sets up a station for hunters in the fall) are the best sites.

A short scramble up a hill is the norm at some access points on the lower river, so be sure you inspect a site before you settle on it for a put-in or take-out. This section of the river is easy to reach from Missoula, not overloaded with white-water chutes like the water upstream, and it stays relatively deep in the late season, making it easier to use hard boats. On the other hand, MT 200 flanks the river at nearly every turn, so you have road noise.

The removal of the Milltown Dam and a smaller blockade near the old Stimson lumber mill in Bonner have opened up the Blackfoot and Clark Fork rivers for the first time in over 100 years. Access points near the junction of these two rivers would make floating from the lower Blackfoot into the main stem Clark Fork a genuine possibility, but for now there is a five-year prohibition of access within a mile of the project. If you're floating, do not proceed past the Weigh Station access.

Hatches and Flies

The Blackfoot River doesn't have the spectacular early-season fishing in March and April like you might find on other southwestern Montana rivers like the Bitterroot. The tight canyons, lack of sunlight, and the area's propensity for colder temperatures make it a tough option before runoff. Rather than gamble with precious vacation time or money, fish the river after runoff or later in the season.

As runoff winds down, Salmonflies and Golden Stones start hatching. These big bugs can come on as early as late May, continue through June and July, and bring some big fish to the surface. Even with just a foot or two of visibility the fish can hone in on these meaty meals and hit like a ton of bricks. Rogue Stones, Stimulators, Lawson's Henry's Fork Salmonfly, Kingfisher's Paranoble, and Thing From Uranus are a few solid choices. "At the beginning of the hatch," Cox says, "they'll take high riders for a week, but then they'll want something that sits low in the water. We like to use the Hammerhead, which looks like a drowned Salmonfly."

In an average year, the appearance of stoneflies and high water go hand in hand. Unfortunately, water conditions can make the river tough to fish despite the abundance of bugs. Wait until the levels start to drop and clarity improves to a slight green or tea color before heading out. John Herzer of Blackfoot River Outfitters says this is one of his favorite times to fish.

"Timing runoff is a gamble, but if you can be in the area as the water is coming down, usually around the last week of June, you can have some good fishing with dry flies and streamers," Herzer says. "My favorite area is between Russell Gates and Riverbend. This is a rough section at this time of year because of all the white water and rocks, but if you have an experienced oarsman, it's a structure-fisherman's dream."

Green Drakes, a variety of caddis, and Yellow Sallies hatch through the middle of the summer. The feeding season for these fish is relatively short, so they get while the getting is good, and it doesn't take huge clouds of bugs before they feed on the surface. If you see any type of hatch activity, tie on an imitation and give it a shot—particularly around fish that are already feeding on the surface. Even if you make a sloppy presentation or misjudge pattern sizes by a size or two, there's still a good chance they'll take a taste.

Lawson's Green Drake Paradrake is one of my personal favorites for the Blackfoot both to imitate the hatch and as a general attractor. It stays afloat in rough water and is easy to see. For caddis and Yellow Sallies, I like to carry an assortment of Stimulators in various sizes, colors, and styles. Make sure to include some with rubber legs.

Skyrocketing summer temperatures mean only one thing on the Blackfoot—hoppers. July and August are perfect for trying a variety of terrestrial imitations, and most anglers opt to use them as part of a dry-dropper rig since most patterns are buoyant enough to support weighted nymphs. I've always been partial to fishing Dave's Hopper on the Blackfoot, but I've also had success with a B/C Hopper, Schroeder's Parachute Hopper, and Kingfisher's Red Legged Hopper. There are plenty of grassy banks and other structure along the river, particularly on the lower half where naturals fall in the water, so the trout become familiar with this food item quickly.

You should also try other off-the-wall attractor patterns this time of year. John Herzer says the character of the river lends itself to good mid- and late-

season attractor fishing not just because of all the structure, but because he believes fish are targeting a nocturnal stonefly as much as they are terrestrials.

"You can camp next to the river, wake up the next morning, and see fresh stonefly shucks on your oars, so I think these fish are keyed in on big bugs other than hoppers. In mid-July through August, I like to tie on big attractors made of foam or something equally buoyant. Something buggy and tan or brown in a size 6 that could pass for a stonefly or hopper and support a large nymph underneath," Herzer says. "From that I'll tie a #10 Copper John or Montana Prince on 30 inches of tippet and fish it as a dropper."

A taut dropper rig is essential for detecting strikes according to Herzer. That's why he uses such large, heavy flies for droppers—they sink quickly and keep slack out of the tippet. To keep the bugs from tangling, he recommends tying a short piece of 2X tippet off the hook bend of the dry fly to which he attaches a 30-inch piece of 4X for the dropper. The short, stiff piece of 2X keeps the rest of the dropper rig from tangling with the dry fly when casting.

Jim Cox is also a fan of the hopper-dropper system, but he says in late summer he'll sometimes use a double terrestrial rig like a hopper and an ant instead of a weighted nymph. "I think this river is one of the best for black ant patterns in the midsummer and fall. A size 12 or 14 is deadly," Cox says.

As the seasons slowly shift from summer to fall, the dry-fly fishing on the Blackfoot slowly nose-dives and nymphs or streamers become the better option. You may encounter sparse patches of October Caddis from time to time, creating a short window of surface action, but stick to subsurface flies if you want to find more and bigger fish.

Rabbit strips and tufts of marabou are my two favorite materials for Blackfoot streamer flies. Every twitch, strip, and movement makes the flies breathe and look alive underwater. Sculpin-style patterns like Kelly Galloup's Dungeon, variations of the Double Bunny, Conehead Muddy Buddies, and Lanier's Deerhead Zonker in earthy colors like olive, black, brown, and yellow are favorites. I've seen fish react to an assortment of other patterns and colors (like pumpkin), however, so don't be shy about pulling something unusual from your fly box.

When it comes to nymph rigs, Jim Cox can't stress one thing enough—keep it simple. "A lot of people concern themselves too much with finding exact imitations for their dry and nymph rigs," he says. "In reality, a lot of basic, reliable patterns will get the job done. You can tie a giant stonefly nymph, big Beadhead Prince, or even a Woolly Bugger on my line as long as the second fly in the rig is a San Juan. They are simple to tie and the fish love them. Some people balk at the worm and say it's not a real fly. I tell them that if they feel that way they should just consider it to be an emerging Royal Wulff."

Most of the Blackfoot is open and easy to navigate; however, some areas require rowing skills. Consult a local fly shop about conditions and hazards before launching your boat if you're not familiar with a particular section of river. JAY NICHOLS PHOTO

Directions

MT 200 follows and intersects the lower and upper portions of the Blackfoot, while Johnsrud Park Road and Ninemile Prairie Road neighbor the middle portion of the river between Johnsrud and Roundup. From Missoula, take I-90 approximately seven miles east to the Milltown/Bonner exit. Follow MT 200 through town (watch the speed limit) and continue northeast. You'll soon see the river along the road, as well as signs for access points intermittently spaced along the drive.

There are several areas to access the North Fork of the Blackfoot. To reach Harry Morgan turn right just after mile marker 44 (near the town of Ovando) onto Ovando-Helmville Road. It will lead you through town and then swerve to the right. Follow it for approximately three miles until you see signs for the access on the right.

To reach the middle portions of the river, continue on MT 200 past Ovando and turn northeast (left) on Dry Gulch Road. A bridge crosses the North Fork approximately 1.5 miles later and offers foot access via a small trail near the southwest corner of the bridge.

To reach the North Fork Trailhead, continue on Dry Gulch Road and turn north on Cooper Blackfoot Road—nearly two miles after the Kleinschmidt Flat Road intersection. It will soon cross the national forest border and lead directly to the North Fork Trailhead and campground.

If you pass the turn at Dry Gulch Road from MT 200, you can also turn left on Kleinschmidt Flat Road a few miles later. An old broken-down combine on the left is a good landmark signaling where to turn. Though these dirt roads are often well maintained and easy to drive on, respect the surrounding residents and drive at a reasonable speed to keep the dust clouds down.

Galloup's Dungeon (Olive)

Front Hook:	#2-4 Daiichi 1720
Rear Hook:	#6 Daiichi 1750
Rib:	Olive saddle hackle
Tail:	Olive marabou with copper Flashabou
Head:	Olive deer hair
Eyes:	Lead barbell eyes painted yellow with black pupil
Connection:	17-pound vinyl-covered wire with one silver-lined ruby bead
Tentacles:	Olive barred Sili Legs

Kingfisher Hammerhead Stone (Salmonfly)

Hook:	#4-6 MFC 7027
Thread:	Dark brown 6/0 Uni-Thread
Tail:	Brown Spider Legs (#3)
Abdomen:	Insect orange and peacock Phoenix Dubbing
Wing Case:	Brown foam
Wing:	Dark dun Medallion Sheeting
Legs:	Speckled brown Centipede Legs (#1)
Eyes:	Black 1/8" tube foam

Lanier's Deerhead Zonker

Hook:	#4-6 MFC 7030
Head:	Black 7 mm cone
Thread:	Olive Nymo thread
Weight:	Lead wire
Rear Body	
Wrap:	Red 6/0 Uni-Thread
Body:	Olive 7 mm Mylar tubing
Head:	Olive whitetail deer
Wing:	Olive/black barred rabbit strip
Eyes:	Gold 3D eyes

Stranahan's Caddis Variant (Tan)

Hook:	#10-16 MFC 7004 or Targus 921
Thread:	Tan 6/0 Uni-Thread
Body:	50/50 mix of hare's ear and squirrel belly Antron dubbing
Wing:	Fine natural deer hair with short black tips
Hackle:	Dark Cree, or mixed grizzly and brown

Clark Fork (Upper)

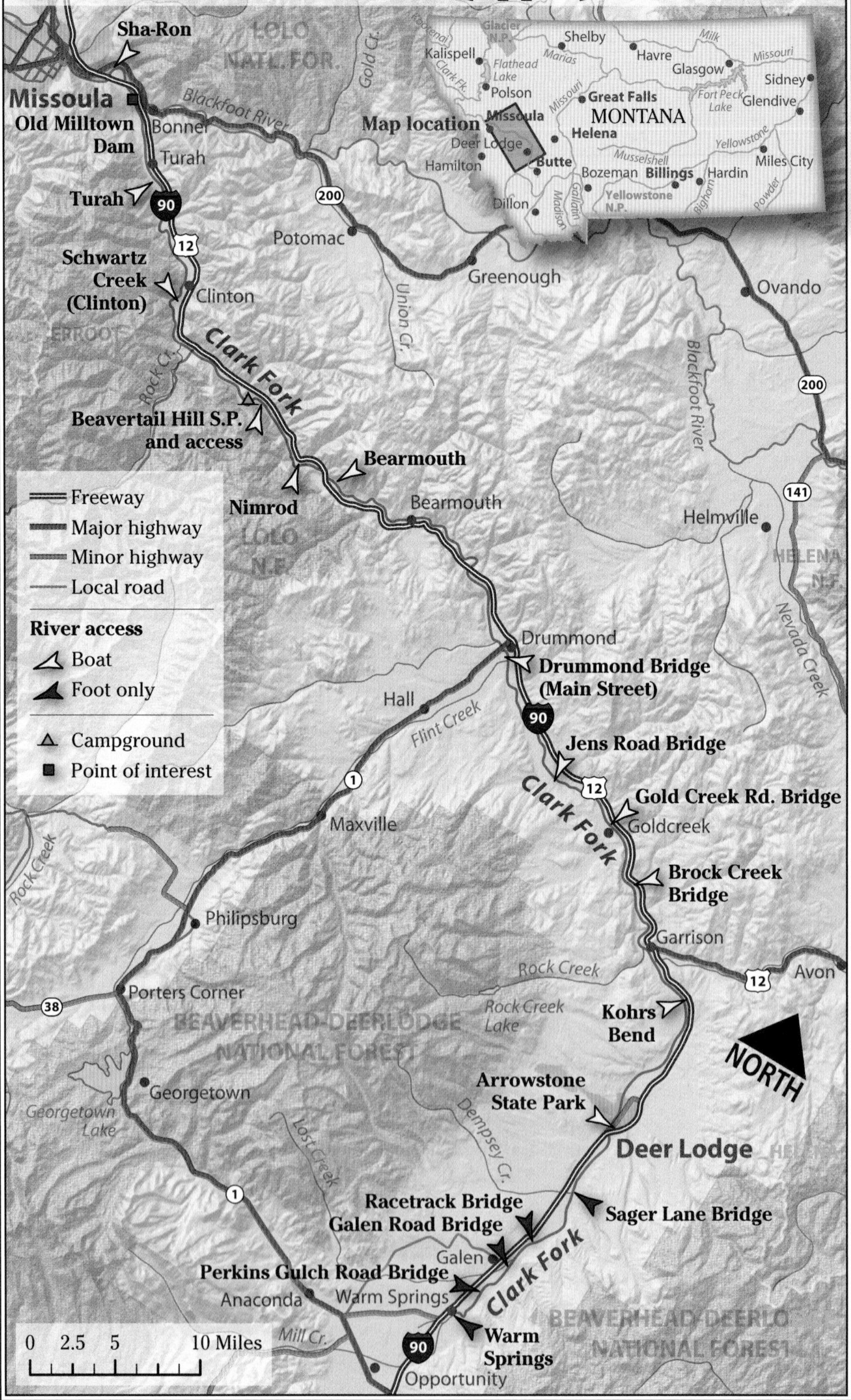

CHAPTER 10

Clark Fork River

Since the early days of statehood, the Clark Fork has been Montana's whipping boy for the whims of progress. Environmentally speaking, I'm hard pressed to think of another waterway in the state that has gone through so much yet continues to give anglers and floaters a quality experience. Just when you think another train derailment, remnant mining waste washout, or other ecodisaster has given the river a final one-two punch, it rises from the ashes like the phoenix.

Year in and year out it's one of the first rivers I look to for consistent dry-fly action, sometimes into November. Despite the great fishing, the Clark Fork has kept a low profile. If you are sick of playing bumper boats on the Blackfoot and Bitterroot, there is ample room to stretch out a line here, with quality fish to match.

Where and When

The Clark Fork actually begins where Silver Bow Creek and Warm Springs Creek meet, not far from the copper-mine pits outside Butte. A virtual toilet bowl for mining waste, many proclaimed Silver Bow Creek dead; however, in recent years Montana Fish, Wildlife, and Parks biologists are seeing wild trout return to the watershed.

The creeks flow into a string of settling ponds near the small town of Warm Springs. The ponds are great places to put in a float-tube and fin for 5-pound trout, but most visit the area to cast into the pond's discharge and the beginning of the Clark Fork River. From the discharge to approximately five miles downstream, the river hosts nearly 1,400 fish per mile, some of which are especially large. The average width of the river here is barely more than two fly-rod lengths, and when the water is low, you can see brown trout lined up shoulder to shoulder in the early morning light just waiting for food.

In fact, early mornings in the summer may be one of the best times to hit the Warm Springs area. Most anglers visit these temperate waters in the winter and early spring for nymphing action—other rivers are frozen or high from runoff—when massive Clark Fork trout scoot up into the discharge pool like herded cattle. Most of what you'll see in the summer fall between 12 and 18 inches, but some real hogs wallow below the discharge.

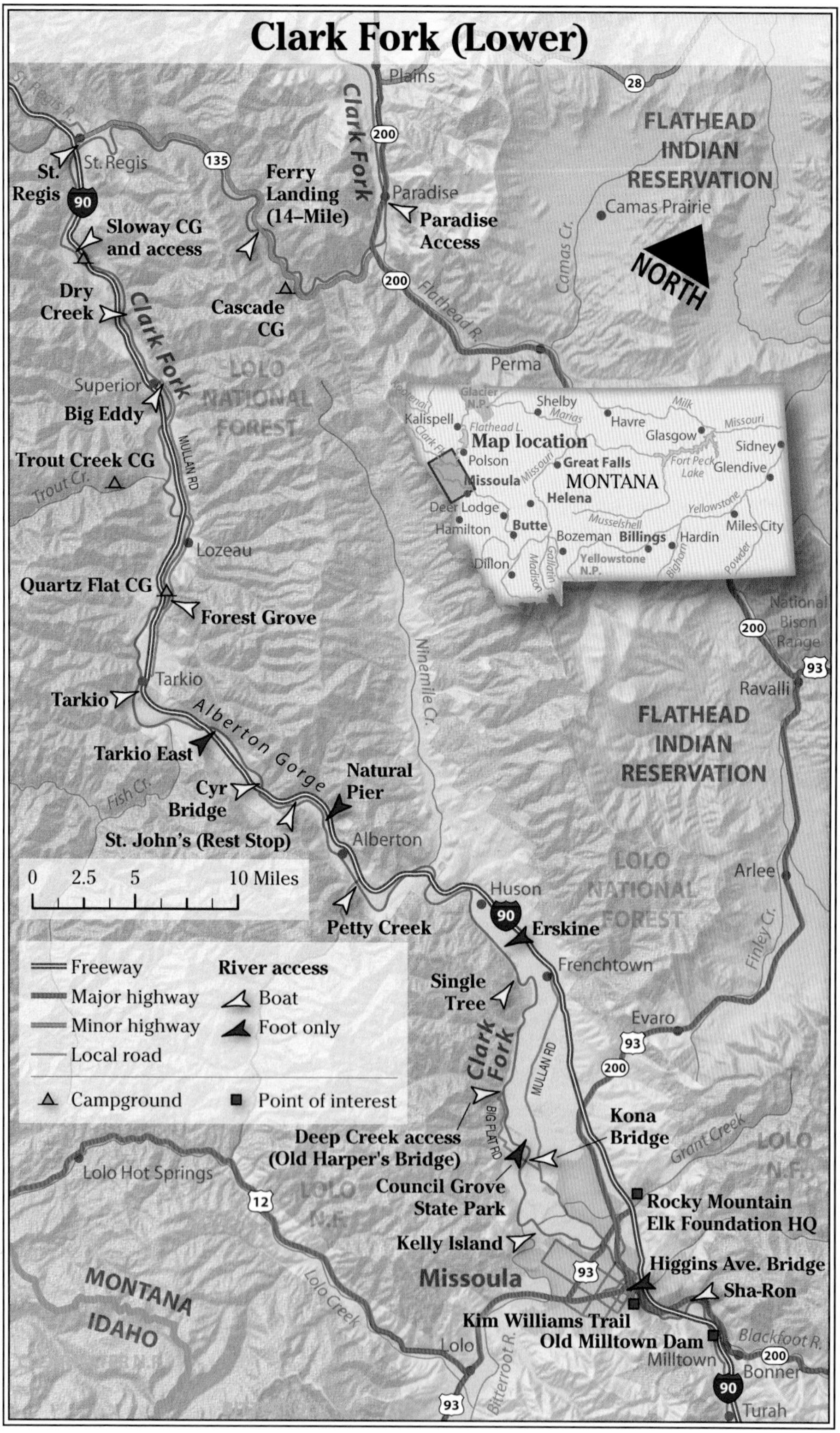

Clark Fork (Lower)
Plains
Clark Fork
28
200
FLATHEAD INDIAN RESERVATION
St. Regis R.
St. Regis
St. Regis
135
Ferry Landing (14–Mile)
Paradise
Paradise Access
Camas Prairie
90
Sloway CG and access
Camas Cr.
NORTH
Dry Creek
Clark Fork
Cascade CG
200
Flathead R.
Perma
LOLO NATIONAL FOREST
Superior
Big Eddy
MULLAN RD
Trout Creek CG
Trout Cr.
Glacier N.P.
Shelby
Marias
Milk
Kalispell
Havre
Missouri
Flathead L.
Glasgow
Sidney
Map location
Clark Fk.
Polson
Great Falls
Fort Peck Lake
Glendive
Missoula
Missouri
MONTANA
Helena
Deer Lodge
Yellowstone
Musselshell
Miles City
Hamilton
Butte
Bozeman
Billings
Hardin
Powder
Dillon
Madison
Gallatin
Yellowstone N.P.
Bighorn
Lozeau
Quartz Flat CG
Forest Grove
National Bison Range
200
93
Ninemile Cr.
Tarkio
Tarkio
Ravalli
Alberton Gorge
FLATHEAD INDIAN RESERVATION
Tarkio East
Fish Cr.
Cyr Bridge
Natural Pier
St. John's (Rest Stop)
Alberton
LOLO NATIONAL FOREST
0 2.5 5 10 Miles
Arlee
Huson
90
Erskine
Petty Creek
Finley Cr.
Frenchtown
Freeway
Major highway
Minor highway
Local road
River access
Boat
Foot only
Single Tree
Evaro
93
Clark Fork
MULLAN RD
200
Campground
Point of interest
BIG FLAT RD
Kona Bridge
Deep Creek access (Old Harper's Bridge)
Grant Creek
LOLO N.F.
Lolo Hot Springs
Council Grove State Park
LOLO N.F.
12
Rocky Mountain Elk Foundation HQ
Kelly Island
MONTANA
IDAHO
Lolo Creek
Missoula
93
Higgins Ave. Bridge
Sha-Ron
Kim Williams Trail
Old Milltown Dam
Bitterroot R.
Lolo
Blackfoot R.
200
Milltown
Bonner
90
93
Turah

To get to Warm Springs, turn east at I-90 exit 201, followed shortly by a turn south to the Warm Springs fishing access site and settling pond discharge. The first mile below the discharge can be crowded, but there are a handful of bridges and parking areas downstream. After exiting I-90, continue heading east and stop at the Warm Springs Bridge (there is a small parking area) or continue to the intersection of Morel Road (Eastside Road) and turn left. This will lead you to a series of connecting roads with bridges for easy access. Look for areas on Perkins Gulch Road, Galen Road Bridge, the bridge southeast of Racetrack, and lastly a bridge between Racetrack and Deer Lodge on Sager Lane.

Fish populations decline somewhat the farther you get from the settling ponds, but so do the crowds. There are some other bridge access points downstream near Deer Lodge, and public areas like Arrowstone State Park. Despite the skinny fish counts, there are some bruisers here, and the reappearance of

Downstream of Missoula, the Clark Fork is a wide body of water well suited for dry-fly anglers who like to spot and stalk pods of rising fish. Check the weather forecast before heading out. Wind can shut down the action fairly quick and in some cases blow a boat back upstream.

Clark Fork fish tend to form pods and schools in various places throughout the system. Once you find fish, you can return time and time again and chances are good you'll find action. JOHN HERZER/BLACKFOOT RIVER OUTFITTERS PHOTO

baitfish means you can slide a sculpin pattern past their noses with some degree of confidence.

"The upper river gets a good *Skwala* and March Brown hatch early in the season," Drew Miller, head guide and outfitter for Grizzly Hackle Fly Shop says. "But the caddis are one of the top hatches. In fact, the upper Clark Fork is where Gary LaFontaine spent a lot of time studying caddis." Farther downstream near Garrison is Kohrs Bend. Exit I-90 at Beck Hill Road (exit 179), then head northwest on the frontage road until you see the site. By mid to late summer this stretch is ideal for wading, and it is floatable early in the season when levels are higher.

The Little Blackfoot meets the river near Garrison, and the cold, clean water breathes life into the river and trout numbers increase slightly. You can access the river via a bridge on the south side of Garrison or head downstream to the bridges near Brock Creek (exit 170), Gold Creek (exit 166), or near Jens Road Bridge (south of exit 162).

Whether it's the effects of irrigation, the impact from mining waste, or just Mother Nature's twisted sense of humor, there are not many trout (some say less than 300 per mile) between Drummond and Rock Creek, which looks enticing as you drive along I-90. "With this Superfund rehab in place, the water between the dam and Warm Springs is being rehabilitated. So I think, as far as the upper Clark Fork goes, things can only get better. Fish numbers are increasing and guides are fishing it more. In the early 1990s people didn't go above Rock Creek, but now you see more people up there," Miller says.

If you feel like the cards are in your favor, and want to give it a shot, there is an access in Drummond, or look downstream to the highway rest stop (for westbound travelers) and the nearby bridge upstream, the Bearmouth area near exit 138, and Beavertail Hill State Park on the south side of the river.

Downstream from the clean, cold contributions from Rock Creek, trout numbers jump up to nearly 1,000 per mile, and aquatic insect hatches become more abundant. One of my favorite short floats early in the Salmonfly season (when water conditions allow it) is to launch a boat from lower Rock Creek (near mile marker 4 or Valley of the Moon) and eventually take out on the Clark Fork in Clinton at Schwartz Creek.

Schwartz Creek to Turah is a popular float once the floating season winds down June 30 on Rock Creek. Stoneflies are hatching on the Clark Fork as high water starts to subside. I like this section because the braids, undercut banks, and overall character are similar to lower Rock Creek. In fact, it's a favorite piece of water among streamer throwers because of the abundant structure and close proximity to Missoula. Try to hit this piece of water on the shoulders of the season to avoid warm water, possible low flows, and the always aggravating algae growth. Also, now that the dam is down and the lower-river fish

The Clark Fork receives less pressure than neighboring rivers, and it's entirely possible to not see another angler all day, especially in the fall as the season winds down. With that in mind, take your time and fish areas thoroughly knowing you don't have to be in a hurry to beat another boat to the next hot spot. JOHN HERZER/BLACKFOOT RIVER OUTFITTERS PHOTO are free to move upstream, there's no telling what you'll encounter in years to come.

"I am convinced we're catching lower–Clark Fork fish up above the dam now," Blackfoot River Outfitters owner John Herzer says. "We caught a lot of 16- to 19-inch fish upstream of the dam when before we would only see this caliber of fish during big hatches like the Golden Stones. Last year we saw them all summer long. Also, there was a more even mixture of browns to rainbows. Historically browns dominated this area. So while I'm not a biologist, I think this is a result of the dam opening up."

After Turah, the river continues to braid and break off into sloughs and backwaters that are a favorite of migratory waterfowl, but until they finish the restoration work at Milltown Reservoir there are no public access areas. Don't miss the Turah ramp if you're floating.

The area around Bonner is the scene of the Milltown cleanup, and until the last rock moves into place and the area is publicly accessible, there is little anyone can offer aside from predictions. At the time of this writing, access is prohibited .5 mile downstream and 2.5 miles upstream from the worksite. When the dam work is complete, the river will flow unimpeded once again. The restoration plans include a public park and the amenities that go with it, so watch for this area to become a popular fishing access and boat launch.

The dam marks the beginning of what most refer to as the lower Clark Fork and the beginning of the "town stretch." "Once the Blackfoot enters the Clark Fork just above Missoula, the water temperatures begin to cool down from the cold water springs and feeder creeks. Also, it completely changes from a brown trout fishery to a rainbow and cuttbow fishery. This is different than most rivers, which are colder in their headwaters," Miller says. Most lower-river fish fall back into the 12- to 18-inch range, and while the likelihood of busting over the 20-inch mark is a real possibility, you may have to work at it. This may mean working deep runs with nymph rigs or pitching streamers in the fall.

The Sha-Ron access in East Missoula is the first pit stop below the old dam site, though the ramp may have a substantial amount of silt around it resulting from the Milltown Dam work upstream. It's a small parking area and boat ramp just northeast of the community near the intersection of MT 200 and Speedway Avenue (MT 533). This is one of the best places to put in if you float the town stretch (you can take out in McCormick Park, though there is no boat ramp and dragging is required), but because the water is relatively deep and swift here (except in lean-water years), I don't recommended it for wading anglers. There are better options downstream. If you decide to float, watch for the large diversion dam just upstream of Jacob's Island near the University of Montana campus. There is usually a boat-size channel on the north side (river right) but inspect the area before you commit.

Once you're into Missoula, there are some solid foot-fishing opportunities, especially as the water drops in the late season. Beginning on the east side of town there is the footbridge near the university (Jacob's Island), the parking area and trail near the Doubletree Hotel, Kiwanis Park near down-

Access is a nice feature of the Clark Fork as it runs through Missoula. Look at the Kim Williams Trail, the Higgins Avenue Bridge, Kelly Island, the Kona Bridge area, and the Deep Creek access if your plans include fishing on foot. JOHN HERZER/BLACKFOOT RIVER OUTFITTERS PHOTO

town, a parking lot under the south side of the Higgins Avenue Bridge, McCormick Park just downstream, and access to the river along the Kim Williams Trail, which runs on the south side of the river between the base of Mount Sentinel to McCormick Park, 1 1/2 miles downstream. If you are fishing near the Doubletree, remember it is artificials only within a 100-yard radius of the mouth of Rattlesnake Creek. These regulations are also in place for other lower Clark Fork tributary mouths like Petty, Fish, Cedar, Dry, and Trout creeks, and the St. Regis River.

As you work downriver, expect some algae growth, especially in the heat of the summer. The algae not only affects your footing, but also fish displacement. In recent years, the nitrate load into the rivers has increased exponentially—some say it is a direct correlation between the area's population boom and the increase in the number of riverbank lawns and golf courses.

"Back in the day, probably when I was in high school, there was a huge push to ban nitrates in detergents, and the sewage plant and Stone Container [paper mill] became very cognizant of the nitrate issue," Cox says. "At that time, the algae buildup all but disappeared. But, the algae issue is rearing its ugly head again. I'm sure that the recent spate of extremely low water and warming temperatures has a lot to do with it, but the past two years in particular have been benign in that regard, suggesting other explanations."

After McCormick Park, shallow, braided channels, diversion dams, and the ever-present odors from the sewage plant near Reserve Street make it a no-go for trout, though lately it is becoming a great place to seek out northern pike if you can stand the stench. You can leapfrog over the town's westward-moving sprawl and land at Kelly Island. This large access area lets anglers see both the Clark Fork and the junction of the Bitterroot River just downstream. From Reserve Street (US 93) turn west on Spurgin Road and travel for approximately two miles (there is a little zigzag at the intersection of Clements Road). The parking area is at the end of the line on the north side of the road. This access is great for a short float to Kona Bridge or a full-day excursion to Harper's Bridge.

For wading anglers, the Kelly Island area is full of shallow-water braids, twists, and turns. However, instead of working the river from the south, go to the Kelly Island foot-access area to the north. There is another parking lot if you take Mullan Road west from Missoula, then turn south on Cole Lane, left (east) on Toby Way, and then another quick left (north) on Council Way. The road will curve in a semicircle, change to dirt, and end in the parking lot. Follow the signs along the way. Once there, cross the small footbridge, follow the trail, and work either upstream or cross to the island to find the channels and braids.

Downstream the river is less intimate and wade fishing is tough. Look for seams, dropoffs, and don't ignore the slow-moving water close to the bank. According to Jim Cox, "the fish tend to hang on tiny seams in inches of water along the bank riffles and runs."

The lower Clark Fork has attractive water around every turn. Unfortunately, not all "fishy looking" water holds fish. Learning where pods of fish congregate comes by spending time on the river.

Though there are some good wading spots, in general you'll fare much better if you can ride on the water rather than walk through it. "Unlike the other rivers around Missoula, which are pretty easy to read, the Clark Fork is bigger so it intimidates a lot of people," Herzer says. "Because there simply aren't many fish per mile, you can cover more water and get into position over areas the trout frequent better than if you are wading."

Chalk it up to natural features in the river or other geological influences, lower Clark Fork trout tend to congregate in site-specific holes, pockets, and runs. After years of fishing the river, tuned-in guides and outfitters know where the fish are holding. "On the Clark Fork, 90 percent of the fish are in 10 percent of the water," Miller says. "They live in pods, isolated in certain areas. They aren't distributed well throughout the river like you'd find on the Blackfoot or Bitterroot. If you can find the pods of fish, they are there all the time. If you get a good cloudy, overcast day with a good hatch of mayflies, the Clark Fork fish will start feeding on the surface. If you mark them, you can go back and catch them on hoppers or something else when they're not visually feeding."

Kona Bridge, Council Grove State Park, and the old site of Harper's Bridge are the next three areas to find the river downstream from Kelly Island and are located within a few miles of one another. Kona and Harpers are good for both wading and floating, but Council Grove is suited for foot anglers—and offers a great look at a side channel of the main river.

To reach Kona, turn west on Kona Ranch Road off Mullan Road. The access and boat ramp are on the southwest side of the bridge. To reach Harpers, continue west on the road. It will turn into Big Flat Road, twist and turn, and eventually switch from pavement to dirt. The road is dusty, bumpy, and has a few blind turns, so drive slowly and cautiously. At the intersection of Deep Creek Road, turn right (northeast) and drive down over the gravel bank (four-wheel drive is sometimes helpful). To reach it from the northeast side of the river, turn south on Harper's Bridge Road from Mullan Road and drive to the end of the line. Council Grove Park is a little over a mile northwest of Kona Ranch Road off Mullan Road.

Single Tree is an unimproved point, and its unmarked location makes it a popular spot for guides and outfitters wanting to hit the terrific water downstream of Harpers. The steep 15-foot bank makes it tough to get boats up to your trailer. If you have a one-man pontoon boat, this stretch is a blast, especially in the latter half of the season. To reach Single Tree, take Southside Road (a dirt road that neighbors the river) from the southwest Harper's Bridge access.

Erskine access on the north bank of the river is not far from Single Tree on the north side of the river. Some trips use the access as an overnight pit stop for a two-day float, but there are a variety of islands and sandbars elsewhere in the river as well. From Frenchtown, take Mullan Road west and look for the access signs about two miles from town. "When the water is low in the summer, there are tons of little islands and beaches to camp on. It's a great overnight stretch," Herzer says.

As the summer winds down, cloudy weather encourages Trico and **Baetis** *hatches. Look for rising fish on the long, flat portions of the river, but be prepared to make long casts with long leaders to avoid spooking fish.*

The area downstream of Erskine is some of my favorite, especially during *Baetis* hatches. The river upstream of Petty Creek doesn't see as much pressure as it used to. If you're able to float this stretch in a one-man pontoon boat or something easier to launch by hand from Erskine, be prepared for a long day and keep moving. The many nice bends, pools, creek mouths, and seams along the bank make it easy to lose track of time. Petty Creek access is on the south side of Petty Creek Bridge, off I-90 (exit 77) just east of Alberton. If you decide to make a go of it, Jim Cox says this is one of the windiest sections on the river. Breezes funnel through Alberton Canyon, and when the weatherman says there's a "hint of wind" in the forecast, expect gale-force gusts.

"The lower river is really one of the best dry-fly fishing rivers in the state as far as consistency goes. The trout seem to key in on dry flies; they love to look up. A lot of the rainbows are in shallow, inside bends and riffles—perfectly suited for hopper-dropper techniques," Miller says. "Clark Fork fish love foam. Anywhere there is a collection of foam, it signifies a collection of food as well, and that's typically when you find a pod of fish."

Natural Pier is on the other side of Alberton and neighbors the frontage road from town. It is mainly a wading access, but since it neighbors a bridge, footing to either shore is an option. Wade carefully though. This portion of the river drops in elevation and is deceptively powerful. In fact, the famous white-water rapids of Alberton Gorge are just around the corner.

If you're floating from Petty Creek, the St. John's access (commonly called Rest Stop) is a mile or two past Natural Pier on the north side of the river (river right). There is a fair amount of rough water between here and Petty, so keep a sharp eye ahead of the boat. Also, don't miss the take-out or you could find your fishing trip turning into a white-water adventure. An added twist is this point is only accessible from the eastbound side of I-90. If you're heading west, get off the highway near Cyr (exit 70), turn left, and reenter heading east. Pull off on the scenic turnout. There is a drive path down to the river where you can use the cobblestone pullout to trailer your rig (four-wheel drive comes in handy).

If you continue heading west on I-90, you'll cross the river and the beginning of a deep gorge. Crossing over Cyr Bridge after exit 70 (westbound side only), then turning left (south) on Sawmill Gulch Road will put you at the Cyr Bridge access—a steep boat ramp meant for white-water rafting groups. The water below Cyr is great for rafters (and a known hot spot for rattlesnake

The Clark Fork near Alberton is full of hazards and only experienced oarsmen should attempt to negotiate it. One miscalculation can lead to trouble even in low-water periods.
JOHN HERZER/BLACKFOOT RIVER OUTFITTERS PHOTO

HISTORY

The Clark Fork is the largest river by volume in the state and drains not only an expansive area of western Montana, but continues into Idaho and on to Lake Pend Oreille, which then dumps into the Columbia River. Lewis and Clark visited the river on their return to St. Louis in 1806 and named the river after the leader of the expedition. As the fur-trading industry grew, the Clark Fork became a highway connecting traders and trappers all over western Montana.

When fur no longer shined, gold, silver, and copper did. In the late 1800s through the turn of the century, mining was the moneymaker. While the copper mines of Butte supported a community, the waste and other side effects nearly destroyed the headwaters of the Clark Fork. There are tales from the turn of the century when the river would run red with waste during high flows, and while many mines are now closed, their ill effects on the region remain to this day.

One of the biggest environmental concerns on the river was the Milltown Dam. Built at the turn of the century to supply power to what was then a relatively small community, it created the Milltown Reservoir where dangerous mine sediments stockpiled. For years, environmental groups denounced the dam as a dangerous, unnecessary concrete wall that was beyond repair, a roadblock to migratory fish like the westslope cutthroat and bull trout, and a reason for the river's rank as the top Superfund site in the United States.

Finally, in 2006, workers began dismantling the dam, but reconnecting a river is not an easy task. They drained the Milltown Reservoir and temporarily rerouted the Clark Fork so they could reach and remove the over 6 million cubic yards of contaminated sediment on the reservoir floor—sediments containing minerals like zinc and lead that are harmful to both fish and humans. In the long run, the removal of the dam will breathe new life into the Clark Fork, but it will be a bumpy road. Anglers, outfitters, and fly-shop owners expect some ill effects on the fishing downstream—the question is how bad and for how long.

"I grew up on this river, and I had some of the toughest fishing I've ever had since they started working on the dam," Kingfisher Fly Shop owner and outfitter Jim Cox says. "I'm not worried. I'm optimistic. We've been down this road before and watched nature heal. ■

sightings) but terrible for anglers, and I recommend avoiding it if you're looking for calmer waters or less traffic (dozens of white-water enthusiasts visit the gorge every day in the summer).

"Not a lot of people fish the gorge section. It's kind of dangerous, a few guys do it, and there can be good fishing because it gets little pressure. But you definitely have to know what you're doing. There are some dangerous rapids in there," Miller says.

While many anglers avoid the white water of Alberton Gorge, there are fishing opportunities. Be prepared to make fast casts to fishy-looking water as you pass by—you may only have a short window of opportunity before it's time to cast into another pocket.
JOHN HERZER/BLACKFOOT RIVER OUTFITTERS PHOTO

Old Highway 10 from Cyr circumvents some of the white-water areas, and the Tarkio East access can put you into some decent fishing water just northwest of the Fish Creek exit (66) on I-90. If I had my druthers, I'd rather visit one of the river's most important tributaries, Fish Creek, reached by heading south on Fish Creek Road, which follows this feeder closely and affords good access. It's full of cutthroat ready to pounce on any number of attractor patterns.

The Tarkio site is the next place you can access the river without running into huge white-water hazards. Take exit 61 from I-90, and then head southeast along the highway for nearly a mile. There is a parking lot and concrete boat ramp at the end. The water downstream from Tarkio is flanked by steep banks and trees, but they provide welcome shade in the heat of summer. With the exception of a handful of fast-water runs, the water is somewhat featureless compared with the rolling stretches upstream, so look to the banks or any other subsurface topography that might hold fish. If you're looking for a calm, half-day float, consider Tarkio to Forest Grove.

Forest Grove is on the east side of the river, across the stream from Quartz Flat public campground. The water downstream of Forest Grove is even more featureless than the water upstream, but it is a good place to hunt heads when *Baetis* or late-season caddis are on the water. Don't dillydally though, since the next take-out is nearly 11 miles downstream and during the short days of fall, you need to budget your time. Take exit 61 from I-90 and head west on the frontage road for 4 miles to reach Forest Grove. Quartz Flat Campground on the other side of the river has over 50 sites available (for both tent campers and RVs) and is easy to reach from the rest area southeast of Superior.

The Big Eddy access is on the north side of the river, just opposite the town of Superior. From here, you can fish through town and down to the Dry Creek ramp. It's a leisurely float, and there are no fast-water chutes or other obstructions to speak of, making this area worth exploring when late-season hatches arrive. In the summer, this sometimes becomes too warm for trout, particularly if there isn't much water coming from the tributaries, so don't fish when the water temperatures push over 68 degrees. Take I-90 to exit 47, then head north on River Street, cross the bridge, then head east on Mullan Road (old Highway 10) to find the parking lot.

"The lower stretch probably has better fish populations than closer to Missoula. I think the reason is you have so many cold, clear mountain streams that keep entering the river so the water quality is a little better, the hatches are better, and the fish can get a little bigger," Miller says.

Big Eddy or Dry Creek to St. Regis are good options for full-day drifts. The first half of this float doesn't change much from what is upstream—it's fairly flat, featureless water. But halfway through this stretch, there are riffles and other fish-holding structure, so if you aren't finding fish in the flat water, push on to the riffles. Dry Creek is near exit 43 (Dry Creek Road). Head north after exiting the interstate, and then head southeast on Old Highway 10 for .2

Some public-access points on the lower Clark Fork are too far apart to reach in a single float. Camping (below the high-water mark) is a great option if you want to reach less-pressured water or maximize your time on the water. JOHN HERZER/BLACKFOOT RIVER OUTFITTERS PHOTO

Clark Fork trout often congregate around fresh, cold-water sources like springs or tributary mouths. Watch for feeding fish as you approach and try to select fish on the outside of the pod first to avoid spooking other fish. JIM COX/KINGFISHER FLY SHOP PHOTO

mile. If you want to shorten it up a bit, look to the Sloway Campground on the east side of the river (river right), but there is no boat ramp here and you may have to drag your boat up the bank. Sloway is near Dry Creek; simply turn northwest on Old Highway 10. Soon after, I-90 will pass overhead and the campground is on the south, between the road and the river.

The St. Regis site is just past the heart of town, and the last lower-river landmark easily reached from I-90. Most drifters use it as a take-out since the next site downstream is nearly 15 miles, an incredibly long stretch to tackle in one day even in high water. Still, what this area does have going for it is the inflow from the St. Regis River, a tributary that winds down from the Idaho/Montana border and dumps cool water into the main stem. The St. Regis in itself is a fun fishery, but like the Clark Fork has received its share of war paint and doesn't hold the huge fish it looks like it should. Take exit 33 from I-90, head northeast on MT 135 for .75 mile, and turn southeast on Two Rivers Road. The parking lot is at the end of the road.

Downstream from St. Regis, the river is broad, flat, and slow in most areas. In fact, if there is even a hint of wind in the forecast, you're better off avoiding it altogether. MT 135 ducks and weaves between the hillsides and the river until it meets up with the Flathead River near Paradise. The only take-out is Ferry Landing (sometimes called 14-Mile Bridge) near the first and only bridge on MT 135 to cross the river. Cascade Campground is a few miles downstream.

"I love this float early season," Cox says. "There is a whirlpool halfway through the float that people need to approach carefully, but I routinely get some of the biggest fish of the year down here. Best *Skwala* hatch I've ever seen was on this stretch, and it's hopper and caddis heaven."

A few miles later, the river merges with the Flathead, takes a northwestern course, and heads to Idaho. There are a few pull-offs and access points downstream, like McKay Landing and Flat Iron Ridge near Thompson Falls, and bridges in Paradise and Plains, but by this point the character of the river has changed from a trout stream to a place more likely to hold bass and pike.

Given the volume of contribution from the Flathead, the river is substantially bigger as well, so if you're floating, be wary of hazards like the fast water near Plains. Typically, this low reach is smooth sailing for even novice rowers, but given the speed and depth, it never hurts to play it safe. Going in to the Thompson Falls area, the river slows down and cascades into a string of reservoirs that extend into the Gem State.

Hatches and Flies

While most anglers who fish the Clark Fork regard it as one of the best caddis rivers in the state, it has many mayfly hatches as well, including terrific Trico hatches. But as much as you might see on the water, you don't always have to go overboard with match-the-hatch fever. "One of my favorite things to do on the river is throw something that's completely the opposite of what the fish are feeding on," Cox says. "If Tricos are busting, and I can't get a fish to save my life, I tie on a big Turck's or foam pattern and throw that into the mix. Typically there's at least one gutsy fish that will come up and smack it. On the shoulders of the season it can get a lot more technical. You're talking fish rejecting Comparaduns for Sparkle Duns. Fish preferring poly-yarn tails over Microfibetts tails, and cripples beating parachutes by a margin of 10 to 1. You have to match color and size."

Unfortunately, the hatches, like the river, are in a state of limbo until the Milltown Dam project is complete and the watershed has time to heal. At present, there is no denying the work impacted the river's aquatic insect ecosystem. "I think the bug activity definitely took a hit," Cox says. "The intensity of the hatches waned, particularly the caddis. Things will come back, it will just take time."

Although recent hatches seem to have temporarily waned, there are still enough bugs to get the fish feeding on the surface. In the early season, just after the ice breaks up and heads downstream, expect to see a variety of midges and smatterings of *Baetis.* These bugs love the dreary, overcast days so common in the Missoula area as winter disappears. Fish will pod up and feed in slow, flat water, making accurate, delicate presentations a must. One word of caution: When the wind starts ripping through the lower river's canyons, hatches can shut down and you're in for a long, cold day on the water.

March Browns and *Skwalas* are meaty meals for fish coming out of the lulls of winter, and because they typically coincide with warmer water temperatures, the fish are a little more active. If the weather patterns are on your side, and the bugs are doing what they're supposed to do, you can have some of the best dry-fly fishing of the year—a time when the rivers are nearly void of angling traffic. "Clark Fork *Skwalas* are a little bigger than the bugs you see on the Bitterroot. I like to use a Rogue Salmonfly, but any of the foam *Skwala* patterns work," Miller says. "The *Skwala* hatch on the Clark Fork typically

During the Clark Fork's Trico hatch, it's not a bad idea to use a large fly, like a Parachute Adams, or in this case, a Gray Drake Paradrake, as a point fly with a spent Trico pattern as a dropper. It makes it easier to detect when fish eat the Trico pattern, and if you're lucky, they'll sometimes fall for the bigger offering.

comes a little later than other streams, more toward the end of April, so it can get blown out with an early runoff. But, when the bugs hatch on the Clark Fork the water is warmer, the air temps are warmer, and the bugs are flying and flopping on the water. Patterns with the appearance of fluttering wings are key."

Around May the caddis begin to appear, but in most years, their fluttering flights are somewhat of a teaser to anglers. Because the Clark Fork encompasses such an immense drainage, high water can come early and stay late. It's not unusual to have off-color water from May to July. It's only an assumption, but I have to believe the Milltown Dam restoration will only amplify these conditions for the next few years until high water flushes any remaining sediments from the system.

As runoff subsides, the big bugs appear, especially near the mouth of Rock Creek. In fact, the water between Clinton and Turah is the go-to spot on the upper Clark Fork if you're into pounding the banks and other structure with #4 foam creations. It's also a good time of year to float this stretch because of the abundant water. If things get slow, rig up a streamer rod and work the same water.

When the river finally settles into its summer groove, Pale Morning Duns (PMDs) are the mainstay, though they aren't as strong as previous years. "We used to see clouds," Herzer says, "and now there's only a handful. I think it has as much as anything to do with the dam guys jerking around with flows before the dam was deconstructed. Up and down, testing this and testing that. We'd get all these flushes of sediment and combined with elevated water temperatures, it just crushed the bugs. I have nothing but confidence that the river will be better than it's ever been in the future; it just takes time to recover."

I like the water between Kona Bridge and Petty Creek when fishing PMDs because the water has a great mix of riffles and smooth, flat water where you can see trout snouts from 100 yards upstream with plenty of time to plan your attack. Despite having to size down my tippet to 4X or 5X, I still like to fish a two-fly rig during this hatch. I like minimal, sparsely tied bugs, especially for fish sitting in that quiet, slow water. For the point fly I use a dun pattern that I can see whether it's a parachute or tan Sparkle Dun. For the dropper I like something just under the surface, not too heavy, like a Barr Emerger.

If you like to fish PMDs, get on the water early before the summer heat puts the bugs and the fish down. It never ceases to amaze me how people spend hundreds of dollars on a guided trip and then sleep in and hit the river after 11 AM. Sunrise to lunchtime is about right and leaves time for a nap and enough juice left over for a return trip in the evening light. You'll see less people and more fish.

Later in the summer, even though the PMDs may still be active, terrestrials begin to move fish. There are plenty of grassy banks, overhanging vegetation, and other places for hoppers, beetles, and ants to fall in the water, and fish do not overlook them. Like the PMDs, terrestrials are another time I recommend covering bases with something on top and underneath. Jim Cox likes to use a variation of tricks.

"The Clark Fork is like a tailwater in character, but in a good year it can rival the Blackfoot in terms of disgustingly large dry-fly productivity," Cox says. "We spend a lot of time in the height of the season throwing junk—big, floating, nasty, foamy stuff like the Rogue Goldens, red Turck's Tarantulas, and Paranobles, which were designed for this river."

Before the dam removal, the Trico hatch on the Clark Fork was one of my favorites, and on a good day, it was as good as anywhere else in the state. If the hatches return to former glory after the dam and water problems are rectified, this is yet another instance of where getting on the water early is in your favor.

When I worked for the *Missoulian,* the window next to my desk overlooked the river running under the Higgins Avenue Bridge. I typically arrived around 6 AM so I could work for a few hours and then take my "lunch break" when I could look out and see mouths sucking down spinners. I didn't even have to get in the water. A friend and I would cast from the side of the Kim Williams Trail into the shadows of the bridge, work downstream toward the Boone and Crockett headquarters, and catch more fish than should be allowed. An hour later, we'd return to work smelling like victory.

"One thing a lot of guys are doing that works is sinking Trico spinner patterns—especially when you get into those pods of fish that are feeding on Tricos and it seems impossible to catch anything because there are so many naturals on the water. They're fishing a bigger bug like a Parachute Adams as the lead fly and sinking a spinner off the back. Just 2 inches under the surface is all it takes," Miller says.

The end of the Tricos signals the end of the tourism season in western Montana, but it's not the end of the fishing season. Mahogany Duns appear in noticeable numbers, but I believe the return of *Baetis* has the fish more keyed up. The cool, partly cloudy days of autumn help bring these bugs to the forefront, and they bring the last few days of solid dry-fly fishing on the river before winter brings things to a halt once again.

"On overcast days, the fish aren't too fussy. But on bright days when the sun is pounding the water, fish are typically harder to come by," Miller says. "Anytime you get an overcast day, we usually get Blue Wings. But in the fall, you'll see hundreds of bugs, especially around Superior and St. Regis."

I enjoy throwing streamers in the stretch between Clinton and Turah, as well as the lower river. Woolhead sculpin patterns, rabbit-strip leeches, or Woolly Bugger–style ties are standard fare. "Black has been a good streamer color on the river. But when the water is a little skinnier, guys use floating lines and throw large mends in the drift so the patterns stay just under the surface. It's like fishing dry flies because you can see the strike," Miller says.

Despite its size and volume, I don't approach the Clark Fork differently than I do many other Western freestones when it comes to gear. A fast-action 4- or 5-weight rod is suited for dry-fly action through the summer, or lightweight nymphing if the Warm Springs discharge is your game. For heavier stonefly nymphs or streamers, I move up to a 6- or 7-weight rod. I like the additional backbone of a heavier rod when I'm fishing heavy flies—and you will too if the famous Clark Fork wind decides to kick up.

Leaders that go 9 to 12 feet are good for summer fishing when water is low and clear and the bugs are one size smaller than what your eyes can see. The fish aren't leader shy, so try to keep tippets above 4X. Occasionally, I'll dip to 5X but have never found the need to go lighter. I'd rather not catch a fish than risk overplaying it. On another note, the terrain surrounding the Clark Fork is somewhat arid and open with little shade through the meat of the day. Use sunscreen and wear good polarized sunglasses for both comfort and health.

Directions

It's difficult to give directions to every access area on a place like the Clark Fork because it travels over such an expansive area. However, I-90 more or less follows the river along most of its course. The state-managed access sites, pull-offs, and boat launches all connect to this highway in one way or another on the upper river. Mullan Road is a key route for the lower river. I've tried to lay out an idea of where to go as I named the access points, but use whatever good references you can find (like a DeLorme *Montana Atlas & Gazetteer*) to help you find your way to the water.

Also, fly-shop employees and outfitters know what's going on with hatches and water conditions and can make some great fly recommendations to boot. The Clark Fork is a big river with many riddles, and if you intend on fishing it for a reasonable amount of time, spending one day with a seasoned guide will get you started on the right foot.

Schlotter's Rogue Foam Stone (*Skwala*)

Hook:	#10-12 Tiemco 200R
Thread:	Black 140-denier Ultra Thread
Body:	Olive closed-cell foam
Wing:	Medical tape over Krystal Flash, and moose mane
Head:	Olive elk hair
Legs:	Black round rubber (medium)
Collar:	Black 140-denier Ultra Thread

Gould's Half-Down Yellow Sally

Hook:	#16-18 MFC 7048
Thread:	Yellow 8/0 Uni-Thread
Egg Sac:	Red Frog's Hair dubbing
Tail:	Yellow Tentacles (#2)
Abdomen:	Yellow .020 monofilament
Wing:	Natural elk over MFC Plain Web
Thorax:	PMD Frog's Hair dubbing
Legs:	Yellow Centipede Legs (mini)
Indicator:	1 mm yellow foam

Furimsky's Hi-Vis BDE (*Baetis*)

Hook:	#16-20 MFC 7048
Thread:	Rusty brown 8/0 Uni-Thread
Tail:	Medium olive EZ Dub
Body:	Medium olive EZ Dub
Thorax:	Peacock herl
Hackle:	Medium dun hackle
Wing:	Gray dun poly yarn
Indicator:	Hot pink Gator Yarn

Harrop's Last Chance Cripple (PMD)

Hook:	#16-20 Tiemco 100BL
Thread:	Yellow 8/0 Uni-Thread
Tail:	Mallard flank dyed wood duck
Shuck:	Rusty brown Antron
Body:	Rusty brown goose biot
Thorax:	Nature's Spirit PMD dubbing
Wing:	Light dun CDC
Hackle:	Grizzly hackle dyed pale yellow

Bitterroot River

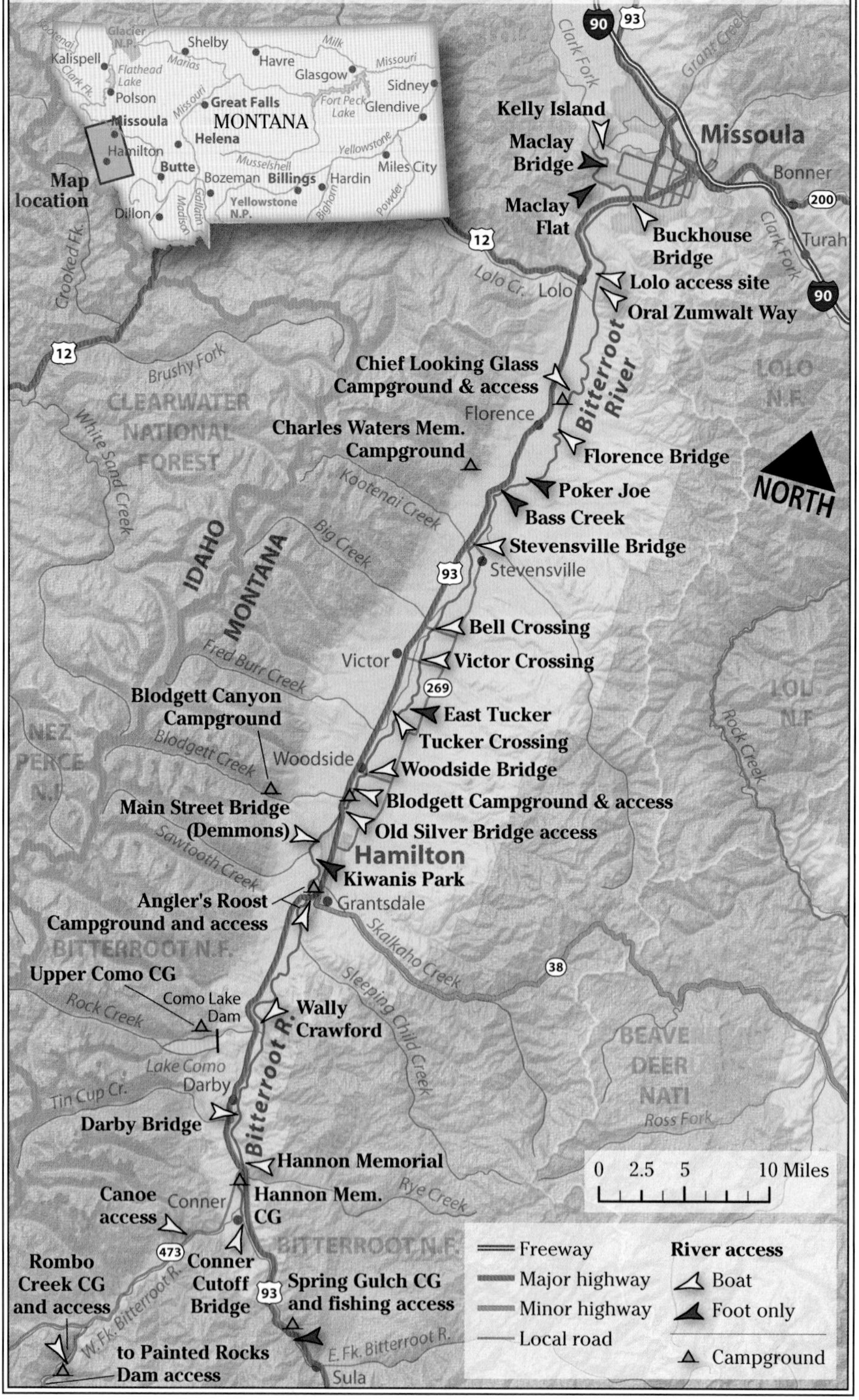

CHAPTER 11

Bitterroot River

The Bitterroot River is so diverse that you can have a vastly different experience each day simply by varying your location up- or downstream by just a few miles; each section is slightly different from those above and below it. It's also a place that produces. The river is full of wild trout and healthy aquatic insect hatches, and at the right time and place, it's ideally suited for those attempting to break the 20-inch mark using nothing but dry flies. "I think the Bitterroot is one of the top three dry-fly rivers in the state," River Otter Fly Shop co-owner Chris McCabe says. "During the prime-time of the season we're fishing dry flies 80 percent of the time."

A few years ago, the Bitterroot River earned a place as the fourth most heavily fished river in the state of Montana. And with good reason. It's a healthy fishery with plenty of access for both the wading or floating angler, and it has some of the best scenery the region has to offer. It's also an area steeped in history. Lewis and Clark made camp near the junction of the Bitterroot River and Lolo Creek before trekking over the Bitterroot Mountains in their continuing search for the Pacific Ocean. And while the valley has morphed drastically since their epic journey, it still has the same essence of adventure and beauty.

Where and When

The West Fork of the Bitterroot begins deep in the Bitterroot Mountains—not far from the Idaho state line. It gains moderate volume from nearby springs and small tributaries and has decent fishing for small cutthroat trout before dumping into Painted Rocks Reservoir. Reaching this portion is easy if you're willing to make the drive. West Fork Road (MT 473) will take you to the reservoir and continue to follow the fork to its upper reaches.

It's the outflow that creates the West Fork fishery as most anglers know it. The cold-water releases keep the water cool and clear throughout the season, making it an attractive haunt for the river's cutthroat populations. While the West Fork's rocky nature and lack of boat ramps keeps most angling traffic on their feet, one popular float is from the Canoe access (near the West Fork Ranger Station) to either Conner Cutoff Bridge or Hannon Memorial less than a mile

Early season fishing on the Bitterroot is becoming increasingly popular, but despite the pressure, the opportunity to catch big fish is still a genuine possibility. If fish aren't interested in larger Skwala *patterns, try smaller mayfly imitations. Mayfly naturals are often more plentiful, but anglers overlook them for the bigger stoneflies.* DOMINIC VALPIANI PHOTO

downstream from the junction with the East Fork. It's a short float (especially when the water is high) that sees more boat traffic than it should, but when the Salmonflies and Golden Stones are hatching it's a tough stretch to beat. West Fork Road (MT 473) follows nearly all the West Fork of the Bitterroot.

The East Fork of the Bitterroot begins in a separate drainage a few miles to the east in the Anaconda-Pintler Wilderness near the Continental Divide. Its upper reaches are intimate, but flowing westward it eventually makes its way into a valley and begins paralleling US 93 after the small town of Sula.

From this point downstream, there are several roadside pull-offs, campgrounds, and intermittent access points where you can park and jump in the water. However, once fishing, be mindful of the high-water line and avoid trespassing. The East Fork is a good option for the wading angler—especially later in the season as cutthroat migrate from the main stem looking for cooler water. Odds are slim you'll hook the trophy of your life, but there are plenty of 10- to 16-inch fish willing to play on the surface. "When runoff is subsiding and Green Drakes and Salmonflies are hatching on the upper main stem, the upper forks are just coming into their own. They continue to get better as everything settles into that summer pattern," Flies and Guides fly-shop owner Chuck Stranahan says.

The two forks combine to form the main stem near Conner. While flows on the upper main stem, from the forks to Hamilton, are low during drought years, sometimes making it tough to float, the river flows along the bases of hills and mountains and is a great option for those looking to mix their fishing with some of the best scenery the river has to offer, including views of Trapper Peak and the Bitterroot ridgeline to the west.

This water generally has a good mix of riffles, soft-water banks, and a few deep slow-water pools. Hannon Memorial, Darby Birdge, Wally Crawford, and the ramp within the Angler's Roost Campground (a private site that requires boaters to register inside the general store when launching or loading) are easy to reach from US 93 and the most popular put-ins and take-outs for floating fishermen.

The West Fork of the Bitterroot generally runs clear before the main stem and offers one of the first opportunities to fish during the famous Salmonfly hatch. Cast along the banks and any other structure, but pinch the barbs before you fish. Large Salmonfly hooks can damage the fish's mouth.

The upper river is more intimate than the lower Bitterroot, so look for fish in textbook holding areas like soft-water seams, along the banks, and in the heart of riffles. HEATHER ROMANS PHOTO

Be mindful that the upper river can hold a logjam or two depending on the whims of the spring runoff. There are also two diversion dams between Wally Crawford and Angler's Roost. There is a newly created channel on the west side of the river near the second and largest of the two diversion dams that takes the pain out of portaging, but inquire at a local fly shop before you launch as seasonal obstructions and water conditions adjacent to these structures change frequently.

"You can almost draw an imaginary line below Hamilton where the river changes and how it functions. The water below the East and West forks has lots of riffles. It's typically colder in the summer and has an abundance of cutthroat," outfitter Jay Dixon says. "As you move from the upper river into the lower river, you'll also see a transition in the bug life based on the stream-bottom habitat. The stonefly masses will go down, and the numbers of mayflies will go up."

Near Hamilton the valley opens up and the river seemingly doubles in size. Contributions from neighboring tributaries like Skalkaho and Blodgett creeks (while somewhat skinny during irrigation season) pump cold, clean water into the river making it a little easier to float. This is also where you can start encountering some of the river's larger, and oftentimes selective, browns and rainbows. Skalkaho Creek is a major brown-trout spawning area. In fact, I remember seeing a dead brown trout wash ashore near Angler's Roost when I was a guide in the area. A photo of the fish even landed in the local newspaper. It measured over 30 inches and apparently died of old age.

The Main Street Bridge access in Hamilton, the US 93 bridge on the north side of Hamilton (downstream of where the Old Silver Bridge once stood), Blodgett Park, Woodside Bridge, Tucker Crossing, Victor Crossing, Bell Crossing, and the access on the east side of the Stevensville Bridge are easy places to reach the river, and like the sites in the upper river are all easily available via US 93. The Main Street Bridge and US 93 bridge sites, however, require a scramble if you're using a boat. The river changes every year, so keep a sharp eye for hazards (often downstream of Tucker Crossing), false channels, or diversion dams (like the one between Main Street Bridge and the US 93 bridge in Hamilton) that sometimes require a portage.

"As the summer heat kicks in, I stay off the lower reaches. I pretty much base myself up- and downstream from Victor in the heart of the catch-and-release water. Then I'll stay in the upper river till the end of August when nighttime temps start cooling things off," Wapiti Waters owner Jack Mauer says.

If you are wading, don't be afraid to put some distance between you and the access. You can often find more solitude and fish that aren't pounded hourly by those unwilling to walk 500 feet.

Look to the sharp banks and inside seams around riffles or structure, especially if there is a substantial drop in depth. Areas like this are attractive because the fish don't have to work as hard fighting the current and they have a perfect vantage point to sight and ambush any food that happens by.

There are also a lot of slow-water sloughs, backwaters, and channels in the lower river—some spring-fed—that stay cold through the summer and are worth exploring. The fish are spooky, but it's an opportunity to sneak up on some big fish. Some channels are easier to access than others, so be mindful of the high-water line to avoid trespassing.

"Some rivers change a little every year, but the Bitterroot is ridiculous. I compare it to rivers in Alaska. If you take an aerial photo every year, you'll see different channels cut and different riffles formed every season. You can be fishing a different trough 200 yards from where you were the season before," Dixon says. "Some stretches stay the same, but most of them are in the upper river. From Woodside or Tucker Crossing downstream is where you'll see most of the changes. I don't know of any other river in the state that changes so much."

From the Stevensville Bridge access downstream to the junction with the Clark Fork River near Kelly Island, just west of Missoula, the Bitterroot takes on

Spring fishing in Montana means expecting any type of weather. Pack clothing for any situation since it may be sunny and warm one moment and cloudy and snowing the next.

Fish congregate in the deepest pools as water levels drop through the summer. Try a dry-dropper or nymph rig at the head of the pool and along the deep edges if fish aren't actively feeding on the surface. HEATHER ROMANS PHOTO

a lackadaisical character. Gentle turns, slow-water flats, and long, flat stretches replace the fast-water riffles and chutes characteristic of the upper river. MDFWP electrofishing data show this area is where the river's biggest rainbows live. There are confirmed (yet fantastic) angler accounts of fish up to 28 inches taken on dry flies, although most fish even close to this size sulk on the bottom through the warm summer months.

You have to fish for them when conditions are right. Try to tackle these areas early or late in the season because of the water's propensity to become too warm in the peak of summer. This is water ideally suited for *Baetis* and Trico hatches where you can see the bulging nose of a trout and have plenty of time to plan your approach and presentation. Runs like this require long, light tippets and steady nerves.

"After runoff, the whole river is good. And until river temps warm up to the point where fishing is fruitless, I think the best mayfly activity is on the lower stretch," Stranahan says. "Then again, in late summer—when the water cools and irrigation needs subside—and into late September and early October you're just as apt to see good PMD activity down there as you are Blue-Winged Olives. There are times in late September, particularly below

Stevensville, where you can see thick, thick, Trico hatches and spinnerfalls. You get big rainbows up on those things. They're like kindergartners eating jelly beans. The more experienced angler can go headhunting and catch large fish."

Stevensville Bridge, Florence Bridge, Chief Looking Glass, Lolo, Buckhouse Bridge, Maclay Flat, and Kelly Island are key access points. There is no boat ramp at the Lolo access, so anglers must carry watercraft from the parking area to the water or use the single-lane boat ramp upstream on the east side of the river off Oral Zumwalt Way (take Upper Miller Creek Road from Missoula, turn south on Trails End Road, then south on Oral Zumwalt). Wading anglers should walk up- or downstream from the Bass Creek, Poker Joe, and Chief Looking Glass areas.

If water temperatures permit, late August through the end of the season is my favorite time to float the lower river. Large Trico hatches bring dozens of fish to the surface, but that doesn't mean they're easy to catch. With so many naturals on the water, you need to bring long leaders, your A-game, and a lot of patience.

"The lower river fishes more like a big spring creek than it does a freestone river because you have those long, broad, flat, slow-moving pools. You need to position yourself above the trout, fish a long leader, and nail the presentation. If you do, you can score," Stranahan says. "And don't forget the late-season *Hecubas* and hoppers. If a morning of sippy rises on flies you can barely see is driving you nuts, relief is on the way with big Brindle Chutes and hoppers."

Hatches and Flies

There's no denying the popularity of early-season fishing on the Bitterroot River. *Skwala* stoneflies, Blue-Winged Olives, March Browns, and the occasional Gray Drakes make their appearance and draw fish to the surface while other rivers in the state remained trapped under sheets of ice. Once regarded as a well-kept angling secret, the months of

Bitterroot trout often wander into sloughs and backwaters and are sometimes easy to spot when PMD, **Baetis**, *or Trico hatches bring them to the surface. Long leaders and accurate casting are essential to catch them.*

March, April, and early May are now a circus of boats and anglers. For those who have enjoyed early-season fishing on the 'Root for decades, the new masses have undoubtedly affected the experience—but the fishing can still be worth the trouble.

"If you get enough warm weather in mid-March without knocking too much snow downriver, you get good *Skwala* fishing. Typically the last two weeks of March and the first week of April," McCabe says. "The crowds haven't been bad in the past few years, but the main push is during the early *Skwala* season. There are a lot of people from out of state that bring their own boats and stuff. But in mid-April, everybody fizzles out on other waters, and that's when the good fishing really starts. You've got March Browns and a host of other mayflies right up until runoff."

The trick is finding a happy medium between the weather patterns and water temperature. For example, the air temperature may be 60 degrees, but if the water is below 40 (like it often is on the upper river on an early spring morning), don't expect the fish to be aggressive. There may be bugs on the water as the air temperatures rise, but until the water temperatures warm slightly, the fish may show little interest. Even a rise of a few degrees makes a big difference.

Gazing up at the views of the upper Bitterroot is a perfect way to rest weary eyes tired from watching a dry fly bob in the current. Take a break from fishing now and again to enjoy the scenery. HEATHER ROMANS PHOTO

Look for the water from Hamilton to the lower river to warm first, but watch out if spring temperatures escalate too quickly. An abnormal warm weather pattern could cause low-level snow to melt and transform the river into a muddy mess.

After a long winter, *Skwala* stoneflies are a welcome sight for both anglers and fish. Before the brunt of the hatch, imitate the nymphs with heavy patterns like a #8-10 Mercer's Skwala Stone. When the fish begin targeting bugs on the surface, look to a #8-12 Gould's Wiggle Skwala and Bugmeister.

"If I'm fishing the *Skwala* hatch, my favorite stretch is the middle river. You can wade-fish or float it, and the habitat is rich with bug life. You are just as apt to see Gray Drakes and Blue-Winged Olives with *Skwalas* being the frosting on the cake. Very often those lesser hatches can save the day," Stranahan says. "Cold water coming from Skalkaho, Blodgett, Mill, and Big creeks causes the *Skwala* hot spots to jump around. The best early-season fishing is typically from Hamilton through Corvallis and Tucker Crossing to Victor or Bell Crossing. The stretches from Victor down tend to peter out as water rises, after an initial bout of decent *Skwala* activity. Some of the best fishing is always from Angler's Roost down to Main Street, most of which is above the mouth of Skalkaho Creek. The same goes for the runs well below Blodgett Creek to the mouth of Big Creek, accessed on several possible floats between Corvallis and Stevensville."

Blue-Winged Olives, Gray Drakes, and March Browns are other mayflies known to appear at the same time—often in heavier concentrations than the *Skwalas.* "There are other important insects during the spring besides *Skwalas,*" Mauer says. "March Browns and early black stoneflies are overlooked. My biggest Bitterroot brown and rainbow both came on March Brown patterns."

If weather permits, the Bitterroot also sees heavy bursts of Grannom Caddis between late April and mid-May. This hatch produces masses of bugs, but whether or not the fish key in on them depends on water conditions. If runoff holds off long enough, fishing can be off the charts.

"Barring a blowout due to early runoff, the Bitterroot can produce a Mother's Day Caddis hatch to rival any. The little gray bugs are especially thick around Hamilton a week or two either side of Mother's Day and active throughout the whole system. At times they cause the trout to get downright reckless on the surface. At such times a gray-bodied version of the Grannom Caddis Variant, in a size 14, seems hardly fair," Stranahan says.

After runoff the *Skwalas'* larger stonefly cousins the Golden Stone and Salmonfly appear. While Salmonfly hatches are not as heavy or notorious as on other waters like Rock Creek, and they generally stick to the West Fork and upper river area, more than enough bugs keep action hot. This is the time to throw large patterns with force and skitter them once they plop on the water. Adding action is realistic and draws the attention of fish. Some of the best days I've had are from twitching a #6-8 Extended Body Foam Golden Stone from Montana Fly Company (MFC) or a #8 Chuck's Golden Stone. Golden Stones are a little more prolific and emergences can span most of the river.

The Golden Stonefly is one of the most prevalent hatches on the Bitterroot, sometimes lasting until August. Use Stimulator-style patterns or foam-bodied creations around riffles and fast water where stoneflies often congregate.

"If the water is clear enough, you can have good Salmonfly fishing from Wally Crawford upstream. However, the Golden Stones are a little more prolific than the Salmonflies. We get the big ones that come off early, and the big nocturnal ones coming off all season. There's Yellow Sallies and everything in between. You can fish stoneflies almost all season," McCabe says.

"If I had to pick one hatch that's my favorite, I'd have to say Golden Stones because they're on the water for such a long time—even until September and October," Stranahan says. "Once they appear in the early season, they're a long-lived bug. And they hatch sporadically."

Another noteworthy Bitterroot hatch, the Green Drakes, show up as Salmonflies taper off. A real treat is being on the water when both Salmonflies and Green Drakes overlap. "We get good Green Drake activity here every year, it's just a matter of having good water conditions to make it fishable or not. It starts late June, and in some years early July. The nymphs live in silt at the edges of slough mouths. If you pinpoint those places, and you're there at the right time, just sit and wait. Soon you see what looks like a freshly shelled pea coming up through the water. Then all of the sudden, poof, wings pop out and this big bug will float for a while and then take off. But, quite often the cycle is interrupted," Stranahan says.

Unless it's a particularly cloudy day, or there is a passing rainstorm dampening the sunlight, don't expect to see a lot of these bugs. Spotting a few here and there is the norm, but it's enough to get fish to key in on them. A #10 Lawson's Green Drake Paradrake and a #10 Nealley's Green Drake are two of my favorite drake patterns. In fact, I caught some of my best Bitterroot fish on a Paradrake long after the hatch diminished—just one example of the fish's ongoing appetite for these bugs. If you want to throw them something different, try a #10 Hookup Green Drake.

Midsummer PMDs are another highlight, but watch water temperatures. In the low-water drought years I've fished terrific PMD hatches on one morning and then returned the next day only to not see a single bug or rising fish because the water temperature increased by a few degrees. Comparaduns (#14-18), simple parachute PMD patterns, and Quigley Cripples (#14-18) should get the job done.

Unfortunately, most of the people who visit the Bitterroot hit the water during the heat of the day in the summer and are off by happy hour. If possible, stay on the water until dark, or take a midday break and fish the evening hours for some terrific caddis action. As the sun fades, these bugs flutter and skate all over the water, and the reclusive fish come out to feed. It's really one of the overlooked and underfished opportunities on the river.

"Throughout the summer, the fastest dry-fly action can occur right around dusk when the caddis hatch and egg-layers from previous hatches are on the water. It might last for 2 hours or 20 minutes—but it's intense. A #12-14 light or tan Caddis Variant usually gets the job done. The light Caddis Variant is especially effective for the first half of the season, as it doubles well for a Yellow Sally. The tan version matches about half of the caddisflies on this or any other stream and is a must for those summer evening caddis grabs," Stranahan says.

The vegetation along the banks of the middle and lower portions of the Bitterroot makes it a perfect place to pound the banks come hopper season. Experiment with a variety of patterns (including buggy-looking attractors) to discover what the fish prefer. In the early evening, I've seen 22-inch browns chase #4 foam monstrosities. This is also a good time to tie on a dropper if you're not already doing so. A beadhead nymph, floating beetle, or ant pattern is a good starting point. Cast your fly as close to grass or structure as possible, mend, and add a few twitches to mimic a natural falling into the water.

The Green Drake hatch on the Bitterroot offers anglers one of the few opportunities to cast big mayfly patterns to big trout. Though they favor cloudy conditions, it never hurts to use a Lawson Paradrake as a dropper from a stonefly pattern.

BITTERROOT RIVER

JAN FEB MAR APR MAY JUN JUL AUG SEP OCT NOV DEC

Midge (Chironomidae)
#16-24 Griffith's Gnat, Disco Midge, Parachute Adams, Palomino Midge

Blue-Winged Olive (*Baetis* spp.)
#16-20 Parachute Adams, Pheasant-Tail Nymph, Sparkle Dun, Rusty Spinner, Furimsky's BDE, Purple Haze

Skwala Stonefly (*Skwala parallela*)
#6-10 Gould's Half-Down Skwala, Mercer's Skwala Stone, Bugmeister, Rogue Foam Stone, Gould's Wiggle Skwala

Brown Dun (*Ameletus* spp.)
#12-14 Parachute Hare's-Ear, Comparadun, Parachute Adams

March Brown (*Rhithrogena* spp.)
#12-14 Comparadun, Parachute Adams, Gray Wulff, Flashback Pheasant-Tail Nymph

Grannom Caddis (*Brachycentrus occidentalis*)
#12-16 Glass-House Caddis, Elk-Hair Caddis, Z-Wing Caddis, Deep Sparkle Pupa, Stranahan's Caddis Variant

Pale Morning Dun (*Ephemerella excrucians* or *E. dorothea infrequens*)
#16-20 Parachute Adams, Quigley Cripple, Pheasant-Tail Nymph, Hare's-Ear Nymph, Harrop's PMD Cripple

Terrestrials (Ants, Beetles, Hoppers)
#14-20 Schroeder's Parachute Ant, Lawson's Hi-Vis Foam Beetle, Gould's Half-Down Ant, Galloup's Ant-Acid; #6-10 Trixie the Hooker Hopper; #8-12 Schroeder's Parachute Hopper, Dave's Hopper

Caddis (*Hydropsyche* and *Ceratopsyche* spp.)
#12-18 Goddard Caddis, Elk-Hair Caddis, Stimulator, Sparkle Pupa, CDC & Elk, Stranahan's Caddis Variant

Salmonfly (*Pteronarcys californica*)
#4-8 Bitch Creek Nymph, Stimulator, Rogue Foam Stone, Romans' Thing From Uranus

Golden Stonefly (*Hesperoperla pacifica*)
#6-12 Stimulator, Elk-Hair Caddis, Pat's Rubber Legs, Bitch Creek Nymph, Clook's Floater in the Pool, Chuck's Golden Stone

Yellow Sally (*Isoperla* spp.)
#14-16 Elk-Hair Caddis, Gould's Half-Down Yellow Sally

Trico (*Tricorythodes* spp.)
#18-22 Polywing Spinner, Griffith's Gnat, Vis-A-Dun, Quigley Hackle Stacker

Green Drake (*Drunella grandis*)
#8-10 Quigley Cripple, Stranahan's Hookup Green Drake, Lawson's Green Drake Paradrake, Nealley's Green Drake

Mahogany Dun (*Isonychia* spp.)
#14-18 Pheasant-Tail Nymph, Quigley Cripple, Rusty Spinner, Comparadun

Gray Drake (*Siphlonurus occidentalis*)
#10-12 Parachute Adams, Nealley's Brown Drake, Stranahan's Brindle Chute, Quigley Cripple, Pheasant-Tail Nymph

Hecuba (*Timpanoga hecuba*)
#10-14 Stranahan's Brindle Chute, Lawson's Brown Drake Paradrake

A dry-dropper rig is one of the most effective techniques on the Bitterroot through the summer, especially when big bugs like Golden Stoneflies or hoppers are present. Tie 18 inches of tippet to the hook bend of the lead fly and tie a nymph or emerger off the tag end.

Tricos signal that another summer is winding down. Coming off in mid-August, these tiny morsels continue into late September in some years. The slow, smooth water of the lower river is where I like to fish this hatch because it's easier to spot fish, plan an approach, and see my fly when I make the cast. If you're having trouble detecting strikes, use a slightly larger fly like a Parachute Adams or caddis as a point fly with a spent Trico dropper. Brown Drakes, Mahogany Duns, and October Caddis come off at this time of year, so by using a lead fly that imitates them you might attract more fish. If a fish rises near your point fly, or it dives under the surface, set the hook.

Tricos aren't the only late-season mayfly. *Hecuba,* a mayfly that resembles Green Drakes, hatches in the latter half of the summer from mid-July to September. You can get away with Green Drake patterns, but a #10 Brindle Chute is a more accurate representation in both size and color. "When they're out, the fishing can suddenly get really good with dry flies. The hatch isn't prolific, they're just here and there, but the fish certainly notice them," Dixon says.

Many anglers confuse the Bitterroot's *Isonychia* hatches with the *Hecuba* because they are similar in size, but *Isonychia* has a maroon body with yellow segments. Fred Arbona makes the best distinction between the two in his book *Mayflies, the Angler, and the Trout.* He says that both appear sporadically and in some cases emergences overlap, but *Hecuba* have orange-brown bodies. *Hecuba* emerges, typically, from late morning or early afternoon until mid to late afternoon, with spinners typically on the water in the evening. *Isonychia* hatches later (late August into early September) with most hatches occurring in the evening.

Though the Bitterroot carries the reputation as one of the finest dry-fly streams in the state, nymphing does have its place. Two-fly nymph rigs produce in the early and late season when surface action is traditionally slow, but don't be afraid to tie a nymph dropper to your dry fly throughout the height of the season. Those fish unwilling to ascend to the surface for a meal may meet you halfway for a Beadhead Prince Nymph.

The dry-fly fishing also overshadows some of the good streamer fishing on the Bitterroot. Most anglers wait until the brown trout are on the prowl in early fall before they start swinging Woolly Buggers and the like, but streamer fishing is good throughout the season and a good alternative if there's not much happening on the surface. "During the dog days of August, the big fish lay at the bottom of those long runs or under the foamy dropoffs along diagonal riffles, and eat sculpins, baitfish, baby whitefish, leeches, crawdads, their grandchildren, or whatever else makes the mistake of swimming into range," Stranahan says.

Fish in the main stem Bitterroot range between 10 and 18 inches long so 4-, 5-, and 6-weight rods with floating lines are perfect. I like to use a lighter rod when throwing small flies like PMDs or Tricos and save the heavier guns for big flies and streamers (that I sometimes pair with a sinking-tip line).

Trico hatches on the lower river can blanket the soft, slow-flowing areas and bring dozens of fish to the surface, but catching them is not easy. Light tippets, precise casting, and a little luck are steps in the right direction. However, don't get frustrated. With so many naturals on the water, fish gain a discerning eye for what to eat and what to avoid.

Big Bitterroot brown trout eat big meals like sculpins and other small trout. However, they also feed on the surface when the river's headlining insects like the Green Drakes or Golden Stoneflies emerge.

"The past few years, with good water flows, we got away with using 2X to 3X earlier in the season, but by mid-July I'm down to 5X," Mauer says. "But there might be a time when you're on a flat piece of water with feeding fish. They can study things a lot more closely in those conditions, so you might want to play the game and downsize your tippet and lengthen the leader. The important thing is recognizing these situations. If you can use heavier tippet, go for it, especially when your flies are large, there is flotsam on the water, or the wind is blowing."

Cutthroat trout occupy most of the river's upper third, while brown trout and rainbows dominate the lower river. Cutthroat aren't as particular as other trout when it comes to flies or presentation, so the upper river is a great place to start if you're new to the area.

Directions

Nearly the entire Bitterroot River is accessible via US 93. If traveling from Missoula, head south toward Lolo, Florence, Stevensville, and Hamilton. Most public access points are clearly marked with signs along the way, but if you have any questions, fly shops can point you in the right direction. Campgrounds such as Chief Looking Glass or Spring Gulch on the East Fork are great if you're looking to maximize your time on the water. Don't expect a primitive experience since they are as popular with swimmers, tubers, and the RV crowd in the summer as they are with anglers.

If you're finding the main river is too crowded for your liking, take a day or two and explore any of the many tributaries that flank the western edge of the valley. Small streams like Blodgett, Lolo, and Kootenai creeks are fun to fish with a 2-weight rod and easy to access (hiking trails or dirt roads parallel most). You won't find trout as large as those in the main river, but the opportunity to explore the wilderness fringe of the Bitterroots makes up the difference.

Trixie the Hooker Hopper

Hook:	#6-10 MFC 7022
Thread:	Pink 6/0 Uni-Thread
Underbody:	Pink foam
Overbody:	White foam
Wing:	Natural cow elk over pearl Flashabou Accent
Indicator:	Pink foam
Legs:	Smoke gray/blue-black Speckle Flake Sili Legs

Gould's Wiggle Skwala

Hook:	#8-10 MFC 7008
Thread:	Dark brown 6/0 Uni-Thread
Egg Sac:	Black foam
Tail:	Brown button thread
Abdomen:	Skwala Frog's Hair dubbing
Rib:	Pearl dyed black High Voltage
Overwing:	Gray calf tail over dun Etha-Wing
Legs:	Black Centipede Legs
Head:	Natural cow elk
Indicator:	Yellow foam

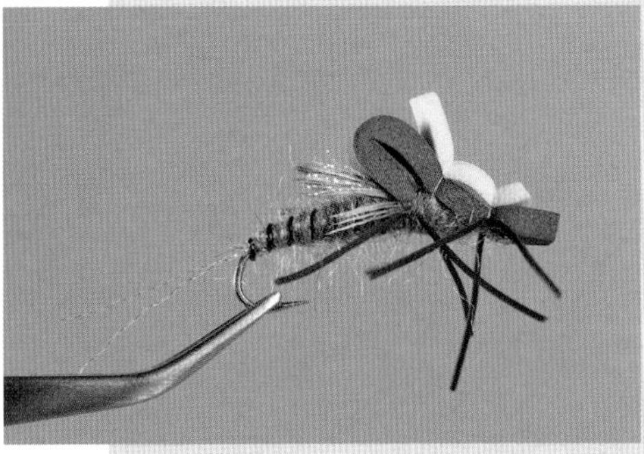

Clook's Floater in the Pool (Golden)

Hook:	#8-10 MFC 7073
Thread:	Tan 6/0 Uni-Thread
Tail:	Pearl Flashabou Accent
Rib:	Brown .060 monofilament
Body:	Golden Stone Phoenix dubbing
Wing:	Natural cow elk over pearl Flashabou Accent
Wing Case:	Brown 3 mm foam
Legs:	Black Centipede Legs
Indicator:	Yellow foam

Fowler's Nervous Minnow (Olive)

Hook:	#4 Tiemco 9395
Thread:	Olive 140-denier Ultra Thread
Body:	Holographic Flashabou
Wing:	Olive Magnum Zonker Strip over 8 strands of Krystal Flash
Overwing:	Six strands of Flashabou and 2 olive Sili Legs on each side
Eyes:	Small Presentation eyes painted red or yellow
Head:	Olive deer hair trimmed flat on the bottom and bullet shape on top and sides

Stranahan's Brindle Chute

Hook:	#10-16 MFC 7000 or Targus 100
Thread:	Tan 8/0 Uni-Thread
Tail:	Golden brown deer hair with long, fine tips
Body:	Olive, orange, and natural hare's ear rabbit/Antron blend dubbing
Post/Wing:	White calf tail
Hackle:	Grizzly dyed golden brown

Note: After you mix the dubbing for the body, add a small portion of gold Sparkle Dubbing or Targus STS.

Missouri River

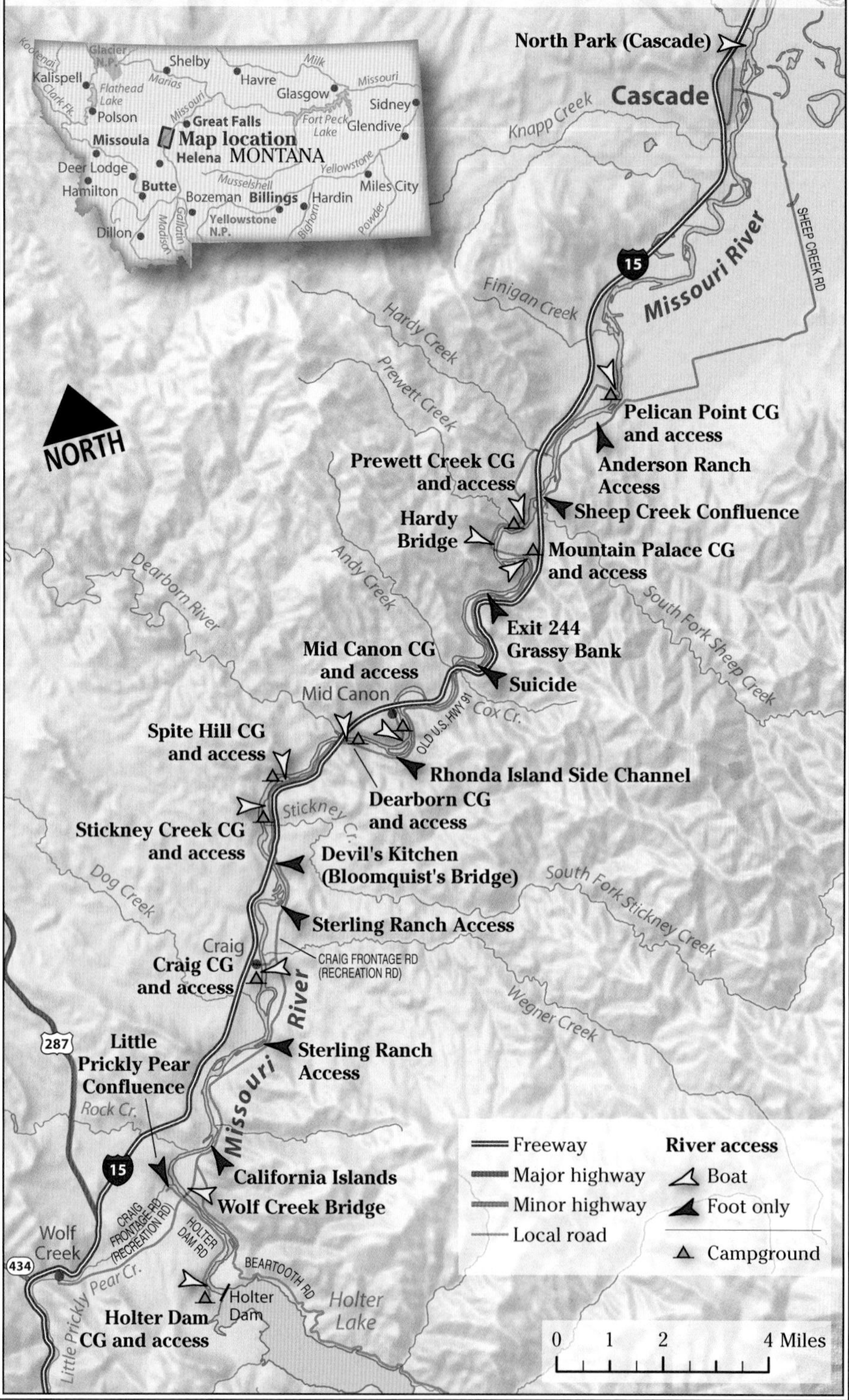

CHAPTER 12

Missouri River

When it comes to fly fishing, there are no absolutes. Weather can change abruptly, hatches may never materialize, or if you're like me and always carrying Murphy's Law on your shoulder, the fishing will only be hot before and after your visit.

Thankfully there are places like the Missouri. While it's not exactly a place that "gives it up" every day of the season, it provides dependable (and somewhat predictable) fishing, solid hatches, and clear, cold water—a rarity during runoff or the later days of the season when the effects of drought take their toll on the state's freestones.

"The Missouri River has just about every personality a trout angler would want. It fishes from 4 inches to 40 feet in depth. It's got some of the finest dry-fly fishing in the country, but if nymphs and streamers are your game, you've got it here as well," Prewett Creek Inn and Fly Shop owner Phil Camera says. "I would say the majority come up for the dry flies simply because it's known as a dry-fly fishery, and when it's hot, it's hot."

While the river's fish can be selective, you can catch them with precise casting and solid presentation—two skills many anglers lack when they make the trek to "the Mo." If you want an edge, go back to the basics of fly casting and presentation and practice, practice, practice. "Once you crack the code on the Missouri, it's probably the best river you'll fish. That means getting two things down: drag-free drift and figuring out what the fish are eating," Montana Trout Syndicate owner Mike Agee says. "When I guide, the number one problem is people don't know how to present that fly so it's the first thing down the river. If you can throw a dry fly with a reach mend, that's a great thing and I want you in my boat."

Where and When

Formed by the Jefferson, Madison, and Gallatin rivers near the town of Three Forks, the Missouri River flows east for over 700 miles, across central Montana and into North Dakota. Famous for transporting Lewis and Clark on their trek westward in the early 1800s, many of the natural landmarks they observed and noted in their journals are still visible today. Those that are not

Depending on the flow, look for fish off the main stem of the Missouri. Trout often swim up and through island channels, sloughs, and slow-water braids to feed.

are obscured by modern man's reservoirs, diversions, and other unnatural formations erected attempting to control Mother Nature. Ironically, it's some of these very structures (specifically the bottom-release dam at Holter Reservoir) that support the river's incredible trout fishery.

After Three Forks, the Missouri makes its way along the Rocky Mountain Front between sandstone buttes, meadows, and dense patches of cottonwoods. There is some good fishing for browns upstream of the dam at Toston, but it gets some traffic from anglers. Living at the mercy of the outflows from three major drainages, however, it's a fickle area in the early season and gets warm in the summer. The best time to fish this water is in the fall when the water temperatures drop and big trout that move out of Canyon Ferry Reservoir between Townsend and Toston take streamers.

Canyon Ferry Reservoir near Townsend is the first pit stop on the Missouri's journey north, followed immediately by Hauser Reservoir. There is some trout fishing below Hauser, but the water is suited more for jet boats. If you're up to the challenge, I recommend hiring a guide (you need a captain's license to run a commercial jet boat in Montana) to see why they call this canyon the land of the giants.

"You can wade-fish it, but to fish it effectively you need a boat. It's a canyon, so it's a lot deeper water than what's below Holter," Agee says. He runs a modified jet boat that he can also row in this 3-mile stretch. "The fishing there is really good. It's the same techniques that we use downriver, it's just bigger fish. There's the same caddis, the same PMDs. During the caddis in July, we were getting 26-inch fish on dry flies. Big, strong, fat browns—and there aren't that many browns, it's mostly rainbows. We also get them on sculpin patterns."

A few miles from Hauser, the Missouri dumps into Holter Lake. The Missouri River as most fly anglers know it begins with the outflow of Holter. Bottom releases keep the next 40 miles or so cold, clean, and clear—perfect habitat for trout and a smattering of aquatic insect species. It is this section, between the dam and Pelican Point (just upstream from Cascade), which some describe as a giant spring creek, that attracts anglers from all over the world. Fine gravel and sparse weeds make up the stream bottom so it's easy to wade, but with such consistent flows, drift boats (with anchors) are the preferred tool for covering water and setting up over feeding fish. "You've got to put it on the money. It's much easier from a boat than on foot," Headhunters Fly Shop co-owner John Arnold says.

Holter Dam is the source for the Missouri's famous tailwater fishery, and not surprisingly, it is the most popular boat launch access on the river. To avoid the crowds, consider visiting the area in the early evening and wade-fish or float between here and Wolf Creek.

Downstream of Cascade the river widens, slows, and becomes too warm in the summer for any consistent trout fishing. Some large trout live beyond this point, but the fish count per mile dives and most fishermen opt to stay closer to the dam.

Of the area between the dam and Cascade, the first few miles of the tailwater to the town of Craig are by far the most popular. Between drift boats, shore anglers, and those carefully wading those last few feet to get within casting distance of a pod of rising fish, the river can be crowded. But the fish are there (up to 4,000 per mile averaging between 14 and 18 inches long with a few over 20) and they are frequently caught, so take heart and enjoy the river for what it's worth. It's huge and there's plenty of room for everyone.

"Crowding is bad in the spring and summer, but especially so in the late spring because all the rivers in the west side of the state are blown out," Agee says, "and this abnormal amount of pressure from all the guides and outfitters who are running their clients from Bozeman and Missoula descends on the Mo."

Most of the Missouri is wide and flat, so the wind can make casting a chore. Knowing how to cast in windy conditions will help minimize frustration levels on the river should gusts pick up.

Though much of the river below Holter Dam is considered a technical fishery, downstream from Craig the fish are more forgiving and tolerant of angling traffic.

For the most part the tailwater portion of the Missouri below Holter is a technical fishery that requires small bugs, light and long tippets, and accurate presentations. If you're easily frustrated, or value quantity over quality, seek other waters. "Either practice before you come to the river or get a casting lesson from a professional just to update yourself," Headhunters Fly Shop co-owner Mark Raisler says.

The uppermost access is directly below Holter Dam on the west side of the river and includes parking and a boat ramp. This is a popular spot with all anglers. One night while fishing with friend and guide Joel Silverman, we talked with a man after watching him land 18-inch rainbow after 18-inch rainbow on a white Woolly Bugger despite the clouds of caddis in the air. He was frustrated because he was after walleye.

During high water (mainly in June), this site is mainly used as a boat launch. However, when levels drop later in the summer, you can launch a boat, row to the other side of the river, and wade. This is great in the evening, and while you can't take your boat past a certain point, there is room to walk all the way up to the dam, though I've had the most success simply fishing across stream from the parking lot.

From here the river flows through a brief canyon and opens into a small valley near the Wolf Creek Bridge and access (another popular put-in and take-out) just a few miles downstream. Little Prickly Pear Creek joins the Missouri soon after, and the slow, deep, and steady river picks up speed and character.

The town of Craig, and the access point many use to launch or trailer their boats, is approximately six miles downstream from the Wolf Creek Bridge. In between there are a few side channels that make for fun fishing. I've burned many hours chasing individual fish in these skinny-water chutes, knowing full well I have to skip other good water to make it out before darkness falls and I can't see the boat ramp.

From Craig to Cascade several access points are perfect for waders and floaters. This stretch also includes inflow from the Dearborn River, an important spawning tributary for the river's rainbow trout. Using I-15 and a few of

WHAT GOES UP . . .

Monitoring streamflows is important if you plan to fish the Missouri. Runoff, the capacity of the reservoirs, and irrigation demands downstream determine how little or how much water is released from the dams, which directly impacts the fishing given the time of the season.

In the summer, if flows from Holter are around 4,000 cubic feet per second (cfs) or lower, the water downstream will be warmer and the fish less enthusiastic. If flows are higher, say between 10,000 and 20,000 cfs, the water is moving faster and can remain cooler for longer distances downstream. The higher the flow, the more difficult it is to wade throughout the river. ■

the neighboring frontage roads, you can easily reach Stickney Creek, Spite Hill, Dearborn, Mid Canon, Mountain Palace, Hardy Bridge, Prewett Creek, and Pelican Point access sites.

While the river between the dam and Craig will run high during runoff, it's almost always guaranteed to be clear. The muddied runoff from the Dearborn, however, can milk up the river from its confluence downstream—something to consider if you're thinking of fishing below it before the spring push of water tapers off.

This portion, known as the canyon stretch, also contains one of the only sets of rough water on the river, Half-Breed Rapids. Located about a mile below the Prewett Creek access, rowers should practice caution and check conditions at a local shop before attempting the float. At one time, the area upstream of Craig was typically the most crowded, but in recent years that seems to have flip-flopped.

"One of the most pressured sections of the river is the canyon. The upper river has seen the quality of dry-fly fishing diminish, and they're not lining the banks like they used to be. The nymphing is always good, but a lot of guys don't want to chase an indicator all day," Arnold says.

After Cascade the water is generally too warm and slow to fish during the height of the season. When temperatures are low at the beginning and end of the season, it's worth taking a trip or two and dropping a streamer in every deep pocket or undercut bank you pass along the way. You may encounter an occasional carp or walleye here as well—both species increasing in numbers as you continue downriver and worth chasing if you need a break from the upper river's crowds.

The river eventually makes its way through a series of canyons and arroyos that while incredibly scenic are difficult to reach on foot and tough to float because of the distance between access points. The Missouri forms Fort Peck Lake, the largest body of water in the state. There is good fishing below Fort Peck Dam for a few miles. While it isn't a place you would plan to take a weeklong excursion, it is something to keep in the back of your mind should you ever find yourself in this country. After Peck, the Missouri meets the Milk

Anglers can sometimes get away with less-than-finesse techniques in the canyon portion of the Missouri, particularly when fishing terrestrial patterns. However, it pays to get out and work feeding fish whenever possible. Conditions can change without warning, so pursue opportunities when they present themselves.

and Yellowstone rivers, enters North Dakota, and continues its way into the nation's heartland.

Hatches and Flies

Aside from the number and size of the Missouri River's fish, the bug hatches are a main attraction for visiting anglers. For the most part, during early spring and fall, small bugs make up the menu. Like most tailwater fish, Missouri River trout have no qualms about choking down a few hundred midges and *Baetis* when conditions are optimal and the bugs are busting. But when unfriendly weather patterns move through the area, it's tough to fish. Wind, especially in the canyon area, can blow a boat upstream and stop a perfect cast dead in the air. If you decide to fish in March or early April, bring plenty of #16-22 midge pupae and *Baetis* imitations (dry flies and nymphs); dress warm; and expect wind-burned cheeks.

Some hatches, like the cloud of Tricos above, fall in blankets on the water, but Missouri River trout sometimes prefer the old, water-soaked pieces of the bugs versus a bug in its entirety. Weathered, used patterns that look like decaying insects often work better than clean ties fresh out of the box.

Since the rainbows spawn in March and April, they'll make their way up the neighboring tributaries and leave the main system to the browns. This is a good time to target some of the fish with streamers, particularly Egg-Sucking Leeches or Woolly Buggers. If nothing else, the constant chuck-and-duck movement will help keep you warm as you pass the time waiting for the nymphing to kick into gear or the midges, *Baetis,* or the occasional *Skwala* to appear.

"We get *Skwalas,* but it's nothing like what you'll see around Missoula. You might find 4 to 40 bugs in a day, but the fish are eating them in March and April. It's somewhat of an unknown hatch for our area. They also hatch on the Dearborn, which is closed at that time of year, but you'll see the bugs just pumping out of the mouth. It's the same time thousands of rainbows are trying to go up there to spawn," Arnold says.

The *Baetis* are an important early-season staple for Missouri River trout, but once the caddis start popping in May and June, hold on. This is one of the most prevalent insect species on the river and one that catches the eye of the angler as well as the fish, probably because the patterns are slightly larger than *Baetis* imitations and a welcome relief to strained eyes. In any case, always carry a selection of caddis patterns in a variety of sizes and colors for both above and below the surface. The one time you don't, you're going to see a fish chowing on them as they can hatch well into autumn.

"The hatches last year were really good, and the caddis came back with vigor. I think the low-water years really took a toll on the caddis, but the past year they were just abundant, and it's going to be even better in the years to come," Agee says. "The good thing is all the high water we've had in the spring cleansed out the river bottom. Now there's this nice, fine, perfect-looking gravel, and that's going to help the mayflies at the same time."

One particular out-of-the-box theory on the Missouri is the fish are enamored with bug parts. Most of the guides and outfitters I've talked to said some of the best action isn't during the height of a hatch, it's the few days afterward when the waterlogged and decaying pieces of caddis congregate in swirling, frothy pools. Some even have evidence for their hypothesis. Stomach-pumped samples revealed nary a whole caddis but instead a gut full of wings, broken bodies, legs, and other pieces and parts. This is something to keep in mind if a simple spent caddis like Lawson's Spent Partridge Caddis isn't getting it done.

"If I'm having trouble figuring out what they're eating, I switch to a spent caddis and it seems like the answer almost all the time," Agee says. "I swear I've seen them eating the dead, spent, floating bug parts. They're not eating the adults, not even the freshly dead ones. They're eating one- or two-day-old bug parts. Hackle-stacker patterns are good imitations for this. They'll eat flies like Elk-Hair Caddis at the beginning of a hatch, but once they get picked on a little bit they switch to barely floating dead bugs."

Casting and mending well are necessary skills on the Missouri River, and most local guides recommend practicing before hitting the water. The ability to place a fly in a specific window and drift it flawlessly can make or break a day on the water.

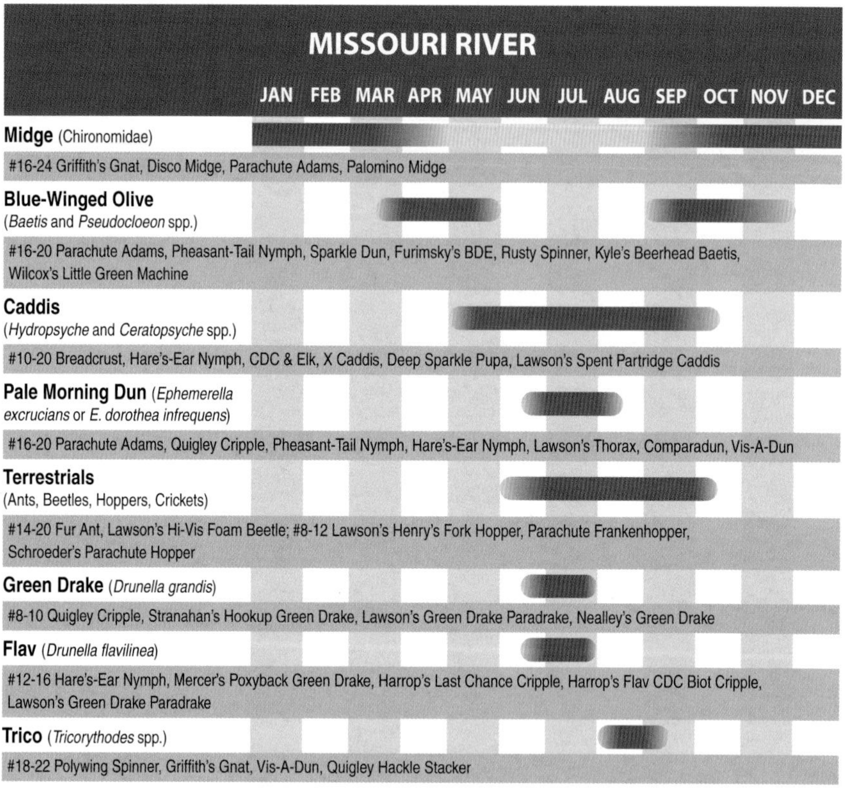

As the season progresses, the action picks up with the appearance of Pale Morning Duns (PMDs). Many of the state's other waters (particularly freestones) are running the color of chocolate milk at this time, making the clear, bottom releases of the Missouri attractive. This hatch brings a lot of fish to the surface at almost any time of the day. Many fish move up into shallower water and are easy to spook (look before you leap off the bank) so long leaders, accurate casts, and drag-free drifts are the rule.

PMD patterns that sit low in the water like Comparaduns and sparsely hackled parachutes are never a bad idea. This is also when the river sees a drastic increase in traffic, so be mindful of other fishermen, principally wading anglers if you're in a drift boat. "PMDs seem to be cyclical everywhere. They're good for a few years and they taper off," Arnold says. "The one thing to note, however, is we don't have a lot of luck on adult patterns. For the most part we fish cripples and spinners."

When the PMDs subside (they sometimes return just before fall), the hoppers rise up. I favor PMD fishing on the Mo over hopper fishing (I enjoy head-hunting individual fish), but that's not to say terrestrials aren't effective. Plop a beefy hopper next to any grassy bank and try a mix of dead-drifting and twitching. Some days the fish prefer one over the other. If you want to increase your odds, tie a small ant pattern off the back.

There are other summer hatches on the river, though many aren't as ubiquitous as those previously mentioned. In fact, now that the silt is flushed from the system, some mayflies starting to gain a foothold may lose a little ground. "We used to only see March Browns trickling out of the mouth of the Dearborn. You now see some huge hatches of March Browns up and down the river. Some of the biggest I've seen were right below Wolf Creek Bridge in May," Arnold says. "Believe it or not, there is a Hex hatch around Great Falls that would blow some Michigan residents' minds. In the years since, the hatch has moved up the river. So while they aren't running hog wild on the upper river, I have had a few rainy, cloudy days where they've come off down by Cascade."

Tricos arrive sometime between mid-July and August. If you are in the right place at the right time, the fishing (and the challenges that go with it) exceeds expectations. One of my favorite sights is a large flying mass of these tiny bugs shimmering in the early morning light. Look for subtle rises, and don't be afraid to use a two-fly rig with an easy-to-see pattern in the lead (like a parachute dry fly) with a spent or sunken Trico tied on as a dropper. There's no doubt the size of these bugs and the delicate takes make it hard to detect strikes, but adding a lead fly, as long as it's not spooking fish, ups the odds in your favor.

Tricos are one of the favored hatches on the Missouri River, but with so many naturals present, it's sometimes difficult to fool fish. While simple spent patterns work well, the fish see many of them through the season. Try variations and sunken patterns for a change of pace.

"We still get good Trico hatches, but the fish don't come up like they used to, probably because of warmer water temps in late summer. People, I think, still remember what it was like in the late 1990s when you could stand in one spot for six hours and smoke 'em. So some of the river's veteran anglers are a little disappointed. Things are just a little more technical, so using a sunken Trico pattern and a spent spinner might be a better plan that just fishing spinners," Arnold says.

Into early fall, *Pseudocloeons* come off, but are often mistaken for *Baetis,* which typically come off later, around mid-October and November. They are somewhat smaller than a true Blue-Winged Olive, so drop your imitations down a size or two and you should be in the ballpark.

While it's fun to spot and stalk specific rising fish on the Missouri, most anglers find greater success under the surface. Nymph rigs with a variety of *Baetis,* scud, PMD, San Juan Worm, and caddis pupae imitations are good choices, though a few select patterns like Kyle's Beerhead Baetis and Wilcox's Little Green Machine have caught on in recent years. The key is fishing the right water. Look for dropoffs, ledges, and any transition areas. Broad and wide, the Missouri can be hard to read at times, especially if you've never fished it before. To many newcomers, it all looks the same at first glance. You have to break it down and look at what's going on under the surface more than what's going on above it. "Nymphing the middle of the river in those weird, soft seams is often better than the banks," Arnold says.

The Missouri can also cure cabin fever. The winter air temperatures combined with the cold water make fish somewhat lethargic, but they will eat.

There is plenty of structure, grass, and other terrestrial-type habitat downstream from Craig, so the fish are sometimes quick to eat an imitation. Cast close to the banks and impart an occasional slight twitch to create the illusion of a struggle.

The few miles of river between Holter and Hauser lakes contain some of the largest fish in the river, but it's a difficult area to reach. Outfitters with jet boats are the best choice if you want an opportunity to catch some very large trout. MIKE AGEE PHOTO

Look for windows of warm temperatures in the afternoon and use small patterns that mimic midges, scuds, or *Baetis* nymphs. You can try a streamer or two, but put it right in front of the fish and strip slow because they probably won't chase it. For my money, a two-fly nymph rig and small indicator is hard to beat.

"Simple, thin mayfly nymphs without flash work better than these modern, sparkly things. Use natural materials so it looks like a bug and not some dang Christmas tree. I tie something I call my natural mayfly nymph, and it's nothing more than pheasant-tail fibers and thread," Agee says. "If I can get away with it, I don't use split shot. I'll use an oversized tungsten bead, especially if I'm using a two-fly rig. It's just my theory, but by getting rid of those lead hinge points, I think you get better drifts. They look more natural when they're being presented. Now, in the spring when the water is deep and heavy, you have to use it. But as soon as it calms down, I use black tungsten. I think it emulates more what's really out there."

Unless you're throwing streamers, a lightweight, fast-action 5-weight rod is the perfect tool for this river. It's light enough to cast small flies delicately but has enough backbone to fight some of the river's larger fish. If you're casting weighted streamers you can use a 6-weight rod and sinking-tip line, though you can often get by with a floating line by adding additional weight to the leader. Leaders on floating lines are almost never shorter than 9 feet, so learn to cast 12-foot-long systems with tippet sizes averaging on the light side, mostly in the range of 4X and 5X.

"I fish a Harvey slack-line leader. I tie the exact same leader formula as George Harvey, though I sometimes make it 11 feet long instead of 10 or $10\frac{1}{2}$ feet," Raisler says. "I believe the first cast is your best cast, and I make a little business plan' for every feeding fish I see. I might cast beside the fish three or four times to understand the feeding line, how the current is going to influence the line, and make sure I have enough line to make a down-and-across presentation—which is what we're doing 75 percent of the time. If you just want to wing it out and hope for the best, that fish is probably going to go down."

Directions

The upper Missouri outside Three Forks is easy to reach from I-90. To reach Trident, briefly take the frontage road on the north side of the interstate and then head north on MT 286. In Trident the road swerves southeast and merges with Clarkston Road. Follow this road if you want to reach the Fairweather access. For the points around Toston, take US 287 north from Three Forks, and turn east on Toston Dam Road or continue to town. Remain north on US 287 to go to Townsend.

Reaching the tailwater below Holter is an easy drive from either Helena or Great Falls. Take I-15 from either Helena or Great Falls, exit at Wolf Creek, and take the frontage road east. This will take you to the Wolf Creek access, but just before crossing the river, turn right on Holter Dam Road to reach the outflow. The towns of Craig, Hardy, and Cascade can also be reached via I-15, but the Craig-Frontage Road (eventually changes to Old US Highway 91) follows and connects with the river at various points from Wolf Creek to Cascade and includes a few roadside access pull-offs. It's also the best way to find the state-maintained accesses, public campgrounds, and boat ramps.

Kyle's Beerhead Baetis

Hook:	#14-20 MFC 7045
Thread:	Tan 8/0 Uni-Thread
Bead:	Root-beer glass
Tail:	Hungarian partridge
Body:	Callibaetis Frog's Hair dubbing
Rib:	Copper wire
Wing Case:	Pearl Mylar
Legs:	Hungarian partridge

Wilcox's Little Green Machine

Hook: #14-24 Mustad 3906
Head: Extra small copper bead
Thread: Black 8/0 Uni-Thread
Tail: Pheasant tail fibers
Abdomen: Pheasant tail Micro Tubing
Rib: Small Ultra Wire, color to match the abdomen
Wing Case: Pearl Fire-Fly or micro Flashabou
Gills: White Antron fibers
Thorax: Olive-brown Ice Dub

Lawson's Spent Partridge Caddis (Olive)

Hook: #14-18 Tiemco 100
Thread: Olive 6/0 Uni-Thread
Body: Dark olive rabbit dubbing
Wing: Dark brown partridge feathers
Thorax: Peacock herl
Hackle: Brown and grizzly rooster neck

Trina's Bubbleback Emerger (PMD)

Hook: #14-20 MFC 7045
Thread: Light cahill 8/0 Uni-Thread
Bead: Gold
Tail: Pheasant tail
Abdomen: Pheasant tail
Rib: Yellow Flashabou Accent and copper wire
Wing Case: Yellow Flashabou Accent over pheasant tail
Thorax: Yellow Wing N' Flash
Legs: Yellow Flashabou Accent

MFC Polywing Spinner

Hook: #18-22 MFC 7000
Thread: Black 8/0 Uni-Thread
Tail: White Microfibetts
Abdomen: White turkey biot
Wing: White Gator Hair
Thorax: Black Frog's Hair dubbing

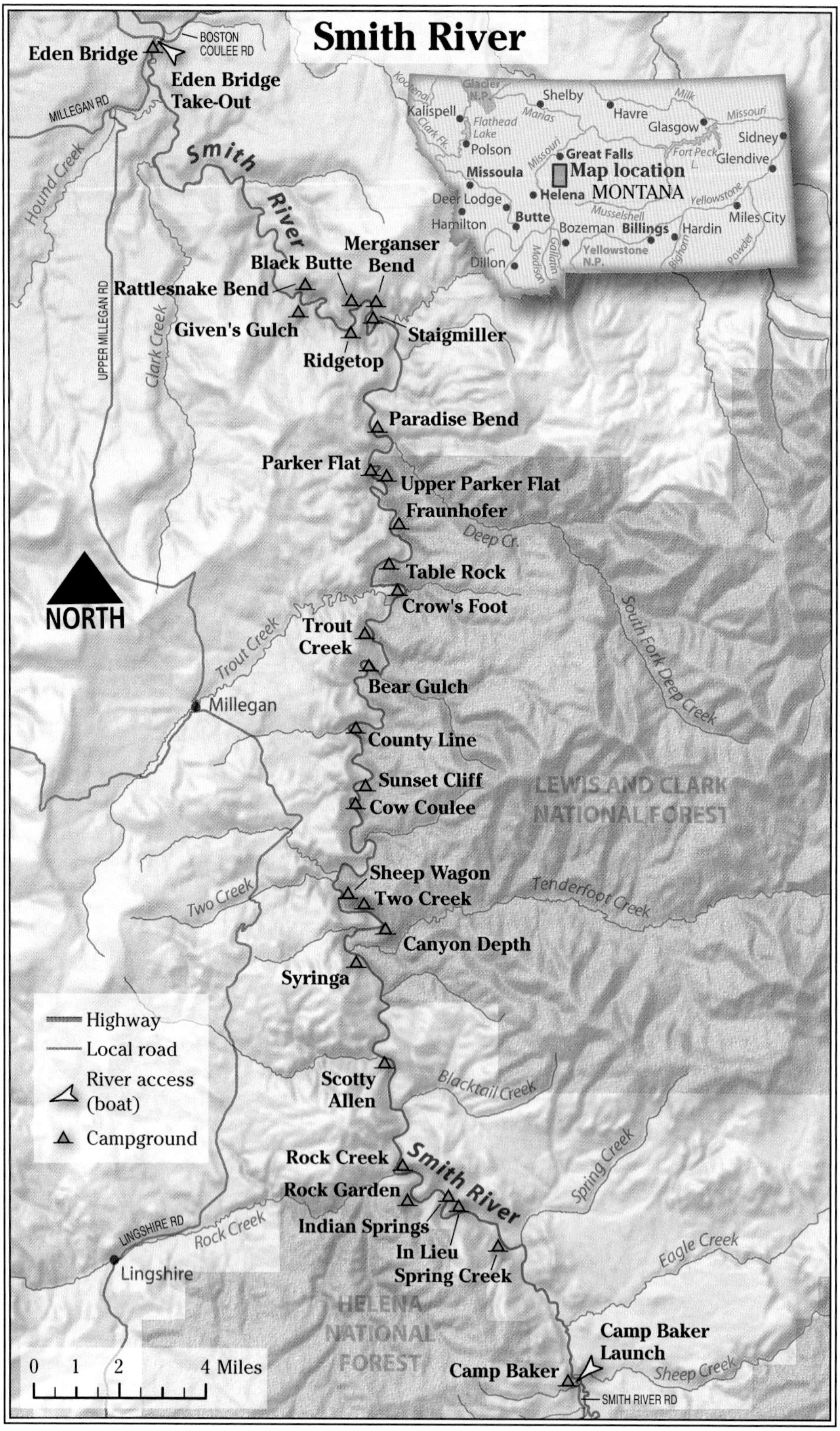

Smith River
Eden Bridge
BOSTON COULEE RD
Eden Bridge Take-Out
MILLEGAN RD
Hound Creek
Smith River
UPPER MILLEGAN RD
Clark Creek
Black Butte
Merganser Bend
Rattlesnake Bend
Given's Gulch
Staigmiller
Ridgetop
Paradise Bend
Parker Flat
Upper Parker Flat
Fraunhofer
Deep Cr.
Table Rock
Crow's Foot
NORTH
Trout Creek
Trout Creek
South Fork Deep Creek
Bear Gulch
Millegan
County Line
Sunset Cliff
Cow Coulee
LEWIS AND CLARK NATIONAL FOREST
Sheep Wagon
Two Creek
Two Creek
Tenderfoot Creek
Canyon Depth
Syringa
Highway
Local road
River access (boat)
Campground
Scotty Allen
Blacktail Creek
Rock Creek
Smith River
Spring Creek
Rock Garden
Indian Springs
In Lieu
Spring Creek
LINGSHIRE RD
Rock Creek
Lingshire
Eagle Creek
HELENA NATIONAL FOREST
Camp Baker Launch
Camp Baker
Sheep Creek
SMITH RIVER RD
0 1 2 4 Miles
Glacier N.P.
Kalispell
Shelby
Havre
Milk
Flathead Lake
Marias
Glasgow
Missouri
Polson
Clark Fk.
Sidney
Great Falls
Fort Peck L.
Glendive
Missoula
Map location
Deer Lodge
Helena
MONTANA
Yellowstone
Butte
Musselshell
Miles City
Hamilton
Bozeman
Billings
Hardin
Yellowstone N.P.
Dillon
Madison
Gallatin
Bighorn
Powder

CHAPTER 13

Smith River

There aren't many places in the Lower 48 where you can float for days on end and feel relatively isolated from civilization. While there is the occasional cabin and resort on the lower river, natural features keep most of the Smith tucked away from the hand of man and help preserve a somewhat primitive experience. The result is an unmatched adventure that takes the five-star lodges out of the equation and returns fly anglers to something simplistic and primordial. It's just you, the river, and the trout during the day and the camaraderie of camp and a blanket of stars at night.

Once you launch there is no turning back, and depending on the size of your group and the ground you cover on any given day, the 60-mile trip through the canyon takes an average of four days. That's four days free of traffic jams, cell phones, and safety nets. It's a wonderful experience. "There is beautiful scenery everywhere, but what makes the Smith experience more nurturing and fulfilling is the isolation of the river. This is an opportunity to take a glimpse of something before cell phones, iPods, and eBay," Lewis and Clark Expeditions owner and outfitter Mike Geary says.

When and Where

The Smith River begins near White Sulphur Springs, and although the 60-mile floatable corridor gets all the glory, there is some fishing on the upper river adjacent to any of the campgrounds upstream from Fort Baker or near Fort Logan on MT 360, or the bridge on Birch Creek Road just west of White Sulphur Springs.

"The upper river flows through the agricultural valley of White Sulphur Springs. Unfortunately, because of over 100 years of ranching and farming practices that pay little regard to the river, the water quality and spawning habitat has been severely degraded," Montana Fly Fishing Connection owner and outfitter Joe Sowerby says. "There are a few habitat projects going on, but the river needs as much help as it can get. There are lots of projects that could be mutually beneficial for the ranchers and the river, so for those that want to help out, get in touch with Montana Trout Unlimited or donate to the Smith River Habitat Project."

The Smith's canyon walls keep the outside world at bay, so plan accordingly. Pack proper clothing and essential gear so that you're prepared, should an emergency arise.
JOHN HERZER/BLACKFOOT RIVER OUTFITTERS PHOTO

The two most important access points on the river are Camp Baker and Eden Bridge—the respective put-in and take-out for the famous 60-mile canyon voyage. Both private and commercial parties are required to register with MDFWP staff at the Camp Baker launch site the day of their float between April 15 and July 15, after which time users must self-register and pay the appropriate fees.

"Most people choose to camp near Camp Baker the night before their launch. When you arrive, you will need to fill out the sign-in sheet or see the ranger on duty. The morning of the launch, the MDFWP official will start boat camp selection about 7 AM. You need to be present or you will be bumped in line," Sowerby says. "There are no designated launch times, so almost everyone ends up shoving off between 9:30 and 11:30 AM. Because of this, the first few miles of river can be crowded until everyone spreads out. One way to avoid this is to plan a short first day and launch around noon. You will have the river to yourself."

Other than simple management of the river (boat identification tags are issued to all watercraft), the Camp Baker registration process allows users to declare their campsites. Despite the fact that there are 54 campsites available, registration helps avoid conflicts downriver and helps preserve a wilderness-like setting for everyone that visits.

"I've been guiding on the Smith for over 15 seasons, and some trips feel more crowded on the river than others, but given the management plan that they have in place, and the size of the canyon itself, you typically get the solitude that you're looking for. A lot of that has to do with the fact that some groups do the trip in five days, others do it in four. So people spread out. You're not stacked up boat to boat. And not everybody floating the river is fishing," PRO Outfitters owner Brandon Boedecker says.

After launching, campgrounds appear after the first four miles. Some have advantages over others in terms of scenery, access to good wade fishing, and privacy. The state made a concerted effort to keep the sites out of sight and sound of each other as best as they could, so several miles separate most campsites, but a few cluster together. Most people on the Smith are there for the same reason as you are, so conflicts are rare and in my experience, most parties are respectful of one another.

"Bring your own firewood but don't overload your raft. There is a fine line between packing light and going prepared. You have to be prepared to handle a winter storm and travel through shallow water," Sowerby says. "Drinkable water is available at various springs along the way (or bring a water-filtration pump). You do not have to haul water for the trip."

After launching, the most notable feature of the Smith is its isolation. Steep canyon walls shelter the river corridor from the rest of the modern world, and it's easy to feel like you're hundreds of miles away from civilization. For those who have fished the river before, it's one of the most relished attributes.

Floating the Smith is not a huge challenge, and even novice oarsmen can make the run without difficulty. The few small white-water chutes are easily

The steep canyon walls of the Smith River cut anglers off from the rest of the world for nearly 60 miles, and although first timers feel like explorers, the pictographs on the rocks are proof that others have passed before us. JOHN HERZER/BLACKFOOT RIVER OUTFITTERS PHOTO

navigable. Just remember to keep a sharp eye for anything ahead like rocks or logjams. "There are several marked rapids on the river, but they are more like rock gardens and rarely present any type of standing waves. The biggest challenge is navigating through shallow rocky runs," Sowerby says. "Always look way ahead and try to go where the most water is going. Since it is a canyon, there are many 90-degree turns that can slam you up against a wall. Just plan ahead and anticipate your oar strokes before you get there."

The Smith is full of twists and turns, and each turn represents new opportunities. Most of the fish hang along the banks or other textbook holding areas like seams, eddies, below riffles, and near structure. In my opinion, calling the Smith a technical fishery is an overstatement, but the lack of cutthroat trout and constantly changing water conditions make you work for the fish. Tributary mouths are one place you can typically find some action. Look to the inflows from Eagle, Rock, Tenderfoot, and Deep creeks for action.

Wildlife abounds in the Smith River corridor. Deer and fowl are the most frequently spotted creatures, but elk and moose are present and the birds of prey populations are as numerous and diverse as anywhere in Montana. Several groups each season have black bear encounters—all the more reason to keep a clean camp area.

The last third of the 60-mile trip, the canyon walls loosen up a little and there are more green meadows, sweeping vistas, and pictographs on the rocks. The river also has more room to spread out because the river widens and there are fewer gravel runs. Joe Sowerby commented that this is where he typically finds himself on day three or four, and where he sees larger rising fish and hatches of bugs like Brown Drakes.

Even though the state allocates certain areas for camping and they're occupied nearly every day during the season, don't ignore basic camping rules like keeping food in a safe, secure area. Wild animals in the canyon, like bears, know where they can find an easy meal.

ADAM DEBRUIN PHOTO

After a few nights and many miles, floaters finally arrive at Eden Bridge. There is one side channel about four miles above Eden Bridge intermittently blocked by logjams, but the ranger working at Camp Baker should inform you of the status before you launch. From here, it's a short drive to Great Falls, or a few miles more to Helena, both with plenty of hotels and restaurants to get a warm shower and a full meal. "We try to time our take-out for just after lunch. This gives people time to fly out the same day if they want, but most people head to Helena, get a hotel and a shower, and leave the following day," Boedecker says.

Like the upper river above Camp Baker, the water below Eden Bridge suffers from a lack of good habitat, and trout numbers drop off. There are a few public access points like the Lower Smith River access 3 miles south of Ulm on MT 330, or the Truly site near the town of the same name, 8 miles southeast of Ulm. "The fishing below Eden Bridge is basically nonexistent. The river loses most of the rocky substrate at that point and flows through rich farmland soils without much structure for trout," Sowerby says.

Most anglers regard the Smith as a brown trout fishery, though there are some rainbows landed here and there. Most fish average between 12 and 18 inches, and a rare fish pushes the 20-inch mark. "Every trip somebody usually catches a brown that's 19 inches or better, and some trips you may catch a half dozen like that. But it's not uncommon to catch fish up to 18 inches. We don't see a lot of rainbows that size. They typically stay below 15 inches," Boedecker says.

Hatches and Flies

Despite the Smith's susceptibility to the nuances of runoff and weather, there is an abundance of food in the river. Plenty of natural items to match, but sometimes the winning ticket is a foam attractor that doesn't look like anything. Keep water conditions in mind because dirty water isn't always the best time to try to force-feed dry flies to trout.

"Trout numbers aren't as high on the Smith as they are on other rivers, and the population is mostly browns. So dry-fly days are much more rare, and since the water is always a little brown, we find ourselves doing much more slow nymphing," Sowerby says. "The Smith has pocketwater, but the canyon walls are often the primary structure we fish around. There are also fish stacked on inside seams and subtle midriver trenches."

Mike Geary, on the other hand, stresses simplicity with his clients, and says that on many days, a simple Stimulator with a beadhead dropper is all you need. Still, a good box should include an array of Parachute Adams, Beadhead Prince Nymphs, Stimulators, hopper patterns, Golden Stones, Bitch Creeks, San Juan Worms, Copper Johns, and black, brown, olive, and yellow streamers. There's no need to get complicated—most of the fish are too aggressive to care if your hook is one size too big or the thorax isn't quite the right shade of dubbing.

PERMIT BASICS

A permit-lottery system regulates access to this river between April 1 and October 31. If you want to float, you can either book a trip with an outfitter or submit an application for a permit. The application deadline for Smith River permits is typically in mid-February, but applications are typically available the first week of January. Contact a Montana Department of Fish, Wildlife and Parks office at (406) 454-5840 for a paper application, or visit fwp.mt.gov/fishing for information on applying online. If you are unsuccessful in the drawing, or want to see about picking up a permit from a canceled party, call (406) 454-5861.

Applications must include a $5 nonrefundable permit drawing fee for both residents and nonresidents, and either a $25 private registration fee if you are a Montana resident or a $50 registration fee if you are a nonresident (both nonrefundable). No individual can submit more than one application. The MDFWP lottery is in early March, and you can check the results on the website or wait for notification by mail. In 2009, 5,702 parties applied for permits. Of that number, 915 received the permit they applied for. That's an average success rate around 16 percent.

There are additional fees at the Camp Baker launch that vary depending on a user's age and residency status. Each resident or nonresident age 6 to 12 is $15, residents 13 years or older are $25, and nonresidents age 13 or older are $50.

If you acquire a permit and are forced to cancel for any reason, notify the MDFWP office at least 48 hours before your assigned launch date. Fail to do so and you are ineligible to enter the lottery for another permit the following year. Any public launch dates remaining after the drawing are available to private parties on a first-come, first-serve basis administered by the MDFWP office in Great Falls beginning around the end of March.

For a complete list of important Smith River dates, requirements, rules, and policies, visit the MDFWP website at fwp.mt.gov/recreation/activities/smithRiver. This page has everything you need to know about planning a trip to the river. ■

Around March and April, the river does see a small *Skwala* hatch but it's mostly a nymphing affair with small Beadhead Prince Nymphs and weighted rubber-legged stonefly patterns. That's not to say dry-fly fishing is out of the question. On warmer days the simultaneous emergence of bugs like *Baetis* creates some surface activity in specific locales.

"We call our primary technique at that time of year the Smith River troll," Herzer says. "Dave Clark, one of my guides from years ago came up with this technique where you use a small indicator and tight-line the presentation through a pocket. Throw it out, mend slightly downstream, give it one long strip, point your rod at it, and just let it run slightly faster than the river."

Trout numbers are fairly high on the Smith, but they are mostly browns. Rainbows are present, but their numbers aren't as strong and on the average they are slightly smaller than the brown trout. ADAM DEBRUIN PHOTO

Rolling into mid-May, traffic on the river picks up as anglers anticipate the arrival of Salmonflies and Golden Stones. The unknown factor this time of year though is high water. It's impossible to predict when the rush of brown water will hit when applying for a permit back in February, but take heart if there is a foot or more of visibility or the flow levels are receding. The Smith fishes well on the drop.

"If the water is dirty, don't give up. Some of the best fish we catch each year are during the 'blown-out' trips. You will have to get out of the boat and do some wade fishing, but just nymphing Woolly Buggers and San Juan Worms on quiet inside seams works well," Sowerby says. "Finding the slow holding water is key. Those fish feed like crazy when the water is up and brown, you just need to get it in front of their face. Sometimes that means using some weight and finding that slot of slow holding water out 5 feet from shore. Other times it's best to go really light and fish right off the edge of the grass in 6 inches of water."

If you're lucky enough to get both good water conditions and launch on a week when the big bugs are ballistic, go out and buy a lottery ticket because luck is certainly on your side. I've never been fortunate enough to hit it on such days, but I've heard enough secondhand stories of 50- to 100-fish days that I continue to roll the dice.

Water conditions vary on the Smith as runoff ends, but when it's clear enough to cast dry flies, try foam attractors or patterns with a Golden Stonefly silhouette. ADAM DEBRUIN PHOTO

"The truth is that the Smith can be a crapshoot no matter when you go. We float from early May through early July. The flows are usually highest from June 1 through June 10, but the river can be too low to float and too warm to fish by the end of June on a low-water year," Sowerby says. "It can also be high and muddy until the end of June on a high-water year. Early to mid May is generally drier (less rain) with lower, clearer water than early June, but you run the risk of colder weather. All that said, my two favorite times to go are around May 14–20 in the hopes of catching the Salmonfly hatch, and then also at the very end of June for Golden Stones and Brown Drakes."

As popular as the Salmonflies are, the Golden Stones appear a little later, often times as runoff levels drop, making them the bread-and-butter hatch for June permit holders. Around that same time, caddis and Green Drakes can appear as well. The Smith is a freestone, so there is a slight degree of unpredictability when it comes to bugs. You never know what you're going to see around the next corner.

By mid and late July, the river becomes too low for most floaters. Having to drag a raft through more shallow-water stretches than you float through is not my idea of fun. If you're up to the challenge, there is good terrestrial and small streamer fishing. Hoppers are plentiful in the canyons and with half the pressure of the early season, the fish are more than willing to move on surface offerings. Later in the season, when irrigation demands taper off and there is a little more water in the system to work with, there are some caddis and *Baetis* hatches worth playing with. You night not see pods of rising fish, but you can coax fish to the surface.

Given the brown trout's predatory and territorial instincts, streamers work well in the spring, summer, and fall. Realistic sculpin imitations, rabbit-strip leeches, and the like are always fun to play with but sometimes simplicity rules. "The fish eat small, brown Woolly Buggers in May, I think in part because they think it's a stonefly," Herzer says. "But I see a lot of little crayfish creeping around in the river. If the water is clear, you can see them just rolling along with the current."

Directions

To reach Camp Baker from White Sulphur Springs, follow Fort Logan Road (MT 360) west from town. It intermittently veers north and west but eventually intersects with Smith River Road. Turn right (north) on Smith River Road, which eventually crosses the river, and the access is just to the northwest, opposite the mouth of Sheep Creek.

Don't mistake the Smith River sign or campground on the left approximately 2.5 miles from Fort Logan Road for Camp Baker. While it is a great area to overnight before driving to the launch the following day, or a place to launch and float in a personal pontoon boat down to Camp Baker, it is not Camp Baker.

The upper river between Camp Baker and White Sulphur Springs is smaller (especially in the summer when flows are low and irrigation demands are high), and access is virtually nonexistent. It eventually splits into forks just west of White Sulphur Springs and becomes an even smaller, shallower version of itself, surrounded by private property.

Eden Bridge is at the junction of Millegan Road (MT 330) and Boston Coulee Road. If you're shuttling a car from Camp Baker, go back to Fort Logan Road (MT 360) and continue west. Then take Lingshire Road (MT 330) north at the intersection near Smith River State Park. Continue on Lingshire as it

Most Smith River trout range between 12 and 18 inches long, but occasionally a bigger fish comes to the net. In the end, however, it's not the size of the fish or how many you catch that you'll remember, it's the experience the river provides. ADAM DEBRUIN PHOTO

SMITH RIVER	JAN	FEB	MAR	APR	MAY	JUN	JUL	AUG	SEP	OCT	NOV	DEC
Midge (Chironomidae)				■	■	■	■	■	■	■		
#16-24 Griffith's Gnat, Disco Midge, Parachute Adams, Palomino Midge												
Blue-Winged Olive (*Baetis* spp.)				■	■				■	■		
#16-20 Parachute Adams, Pheasant-Tail Nymph, Sparkle Dun, Furimsky's BDE												
Caddis (*Hydropsyche* and *Ceratopsyche* spp.)					■	■	■	■	■			
#10-20 Breadcrust, CDC & Elk, X Caddis, Deep Sparkle Pupa												
Skwala Stonefly (*Skwala parallela*)			■	■								
#6-10 Gould's Half-Down Skwala, Rogue Foam Stone, Gould's Wiggle Skwala, Bitch Creek Nymph												
Pale Morning Dun (*Ephemerella excrucians* or *E. dorothea infrequens*)							■	■				
#16-20 Parachute Adams, Quigley Cripple, Pheasant-Tail Nymph, Hare's-Ear Nymph, Lawson's Thorax, Copper John												
Terrestrials (Ants, Beetles, Hoppers, Crickets)						■	■	■	■	■		
#14-20 Schroeder's Parachute Ant, Lawson's Hi-Vis Foam Beetle; #6-10 Trixie the Hooker Hopper, Kingfisher's Red Legged Hopper; #8-12 Parachute Frankenhopper, Lawson's Henry's Fork Hopper												
Salmonfly (*Pteronarcys californica*)					■	■						
#4-8 Bitch Creek Nymph, Stimulator, Rogue Foam Stone, Romans' Thing From Uranus, Bitch Creek Nymph												
Golden Stonefly (*Hesperoperla pacifica*)							■	■				
#6-12 Stimulator, Elk-Hair Caddis, Pat's Rubber Legs, Bitch Creek Nymph												

heads west and north and eventually changes to Upper Millegan Road. It eventually hits Millegan Road, and a few miles north is Eden Bridge. The entire route is long and full of twists and turns. If you're coming from Great Falls, take I-15 to Ulm, then follow Millegan Road (MT 330) south to the access.

Planning a Trip

For those lucky enough to draw a permit or book a trip with an outfitter, the Smith River Management Plan allows nine launches per day (eight private and one commercial, except two days per week when the state permits two commercial launches). Each permit allows that party to include up to 15 people, but there is no limit on the number of boats. If you don't draw a permit and don't want to hire an outfitter, you can pick up a permit from a canceling party by calling (406) 454-5861, but your group is limited to a maximum of eight people.

This might seem like a lot of people launching at once, but some days are better than others, and of course the number of boats and people on the water jumps up and down depending on how pleasant or uncomfortable the time of the year. According to MDFWP statistics, use of the river has gone up across the board (outfitters and private parties) over the past few seasons. The state hands out the same number of permits each year, but the average size of

When applying for a Smith River permit, consider factors like the time of year, weather conditions, and the demand for certain launch dates. While there are typically many open slots in the early season, conditions are sometimes unpleasant. Apply for a time too late in the season, and you may need to deal with low water. JIM KLUG PHOTO

participating groups has become larger. Some like to point fingers at the commercial industry, but outfitters and guides only have access to approximately a tenth of the river's overall use.

"The average size of groups has increased in the last 10 years," Blackfoot River Outfitters owner John Herzer says. "The average party used to be around 4 anglers. Now it's near 10 or 12. That's one thing that has contributed to the 'crowded' feeling. And it's not all outfitters. Every year they publish statistics on the river's usage, and out of the 76 launches outfitters are allowed a year, the most we've ever used is 57 or something like that. In fact, I know some outfitters donate their unused dates back into the pool so private parties can scoop them up."

If you're attempting to organize a float trip on the Smith, the key is planning—and even then, Mother Nature can toss any well-laid strategy out the window. Before you submit an application, settle on days that you and your group are comfortable with, keeping in mind the climate and sudden weather shifts typical in the early season. If the idea of awaking in frosty conditions, sitting through a summer thunderstorm, or going a few days without bathing makes you flinch, this trip probably isn't for you.

"If you're organizing a trip on the Smith, you have to expect anything," Herzer says. "I've turned down numerous people who want to go, because it's not in their personality. You can just tell you don't want to be on the water with some folks when it decides to snow hard for three days. They just won't like it. You have to be ready for anything and expect the very worst, because once you launch, you're committed."

One of first things to consider when planning a Smith trip is that the fishing season is relatively short. Between the winter thaw, high water during runoff, and then a slow-and-steady drop to nearly unfloatable late-summer flows, there are only a handful of weeks in a season when visitors can see the

Smith in all its glory. MDFWP rates June 10 to July 10 as the busiest time on the river.

Most applicants shoot for dates between mid-May and mid-July. Typically, the water is high and off-color but clear enough to fish, and the late spring weather is pleasurable. Apply for a late-summer launch date and you run the risk of low flows, especially in years of drought, which makes the trip a little more arduous from dragging over shallow areas. "When low flows and warm weather hit the Smith, the fishing just shuts down, and the fish go deep. We start floating it in mid-May and we're usually done the first week of July," Brandon Boedecker says.

Early birds willing to tough out an occasional snow squall or cold temperatures can apply for an early departure sometime around mid-April, but you better know what you're doing. A fluke weather front can throw a wrench in anyone's gears, making it tough for someone without the skills or the gear to complete the journey. "We advise our clients to bring winter-weather gear until June 20 or so. I have seen too many late-spring snow squalls. I would get the 10-day forecast just before you go and adjust accordingly. The first two days and nights are generally colder because you are at higher elevations," Joe Sowerby says. "We always bring a wall tent and wood-burning stove for our guests. It is a lot more work, but if the weather goes south, at least you have a warm common area in which to socialize instead of everyone going back to their own tents."

"One of the problems is that MDFWP releases the drawing statistics for the previous year. Applicants look at the chart, see that fewer people apply in the early season than in June, for example, and they draw a permit in April. They don't factor weather, conditions, or anything like that. They're just excited to have a permit," Herzer says. "I know guys who were iced-in at Syringa camp for four days one year. It looked like a picture out of the Shackleton adventure. They get in and the temperature just kept dropping. During one night, it got down to 8 degrees and they could hear the river icing up. The river locked and they couldn't drag around. The group was prepared but lesser folks couldn't handle it."

The safest bet is to go with an outfitter. It costs more money than planning a trip on your own; however, you won't have to worry about anything but fishing. They handle the boats, shuttles, food, camps, and everything else that goes with planning such an outing. And, because they dedicate one, two, or three boats specifically for gear and essentials, you don't have to worry about fishing in tight quarters inside an overloaded raft. Everything is taken care of.

Every year Montana Department of Fish, Wildlife and Parks receives comments from Smith River users. At the end of the season, they post the comments on the website for all to read. I highly recommend reading this document if you want unbiased opinions and thoughts from those who recently traveled down the river. Not only does it give an idea of what to expect, but it may clue you in on some activities and behaviors to avoid.

Mercer's Biot Epoxy Stone (Golden)

Hook: #8-14 Tiemco 2302
Thread: Tan 8/0 Uni-Thread
Tail: Sulphur-orange turkey biot marked with brown marker
Abdomen: Sulphur-orange turkey biot marked with brown marker
Thorax: Golden Stone Buggy Nymph dubbing
Wing Case: Turkey tail coated with epoxy
Legs: Brown hen hackle
Collar: Golden Stone Buggy Nymph dubbing marked with brown marker
Head: Gold bead
Antennae: Sulphur-orange turkey biot marked with brown marker

Muddy Buddy (Olive)

Hook: #2-6 MFC 7008
Cone: Gold 7 mm cone
Thread: Olive Nymo thread
Weight: 1 mm lead wire
Tail: Olive Flashabou Accent
Body: Chartreuse Wing N' Flash
Wing: Light olive rabbit strip
Throat: Red High Voltage
Collar: Olive deer hair
Legs: Speckled-olive Centipede Legs

Trina's Stimi Stone

Hook: #8-10 MFC 7009
Thread: Dark brown 6/0 Uni-Thread
Rib: Copper wire and brown saddle hackle
Body: Yellow 4 mm tube foam
Wing: Natural cow elk
Thorax: Peacock herl
Legs: Copper-brown Super Floss
Hackle: Grizzly saddle hackle

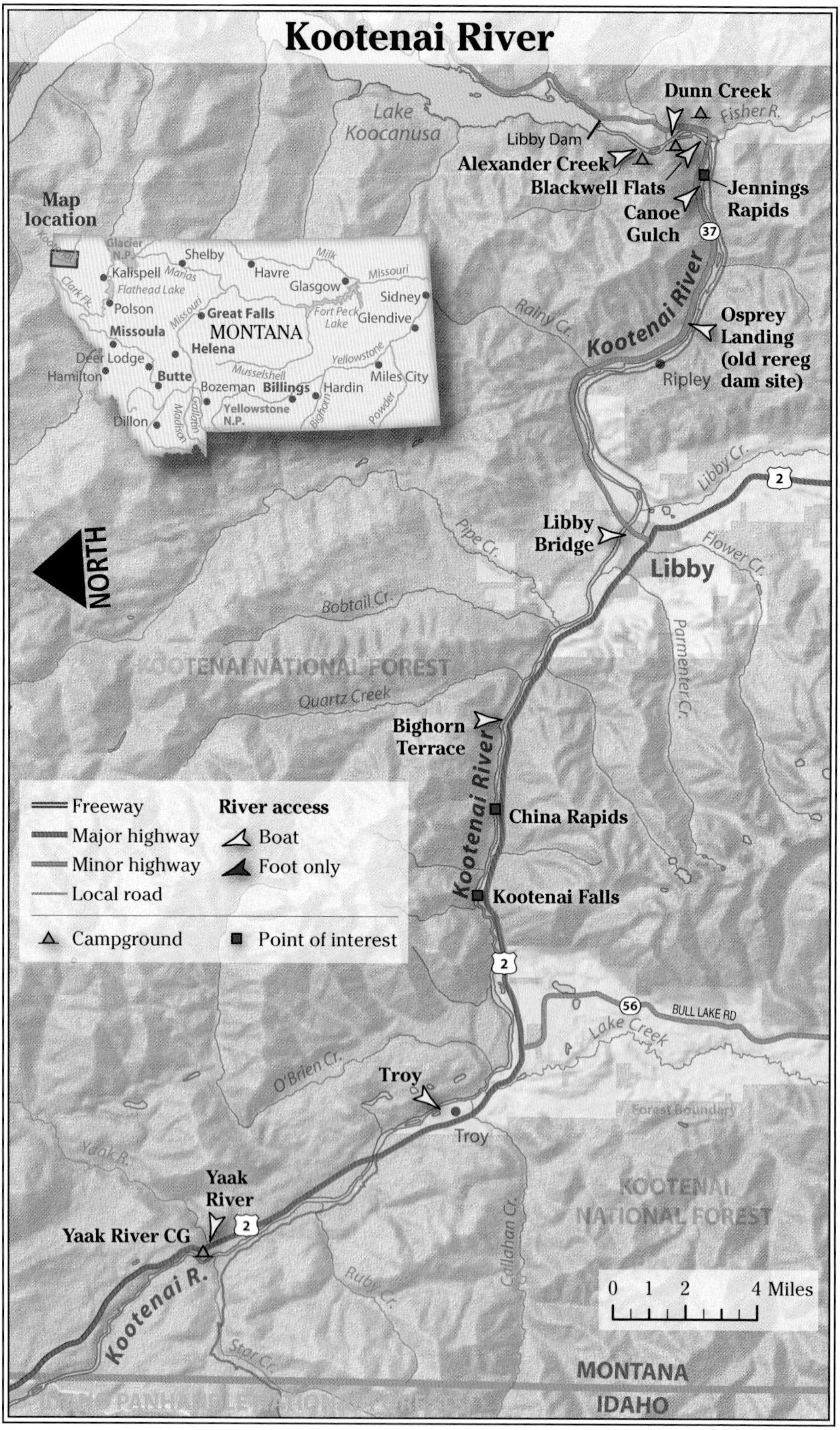

Kootenai River
Dunn Creek
Fisher R.
Lake Koocanusa
Libby Dam
Alexander Creek
Blackwell Flats
Jennings Rapids
Canoe Gulch
37
Map location
Glacier N.P.
Shelby
Kalispell
Marias
Havre
Milk
Missouri
Glasgow
Flathead Lake
Sidney
Clark Fk.
Polson
Great Falls
Fort Peck Lake
Glendive
Missoula
MONTANA
Helena
Deer Lodge
Yellowstone
Hamilton
Butte
Musselshell
Miles City
Bozeman
Billings
Hardin
Yellowstone N.P.
Powder
Bighorn
Dillon
Madison
Gallatin
Rainy Cr.
Kootenai River
Osprey Landing (old rereg dam site)
Ripley
Libby Cr.
2
NORTH
Libby Bridge
Pipe Cr.
Flower Cr.
Libby
Bobtail Cr.
Parmenter Cr.
KOOTENAI NATIONAL FOREST
Quartz Creek
Bighorn Terrace
Kootenai River
Freeway
Major highway
Minor highway
Local road
River access
Boat
Foot only
China Rapids
Kootenai Falls
Campground
Point of interest
2
56
BULL LAKE RD
Lake Creek
O'Brien Cr.
Troy
Troy
Forest Boundary
Yaak R.
Yaak River
Yaak River CG
2
Callahan Cr.
KOOTENAI NATIONAL FOREST
Ruby Cr.
0 1 2 4 Miles
Kootenai R.
Star Cr.
MONTANA
IDAHO

CHAPTER 14

Kootenai River

Before the construction of Libby Dam, the Kootenai was as fussy as a teething child, running as high as 70,000 cubic feet per second into September, which made fishing all but impossible some years. Since the dam's construction in 1972, fish numbers have leaped and flows have stabilized. Now anglers can visit the river nearly any time of the year and find action.

The Kootenai is also famous for dishing out surprises. In 1997, an angler caught the state-record rainbow trout (33 pounds) just below the dam. Ten years earlier a whitefish weighing just over 5 pounds came to the net from the same area.

Like any of the other big waters in the state, you have the chance to catch a big fish on the Kootenai. But if fishermen were making trip after trip and catching 20-inch fish with some regularity, the fly-fishing world would know about it—and they would descend upon the river in droves, despite its remoteness. That simply isn't the case here. Yes, there are big fish in the Kootenai—there are photos in fly shops and state records to verify that. But I have to believe the big fish (above 18 inches) are the exception and not the norm.

"Everybody knows about the state-record rainbow, and once in a while I get a call from a guy who says he's interested in fishing below the dam and wants one big fish, and I have to tell them they have the wrong outfitter," Linehan Outfitting Company owner Tim Linehan says. "I don't mention the fish below the dam much. They aren't a fair representation of the river. If you look below every dam in the country there is probably 20 huge fish of some type. It is not a bug factory, so the bread and butter is 12- to 14-inch fish, but they're shaped like a fist and solid muscle."

So aside from the fishing, why do so many people visit the Kootenai? The answer is simple—solitude and scenery. "The Kootenai is a little harder to get to than most state rivers," says Dave Blackburn of Kootenai Angler. "It's helped protect the resource from the constant pounding of boat after boat. People don't mind seeing other folks on the water, but my repeating customers like the lack of crowds, the solitude, the Glacier Park–like scenery, and the dependable dry-fly fishing."

Upstream of Kootenai Falls, the China Rapids area is a hazard for boaters, but it's a great place for wading fishermen to explore during the low flows of summer. Present a hopper or attractor pattern in the slow-water seams off the main channel and any other pockets created by the hundreds of boulders in the river. JAY NICHOLS PHOTO

The river is off the beaten path, which makes it perfect for anglers that care more about the challenge and experience and less about the size or number of fish they catch. While it is neighbored by an improved highway and close to modern service, the river is tucked away so far in an overlooked part of the state that the surrounding forests, high mountains, and abundant wildlife make it feel like you've ventured into the unknown at times.

"Our idea of a busy day on an 8- or 9-mile float is to see a half-dozen boats or less. Compared to other tailwaters like the Missouri, that's pretty light," Kootenai River fly-fishing guide Kelly Palmer says. "I don't think the

Kootenai is ever going to be a 'premier' destination. Some guys will trade the size of the fish for the opportunity to fish a river where you're not playing bumper boats."

Aside from the solitude and scenery, the Kootenai is also the last stronghold of native redband trout in the state. Many of the fish in the river are a strain of Kamloops, but every now and then you can find a pure redband. At one time, these fish spread throughout the Northwest but now occupy only a handful of streams. Like most of the Kootenai River fish, the redbands aren't known for their size, but even the smallest fish put up a fight and take to the air like their Kamloops brethren.

"Most rainbows made their way into Montana's Rivers via railroad in the '40s and '50s, so they're pretty much stocked statewide. The trains didn't make it up here, so we have a strain of pure Columbia redband rainbows in the system," Blackburn says. "They did, however, put a Kamloop-strain of rainbow in the reservoir, which eventually made it into the river as well, so there is also a mix of the two."

Where and When

The headwaters of the river reside in Canada, but it flows into Lake Koocanusa—a massive man-made body of water much longer than it is wide—near the international border. The reservoir is one of the largest and deepest in the Northwest, and since it's filled with snowmelt, the water spewing from

In 1997, an angler caught the Montana state-record rainbow trout below Libby Dam. It weighed 33 pounds. Big fish continue to stack up in the few miles downstream of the dam, but anglers should expect to encounter more of the river's 12- to 14-inch fish. JAY NICHOLS PHOTO

the dam is extremely cold. In fact, the low mean water temperature and lack of nutrients are two side effects of the dam that some credit for the stifling of many aquatic insect species and the slow growth rate of the Kootenai's fish. Guide Kelly Palmer puts the growth rates in perspective and says the 3- to 5-year-old fish in the Kootenai are typically the size of 2-year-old fish living in tailwaters like the Missouri or Beaverhead.

Primary nutrients of nearly any system, like phosphorous and nitrogen, are a derivative of woody debris, and they find their way into the system from tributaries. Unfortunately, those elements are prone to bond with the clay in the soils that enter a lake's feeder streams with runoff and precipitate to the bottom of a reservoir. Because of the Libby Dam design, the nutrients fall to the bottom of Lake Koocanusa, never wash through the dam's turbines, and thus never reach the Kootenai River downstream of the dam, impeding the growth of many aquatic insects.

It's a chain reaction. The nutrients help the algae loads, which in turn help the aquatic insects, which help grow the fish. When a link in that chain is missing, growth rates are affected. Some local outfitters put it best when they say the river is just too clean.

To make matters worse, the 2006 season saw an unprecedented amount of water spill through and over Libby Dam. Rapidly melting snow and poor water-release management led to a huge push of water, and it's likely that the river's fish numbers and bug life took a hit.

The first few miles below Libby Dam is famous for its large rainbow trout, but they often hold in deep water. Use sinking lines and heavily weighted streamers to get your fly in front of fish. DAVE BLACKBURN/KOOTENAI ANGLER PHOTO

"The top section of the river used to be where you would catch the bigger fish. But we had a monster spill in 2006 that some of us feel took a toll on the rainbow populations," Palmer says. "We already have a relatively nutrient-deprived river. Combine that with the effect of a spill where you get a saturation of nitrogen, and it's going to take a toll. In 2006, they were running 28,000 cfs through the turbines, and they spilled another 27,000 cfs over the face of the dam, so you have this thunderous 55,000 cfs on the top end of the river blowing out whatever was in its path."

While the push of water was a sincere concern to those that make their living on the water, Montana Fish, Wildlife and Parks biologists assured anglers the outcome was not as bad as perceived. "We didn't see anything bad happen to the fish," Montana Fish, Wildlife and Parks biologist Ryan Sylvester says. "Right now, the Libby section is averaging 2,000 to 2,500 per mile. Our studies show these fish are smaller than the fish before the dam was in place, but there are certainly more of them. The Osprey Landing section started monitoring in 2001 and it's been averaging 1,000 to 1,500 a mile, but they're a little bigger in that section compared to the Libby section. A population estimate was performed this fall [2008] below the dam and yielded an estimate of about 1,500 per mile."

The Kootenai is quite possibly the biggest river in terms of flow that a fly angler can tangle with in the state of Montana. Even at low flows (anywhere between 4,000 and 6,000 cfs) this tailwater is moving fast enough to sweep the legs from under even the sturdiest waders. There are many deep whirlpools and undertows along the dropoffs—dangerous terrain for inexperienced floaters and waders.

While the upper river is tough to manage on foot, it is easily accessible. The 15 miles or so between Libby and the dam are paralleled by MT 37. There are no state-managed fishing-access sites on the Kootenai, but there are plenty of areas managed by the U.S. Forest Service and the Army Corps of Engineers that are just as good. Some include boat ramps and parking lots, while others are roadside pull-offs where you can park and scramble down to the water.

The many public-access points in the first few miles of river make it easy to plan a float over different water depending on what's hatching and the time of day you are fishing. The first and probably most popular areas are from Libby Dam to Canoe Gulch nearly four miles downstream. In the space between, you'll fine three campgrounds (two on the eastern shore and one on the west) and a day-use area that are all easy to reach via automobile.

Alexander Creek and Blackwell Flats campgrounds are on the western shore. Turn north on Forest Road (FR) 228 about three-quarters of a mile past Dave Blackburn's Kootenai Angler near the sign on the north side of the road marking the distance to the dam. Blackwell Flats is on the right, between the road and the river after making the turn, but Alexander Creek is another two miles down the road. Both areas have campsites, restrooms, and boat ramps.

If you want to launch your boat or fish even closer to the outflow of Libby Dam, turn east off FR 228 into Alexander Creek Campground, drive through the campground, past all the sites, and continue toward the dam and David Thompson Bridge. Cross the river and continue downstream along the eastern shore. There is a one-lane road to the Libby Dam access a few hundred yards downstream of the bridge. This day-use area has a restroom, picnic areas, parking, and unimproved boat ramps.

While I have had good luck fishing to rising fish with dry flies, the upper river near the dam is the best place to try streamers. Use a sinking line, weighted flies, and get as low as you can go. The dam turbines suck in kokanee salmon from Lake Koocanusa, turn them into chum, and spew the chip-chop into the river for any rainbows willing to belly up to the plate. Patterns that imitate injured fish, like kokanee, are a good starting point for fly selection. This is much easier said than done depending on the release flows, but the suspense of streamer fishing keeps things interesting. This also means you may accidentally catch one of the river's many bull trout, so if you do, release it gently, since they are a threatened species.

Also on the eastern shore, not far from the Libby Dam Access, is Dunn Creek Campground. This facility also has restrooms, parking, camping, and a boat ramp. Dunn Creek is easy to reach from MT 37. If you're heading north on the highway, look for signs and a left-hand turn (west) approximately one mile after crossing the river.

These access points create somewhat of a loop around the first 4 miles of river, and Canoe Gulch is the westernmost anchor point. Because Canoe Gulch is not marked with signs and the boat ramp is nearly invisible from the road, this is a tough one for first-time visitors to find. The best landmark is Canoe Gulch Ranger Station on the north side of MT 37. The boat ramp and parking area is an overgrown pull-off just across the street between the road and the river. I don't recommend the boat ramp for rigs without four wheel drive. It's unimproved and has a fairly steep gradient.

If you can't find or are unsure about loading or unloading your rig at the Canoe Gulch ramp, look to Osprey Landing about four miles downstream near mile marker 9. This facility has a concrete ramp, plenty of parking, restroom, and access to MT 37.

The town of Libby, and the city's boat access site, is about eight miles downstream from Osprey Landing. This stretch of river is popular with floaters because the distance between access points is perfect for a full-day float, and the ramps are improved and easy to use. Look for the turnoff on the northeast side of town next to the MT 37 bridge across the river. Turn north on City Service Road, and you'll see the boat ramp, parking area, playground, and other public accommodations.

The water downstream from Libby is also a popular area to fish, especially during the summer when hoppers are out. There is a good deal of overhanging vegetation so terrestrials constantly fall into the water, and riffles and fast-water seams are where you can throw big bugs and catch fish. It's a refreshing break from the flat-water presentations and refusals from discriminatory fish you find elsewhere on the river. Since there is so much water, break it down

Most of the fish in the Kootenai range from 10 to 14 inches long, but they don't come easy. Clear water and keen senses help the fish discern between a real or natural before striking, so flawless presentations are a must in some areas. JAY NICHOLS PHOTO

and fish it systematically. "The Kootenai is so big it intimidates a lot of anglers sometimes, but there's no need to adjust what anglers are used to. Just as an angler might on a smaller stream, focus on fishing the banks, or gravel-bars, or the lee side of islands, looking for structure and seams," Palmer says.

I like this area because the character of the water changes around every bend. For a few hundred yards I may be in textbook streamer water, but then switch to a dry-fly rod when I see rising fish, then move to a dry-dropper rig when I want to jump out and really work a riffle. It's scenic (despite the presence of residential areas) and a good area to fish if you're staying in Libby.

If you're floating from Libby, Bighorn Terrace (sometimes called River Road) is the next ramp downstream at the end of Kootenai River Road with a nice ramp, restroom, ample parking, and a trail that heads downstream in case you want to park and explore on foot. From Libby, take MT 37 north out of town. After crossing the bridge turn left (west) on Kootenai River Road. The road ends at the access site approximately seven miles later. This is the last public take-out before China Rapids, so you don't want to miss it.

Even though Bighorn Terrace is the final stop for floaters, the water from here to the falls is ideal for wade fishing and easily accessible from US 2. In fact, some of the same water most people float between Libby and Bighorn Terrace is easily reached from the road. As long as you're mindful of private property, it's perfectly fine to park in any of the several pull-offs, scramble through the grass, over the railroad tracks, and down to the water. The mile or two upstream from the falls is especially fun to fish when flows are low (otherwise, I don't advise it). This run, known as China Rapids, is full of boulders, seams, pockets, and other structure that hold fish.

Kootenai Falls is a spectacular natural feature that separates the upper river from the lower river. Long considered a sacred place by native tribes, it's now a pit stop for tourists complete with a walking trail, scenic viewpoints, interpretive signs, and a suspending footbridge over the white water. It's easy to find near mile marker 21 off US 2, so stop and enjoy this terrific sight if you have time, especially if you have your family in tow.

"We know fish go over the falls, and a few fish move up over the falls—as difficult as that is to believe," Sylvester says. "I've documented a 25-inch bull trout tagged below the falls that ascended Kootenai Falls, went up Quartz Creek to spawn, and then returned to the Kootenai River. I guess if a bull trout can do it, the rainbows can too. We don't know how often it happens, but it does happen occasionally."

There certainly aren't as many fish per mile below the falls, and there are some other species like brown trout mixed in. "Brown trout were illegally introduced to Lake Creek a number of years ago. We are starting to see a few more browns in the lower river—my clients are catching less than six a week," Palmer says.

Fishing tactics aren't any different than for the upper river, but populations aren't as strong. "Downstream of the falls we switch to bigger attractor patterns and streamers. There aren't a lot of heavy hatches and the fish are more opportunistic," Blackburn says. "These fish are football shaped and I've never caught a wild fish like them. Even the small fish jump five or six times," Blackburn says.

The Troy access is the first public access point downstream of the falls, but some outfitters have private access points in between. Though the price of admission into these private areas is hiring a guide for the day, it's worth it, and you can see water that some Kootenai anglers never see. The Troy site is easy to get to, and the float from here to the Yaak River confluence has some great water. From US 2, turn northeast on 3rd Street. After crossing the railroad tracks, turn left on Riverside Avenue and continue until it dead-ends into the parking lot and public park.

Yaak River not only provides a much-needed influx of cold, clean water to the main stem Kootenai, it's a spawning sanctuary for the native redband rainbows and also has brookies. "The Yaak is a pretty little 3-weight stream. It doesn't hold a lot of large fish, and I attribute that largely to the introduction of brook trout, so you've got that crowd-and-stunt dynamic going on," Palmer says. "There are native, pure-strain redband rainbows in the system above the falls."

"The one thing I tell people about the tributaries is to keep moving. Don't get concrete feet," Linehan says. "This is fairly mountainous country so carry some attractor patterns, make a few casts, and move on."

Follow US 2 from Troy for 7.5 miles. Yaak Campground, which is split in two (half on the north shore of the Yaak, half on the south shore), is on the west side of the highway and flanks the Kootenai River. Aside from camping, this is also a popular take-out, but floaters should be aware that the water is turbulent.

"Early in the season, down by the Yaak-Kootenai junction, you really have to pay attention. These are two big volumes of colliding water. It wants to push you into this huge, dark, abysmal back eddy. Anytime you fish through that area, pull river right and get as far up into the Yaak as you can and scratch along that bank," Linehan says. "If you're not paying attention you'll get into trouble. It's not anything you can't handle if you've been on the sticks for a while, but the idea is to scoot along through the mouth of the Yaak. It's totally confused water."

You can float from the Yaak access and polish off the remaining few miles within the Montana borders, but the next take-out is in Idaho. If you plan on working downstream, carry a fishing license from each state or stop fishing at Leonia Bridge. The river flows through a canyon, so there is no other access until the take-out.

Even during the low flows of summer, the Kootenai runs an average of 4,000 to 6,000 cfs, and floating the river offers more advantages over wade fishing. Most of the water is calm, flat, and not a problem for novice oarsmen, but talk with locals about specific rough areas before launching to avoid trouble. JAY NICHOLS PHOTO

Once in Idaho you can take out at the Twin River Resort in Moyie Springs. The resort owner installed a sandy boat ramp and charges $3 per day, per car, for anyone using it. There is some good fishing down here, but only float this long stretch if you are willing to put in a long day on the water.

Hatches and Flies

While the record books and archived photos prove there are bigger fish in the system, most of the specimens I've caught and seen are rainbows from 8 to 12 inches long. Anything stretching longer than that (not counting the river's bull trout) is a large fish for the Kootenai. They are beautiful, however. Chrome-bright like steelhead fresh from the sea with more spunk and fight in them than a fish twice their size. And, make no mistake, they are selective. I'm hard-pressed to remember another time when such moderately sized fish required long leaders and perfect drag-free drifts.

Fishing from a boat is much easier on the Kootenai than trying to attack it on foot. The water is wide, deep, and swift, and having the ability to either anchor up over a pod of rising fish or scoot across stream to hit the tailout of a pool where you see fish rising is much safer in watercraft than trying to brave a crossing on foot. Lastly, a boat makes it all that much easier to get a good presentation. The current is deceivingly fast (even at late-summer low flows of 6,000 cfs) and having the ability to move the same speed, or slightly slower, than your presentation helps bring more fish to the net.

A boat also helps you fish to the structure. "If you just pound the banks, you won't always find the bigger fish. When the water is lower in the summer, we're fishing behind big boulders, over dropoffs, and out in the middle of the river. Unlike some other rivers, Kootenai fish will hold in heavy water. I think it's part of their biological nature. So when anglers are just looking for soft-water holding areas, they're probably floating over the fast water where the bigger fish sometimes hold," Blackburn says.

Most of the river is easy to navigate, even for novice oarsmen. There are a few sets of white-water runs like those upstream of Canoe Gulch and the Yaak River confluence that floaters should be aware of. Stay in touch with fly shops for information on flows, hazards, and general fishing conditions.

Because Libby Dam is able to draw water at various depths, the water temperatures remain fairly consistent throughout the year, and the fishing season can sometimes begin long before some other rivers thaw. At this point, it's mostly a nymphing and streamer game, but the rainbows are preparing to spawn and eager to eat. *Baetis* and midges make up most of the bug life, but egg patterns work well too.

From March to April, bug activity picks up as weather patterns change from winter to spring. March Browns will show up, but because the Kootenai basin drains such an immense area, watch streamflow levels and weather forecasts. You never know when a flush of snowmelt coming down the Fisher River (a large tributary in the upper river) will shut things down for a few

Offset from many of the state's other fly-fishing hot spots, the Kootenai offers an element of solitude that returning anglers appreciate. Though relatively unpressured, the best fishing is still in the early morning and evening hours when insect activity is greatest.

days. Most times, you can fish the first few miles below the dam, but below the MT 37 bridge, the Fisher River can mess things up. If in doubt, call ahead and talk to a fly shop or outfitter about current conditions and predictions. It's a long way to travel if fishing conditions are questionable.

As the summer fishing season commences, stoneflies crawl to the shoreline. There are Salmonflies on the Kootenai but not in masses like they appear on freestones in the southwest part of the state. Fish will target them, so bring some #4 patterns as well as some smaller, paler versions in case you also encounter Golden Stones. Typically, Green Drakes hatch during this window as well, but from what I gather, hatches are sporadic and their numbers are seemingly decreasing year after year.

Blue Quills are one of the most important hatches on the river because they can appear at any time from the spring to the fall. Dave Blackburn recommends #16-20 short-shank parachute and thorax-style flies not just because

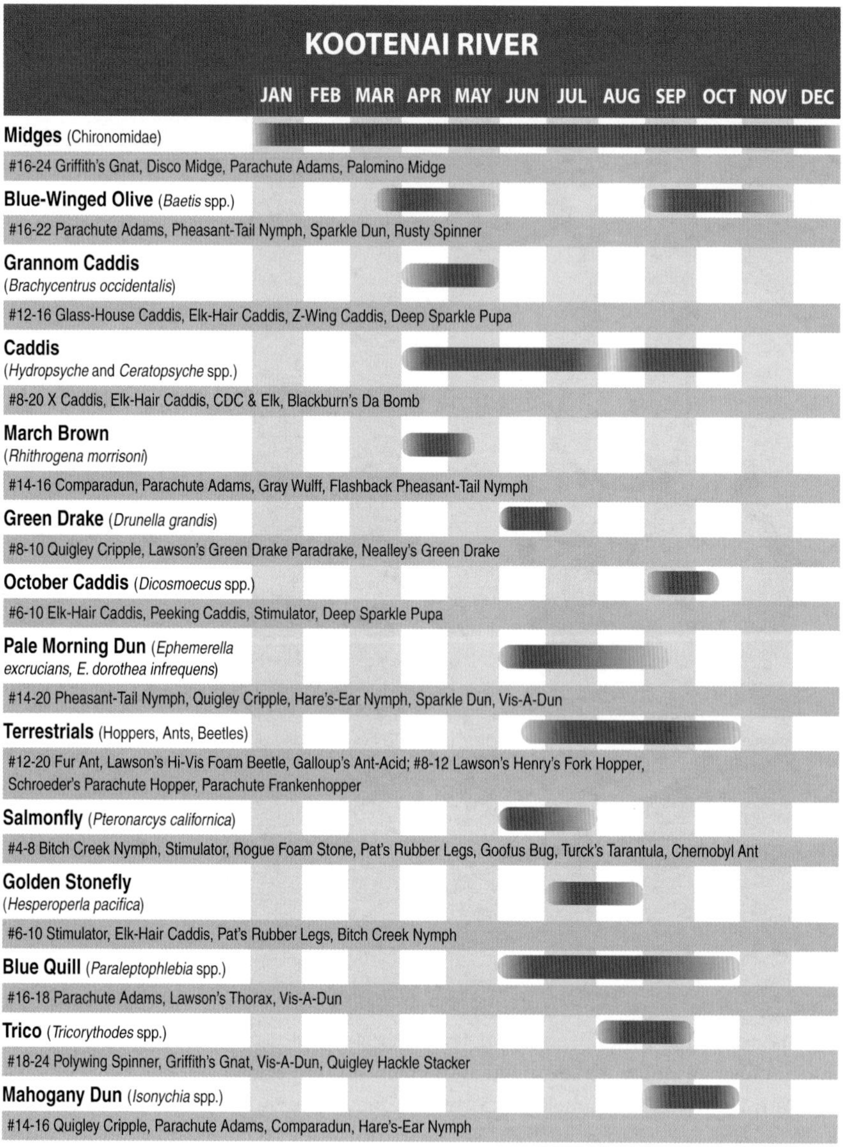

they're realistic, but because a smaller, stouter hook gets a better bite on the fish. "When the fish are taking Blue Quills (*Pseudocloeon*), they won't take anything else," Blackburn says. "You'll move from one section to another, and one school of fish may be taking quills, and the next caddis pupae. If you pay attention to what is on the water, you can figure things out."

Pale Morning Duns are the meat-and-potatoes hatch. In the beginning they'll be large (#14), but as the summer progresses, you may need to downsize your patterns to #18s. When PMDs are hatching, sometimes it's better to select a shorter float and hit the side channels. Anchor the boat and wade-fish these spots, especially in between the dam and Canoe Gulch, and you may find some decent fish.

A range of caddis species is another important Kootenai River staple. Grannom, Spotted Sedges, and other caddis of varying sizes and colors come off throughout the season, particularly in the evenings. In late summer, you can often spot fish from a high vantage point. One night Jay Nichols and I stood on the shoulder of MT 37 looking down into the water and could see fish ascend from the bottom, eat a caddis, and then retreat. Suffice to say, even though we could spot the fish, it took a few pattern changes before we found what these fussy 12-inchers would move for. Some patterns to carry for caddis include Mathews' X Caddis, CDC & Elk, and a few pupae patterns that sit just beneath the surface film.

"There is little in the way of unique patterns needed on the Kootenai. We fish a lot of Elk-Hair Caddis, parachute patterns, familiar nymphs or soft hackles underneath, and even big terrestrials depending on the time of year," Palmer says. "Most people drop down in fly size, but I oversize my flies a lot of the time."

Around the same time, the terrestrials begin to stir. For many, the hopper fishing is the main attraction. Late-summer flows on the river are typically at their lowest, so fish are concentrated in easy-to-read positions as opposed to when the river carries three or four times the volume and seems relatively featureless. Try a variety of patterns because these fish seemingly change their preferences on a whim. They may want a realistic pattern one minute and then a large Chernobyl Ant–style fly the next.

With the exception of a fish crashing after a fallen terrestrial, I've noticed trout feeding in pods rather than sporadically by themselves. For floaters this may mean going hundreds of yards without seeing any activity and then stumbling on a dozen or more fish feeding along a rocky shoreline. Their fussy nature makes it hard to target a specific fish, but in most cases, it doesn't matter since they're all about the same size anyway.

"I don't think these fish are as fussy as, say, Missouri fish or Henry's Fork fish," Linehan says. "The challenge is this water is so clear that it makes the fish especially spooky. If you can see them, there's a good chance they can see you. They're less picky from a pattern point of view, but it's much more necessary to get long drifts on light leaders."

"As the glacial silt filters out of the river, you have to lengthen your leaders and drop a size. I never go below 6X and typically stay with 5X. The water is so clear it becomes a spring creek–like scenario. Into September, we get a small green chironomid in a size 22. We fish a big Wulff in front as an indicator and a tiny green midge larva as a dropper," Blackburn says.

A 4-weight rod and floating line is a good match for the Kootenai's rainbows. Leaders may need to be slightly longer than you may be accustomed to using. It lessens the likelihood of lining a fish and allows for a longer drift, especially with lighter, supple tippets like 5X and 6X. A stiff 6-weight and sinking line is a must if you plan on passing streamers in front of the fish below the dam.

Streamers also have their place if you're looking for some of the river's larger rainbows. Some local favorites include black and purple articulated Marabou Leeches, olive and yellow Double Bunnies, Conehead or Kiwi Muddlers, and black Woolly Buggers. Of course, going deep with meaty offerings may entice one of the river's bull trout, and while their numbers are seemingly stable in the watershed, they remain a protected species and cannot be specifically targeted.

"I think bull trout are coming back. They took a hit during the spill of 2006, but last fall I think we had the highest counts of bulls on the river. The last count turned up something like 500 bulls that were 20 inches or longer between the mouth of Fisher River and the Libby Dam," Blackburn says. "We don't target bulls, but we use sinking tips and shooting heads that get 15 to 20 feet down. Twenty years ago, we'd catch 90 percent rainbows. Since the spill, we've seen close to a 50-50 mix. These days it's fairly common for bull trout to attack a small rainbow on the end of your line."

Studies from MDFWP confirm Blackburn's observations to a degree. "We started estimating the number of bull trout from Libby Dam to Fisher River confluence in 2004, but it's been all over the map. In 2004 and 2005 it was right around 1,000 fish. Then it dropped in 2006 (prespill) to around 175. Since 2007, the population estimate has been around 350 or 400 bull trout," Sylvester says. "We don't know what's causing the fluctuation in bull trout numbers. It may just be the fish moving throughout the system and a function of entrainment through Libby Dam."

Directions

US 2 and MT 37 neighbor the Kootenai River from Libby Dam to the Idaho border. To get to the river from Missoula, head north on US 93 and then west on MT 200. After Noxon, turn north on MT 56 (Bull Lake Road). MT 56 runs into US 2 just a few miles east of Troy, but you can turn right (east) and head toward Libby. If you're coming from the Flathead Valley, follow US 2 west from Kalispell into Libby.

To reach the upper river above Libby, follow MT 37 (California Avenue) north. This road crosses the Kootenai on the north side of town and follows the upper river to the Libby Dam and Lake Koocanusa. To reach the upper access points (like Thompson Bridge below the dam) and campgrounds on the west shore near the dam, turn left (north) on FR 228 before crossing the river near the Fisher River.

From Libby downstream, US 2 follows the lower river to Troy and on to the Idaho border. There are some public sites like Kootenai Falls and other fishing points, as well as roadside pull-offs along the way, but be mindful of private property.

Mathews' X Caddis

Hook:	#14-18 Tiemco 100
Thread:	Olive 8/0 Uni-Thread (color to match body)
Body:	Olive Sparkle Blend dubbing
Tail/Shuck:	Brown or olive Z-lon
Wing:	Dark deer hair

MFC Chernobyl Ant

Hook:	#4-12 MFC 7022
Thread:	Black 6/0 Uni-Thread
Hackle:	Brown
Overbody:	Black foam
Body:	Chartreuse Wing N' Flash
Underbody:	Chartreuse foam
Indicator:	Yellow foam
Legs:	Barred olive/black Sili Legs

Lightning Bug (Copper)

Hook:	#12-18 MFC 7076
Bead:	Copper
Thread:	Rusty brown 6/0 Uni-Thread
Tail:	Pheasant tail
Rib:	Copper wire
Body:	Copper High Voltage
Wing Case:	Copper High Voltage
Thorax:	Peacock herl
Legs:	Pheasant tail

Parachute Hopper (Tan)

Hook:	#8-14 Tiemco 5212
Thread:	Cream 6/0 Uni-Thread
Post:	Natural calf tail
Rib:	Dark brown floss
Legs:	Knotted pheasant-tail fibers
Hackle:	Grizzly
Abdomen:	Golden brown Antron

Flathead River (Upper)

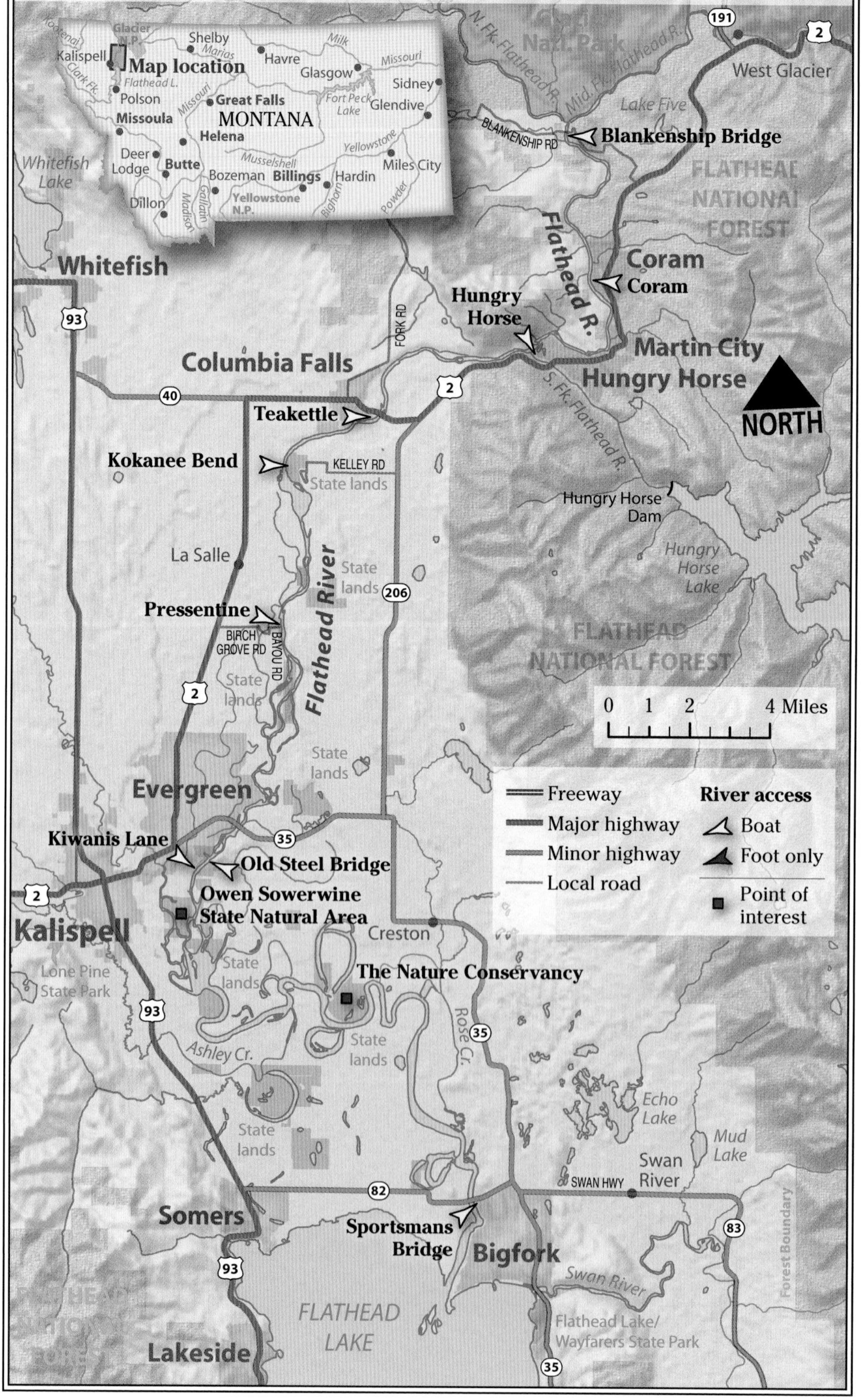

CHAPTER 15

Flathead River

Finally, after wandering through all those miles of wilderness, crossing international borders, and working their way along the borders of one of the nation's most visited national parks, the three forks of the Flathead converge and form the main stem near Hungry Horse. But the celebration is short-lived. The big body of water only works through the valley (some of it tough to reach because of private property) before plunging into Flathead Lake, an enormous body of water pitted between the towns of Bigfork and Polson.

While there is fishing in this stretch, it's a tough proposition for the wading angler. Modest gradient and little structure make it a wide, swift, and flat place to fish—not terribly exciting compared with the wild water on the three forks. The good news is most of the fish that are here migrate back and forth from the lake and are typically larger than the average fish in the forks upstream.

"The window of opportunity for trout on the Flathead isn't quite what it is on the state's other rivers," Bigfork Anglers fly-shop owner Jason Lanier says. "But we get some good spring fishing with nymphs and dry flies. Actually, it's one of the best opportunities to catch the lake-run cutts, which are huge. A guide from Glacier Raft Company caught a legitimate 27-inch cutthroat in the main stem last year. I would have never believed it if I didn't see it. It was probably one of the fish that moves between the lake and the river."

Blankenship Bridge is the first access after the North and Middle forks join, though most locals, guides, and outfitters refer to this area as the Middle Fork and the area downstream of the junction with the South Fork of the Flathead as the main stem. Generally, this area sees some swimmers and rafters in the summer, but the water downstream has some solid fishing opportunities. Most of the crowds stick to the lower Middle Fork's whitewater chutes.

Downstream, the main stem gains considerable volume from the South Fork of the Flathead near Hungry Horse. From here to the lake, the river is big water. "The main stem Flathead is big water, and wade fishing is probably limited on this river more than any other in the state," Westslope Troutfitters co-owner Brendan Friel says. "In addition to that, there are a lot of places that don't hold fish. Even some of the fishiest-looking water can be empty."

Flathead River (Lower)

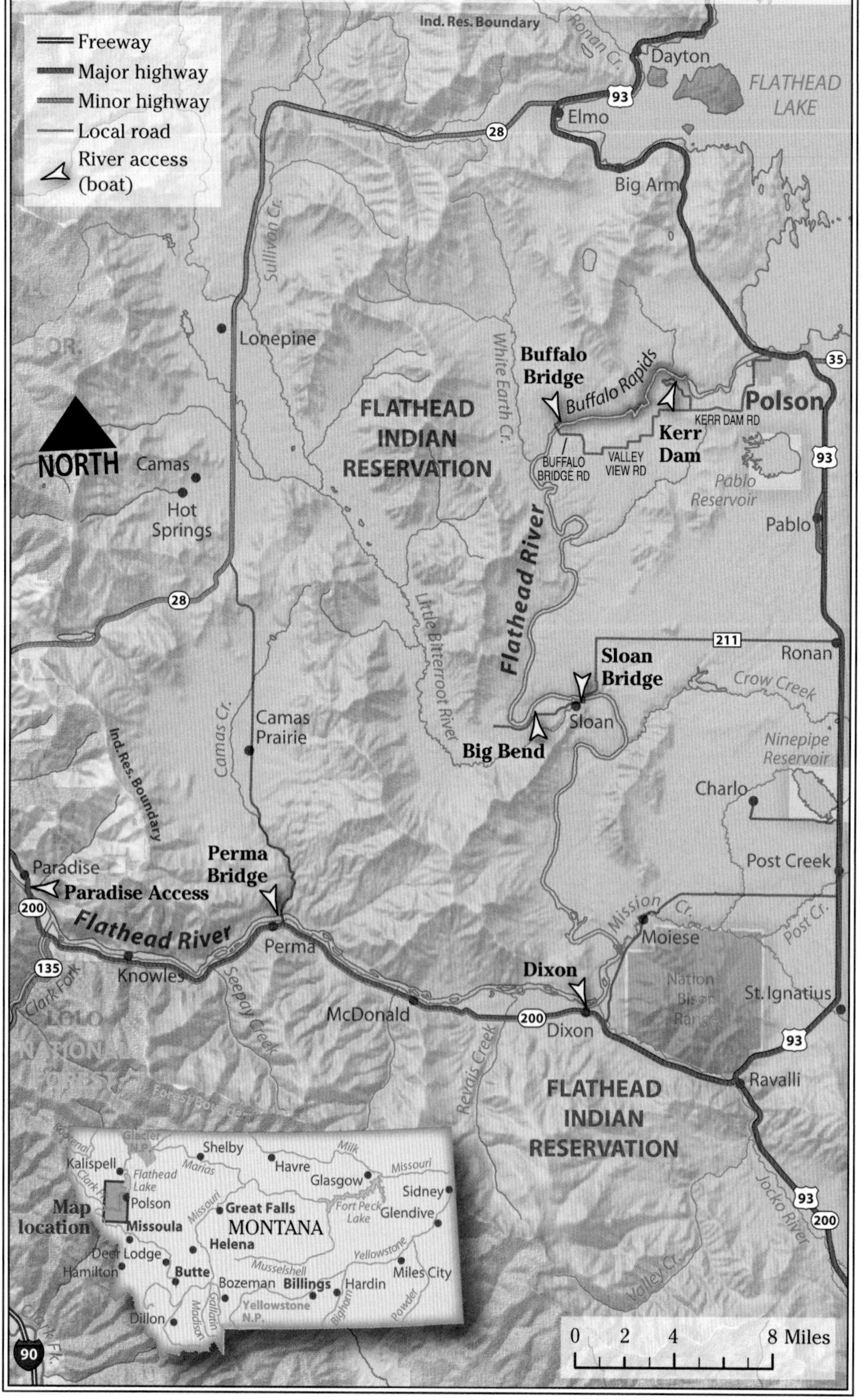

As time goes by and you become more familiar with the best areas in the river to fish, a boat becomes even more handy. Rather than waste time in unproductive areas, it's easy to push through slow spots to get to more productive water. "You can use a boat as a vehicle to reach different wade-fishing areas. You don't have to cast from the bow all day long," Arends Fly Shop owner Bob Arends says.

The Teakettle access is just off the US 2 bridge on the east side of Columbia Falls. "Right above Teakettle Bridge," Lanier says, "a huge riffle everyone calls Old Faithful stretches across the whole river and has really good wade fishing if you don't have a boat."

For a short float, you can take out on the east side of the river at Kokanee Bend just a little over two miles downstream from Teakettle. To reach it from US 2, turn southwest on River Road on the east side of the bridge outside Columbia Falls, and then follow Columbia Falls Stage Road south. The road angles west and intersects with Hellman Lane. Head north on Hellman and then west on Kokanee Bend Drive. The parking lot is at the end of the road.

The lower Flathead River is off many anglers' radar screens because of the lackluster trout fishing. However, it's an excellent pike and bass fishery and a great place to cast Clouser Minnows or large rabbit-strip pike flies. JAY NICHOLS PHOTO

Below Kokanee Bend, the river goes through a series of braids and island channels that present a good opportunity to use a boat to access some wader-friendly water—a relative anomaly on this big river. It's worth anchoring the boat and exploring shallow riffles and undercut banks with attractor patterns. "For the most part, look for the typical trout-holding spots first like islands points, seams, and any other structure in the river," Lanier says. "When you get to the long stretches that look void of fish, you just have to look for them in the buckets and pools."

Pressentine access on the west side of the river is next. Turn east on Birch Grove Road from US 2 and continue southeast at the intersection of Bayou Road. Bayou Road snakes past a few houses, but at the next intersection turn north and follow the road to the parking lot.

Like the water upstream, the river below Pressentine has plenty of braids, islands, and channels. If floating, you'll go under the MT 35 bridge and encounter the Old Steel Bridge access soon after on the west side of the river. Brendan Friel says it's one of his favorite stretches of the river because there's good water and side channels to explore but not as much pressure as House of Mystery to Teakettle or Teakettle to Pressentine. This area is more popular as a take-out than a put-in since the river turns broad and slow about a mile and a half downstream. It's a shame because there are dozens of islands and sloughs between here and Flathead Lake that are home to fish other than trout.

The upper Flathead River is suited more for floating anglers than waders, but there are plenty of braids, channels, and islands worth exploring. Anchor the boat and fish the soft water in and around these landmarks for shots at fish other fishermen may be floating past. DUNCAN OSWALD PHOTO

The closer you get to Flathead Lake, the wider and slower the upper Flathead becomes. If you fish the river this far down, don't be surprised to find more pike and even largemouth bass than trout, especially if you're fishing in and around the backwaters and sloughs.
DUNCAN OSWALD PHOTO

"There are a few seams, pockets, and backwaters in the lower Flathead just before it goes into the lake that hold largemouth bass," Lanier says. "The biggest ones you get are about four pounds, but in the summertime they'll eat poppers on top. There's a few sloughs we found last year that had some nice fish."

You can access some of the sloughs and backwaters on foot through Stillwater State Forest, but the action is better if you're able to maneuver through the water by boat. In fact, jet boats, which come up from Flathead Lake, have an easier time negotiating the maze of water than drift boats.

"There are quite a few fish species other than trout between the lake and Kalispell. I once even saw a pike right above Teakettle Bridge in a little side slough. I talked to a local biologist who said that is the farthest they've heard pike swimming up the system from the lake," Friel says. "Most of the pike stay in the lower river."

The Sportsmans Bridge access is the last one on the upper Flathead main stem. It's near the MT 83 bridge southeast of Kalispell on the eastern side of the river. This is a better site for powered watercraft than drift boats or wading anglers since by this point the river looks more like a deep, slow-moving Midwestern river than a trout fishery.

Hatches and Flies

In the past, the Flathead River was labeled as a sterile system with little or no bug life or fish. That has changed in the last decade with the help of new angling regulations and a little help from the South Fork. "The main stem has been doing really well for about 10 years now, ever since they put catch-and-release regulations on the cutthroat," Stumptown Anglers fly-shop owner Dave Brown says. "But another key has been the dam on the South Fork. It has a selective draw on it so they can pull water from different levels in the reservoir depending on temperature. Essentially, they've been trying to mimic the normal flows and temperatures depending on the time of year. It's not perfect, but it's being handled for the betterment of the fishery, and we're seeing some better hatches than we used to, especially within the last 3 years."

The prime season on the Flathead system is relatively short. A late spring, snowmelt, and an early fall make July, August, and September the best months to time a trip. "We have the golden three weeks (generally the first three weeks of July) when the river is dropping and clearing, the big bugs are going, and the fishing is some of the best of the season," Brown says. "There are only a few months to fish the river, so you can expect to see more people

Damselflies and Dragonflies are sometimes just as popular with Flathead River fish as terrestrials and stoneflies—proof that you shouldn't overlook any food sources when trying to figure out what the fish will key on. JAY NICHOLS PHOTO

on the water than other months. But pressure is still relatively light. We're blessed by our location because it's not within easy reach of other high-traffic waters. Most people end up fishing here because they're on vacation with their family around Glacier."

Golden Stones are one of the most prolific bugs on the river when water conditions begin settling down after runoff. Foam-bodied patterns and other low-riding imitators work well, but don't be too concerned with realistic imitations. Cutthroat are opportunistic and typically presentation outweighs the need to realistically match the bugs.

Soon after, hatches of PMDs and Green Drakes work up and down the river. Again, you won't see clouds of bugs in the air because of the low-nutrient water, but they will provide you with clues for choosing the right pattern. "When the summer comes we get decent PMDs, Green Drakes, a few Golden Stones, and some decent caddis hatches, but it's pretty spotty. We end up using a lot of attractor patterns," Lanier says. Some grass banks along the main stem stretch for hundreds of yards, so when the season steps into late July and August look to terrestrial patterns. "Terrestrial fishing is good, especially with little black stuff like beetles and ants," Lanier says. Since much of the fishing is best with attractor-style dry flies, a 5-weight rod coupled with a floating line and 9-foot, 2X to 4X leaders are good for the main stem.

Lake Whitefish

In the late fall, lake whitefish, a cousin to the river-dwelling whitefish so often despised by fly fishers, make their spawning runs upstream from Flathead Lake. Originally planted in the lake with the intention of kick-starting a commercial netting operation, these fish are hefty (up to 3 pounds) and make good table fare.

Those who have fished for shad will be familiar with the technique for catching whitefish. Bounce conventional jig heads wrapped with chenille or marabou (chartreuse is the most effective color) through the deep eddies and pools. Granted, this technique is better suited for conventional fishing gear, but the fish are fun on a fly rod and catchable from shore. It's worth a shot. With liberal daily limits, feel free to keep a couple for the smoker or barbeque.

"We have a lot of Lake Superior whitefish, which is totally different from a mountain whitefish. They look more like a shad, fight hard, and are larger. They're not in the river in the summer. They make their way up in the fall around late October. You can float down the river and the water is so clear you'll see this big, dark mass of fish. I bought a 5-weight Spey rod and nymph with it and just crush them. Plus you get a few trout mixed in," Lanier says. "They're really good to eat. In fact, a lot of restaurants up here serve them. There's a commercial market for them, and if you buy a $5 commercial license, there's a few middlemen that pay around $2 a fish. So if you go out, catch 30 of them, you've got the gas and beer for you and your friends covered for the day."

FLATHEAD SYSTEM

JAN FEB MAR APR MAY JUN JUL AUG SEP OCT NOV DEC

Hatch	Patterns
Midge (Chironomidae)	#16-24 Griffith's Gnat, Disco Midge, Parachute Adams, Palomino Midge
Blue-Winged Olive (*Baetis* spp.)	#16-20 Parachute Adams, Pheasant-Tail Nymph, Sparkle Dun, Rusty Spinner
Caddis (*Hydropsyche* and *Ceratopsyche* spp.)	#12-16 Sparkle Pupa, Elk-Hair Caddis, Goddard Caddis, Stimulator
Pale Morning Dun (*Ephemerella excrucians, E. dorothea infrequens*)	#16-20 Parachute Adams, Flashback Pheasant-Tail Nymph, Rusty Spinner, Quigley Cripple, Vis-A-Dun
Terrestrials (Ants, Beetles, Hoppers, Crickets)	#14-20 Schroeder's Parachute Ant, Gould's Half-Down Ant, Fire Beetle; #6-10 Trixie the Hooker Hopper, Kingfisher's Red Legged Hopper; #8-12 Lawson's Henry's Fork Hopper, Parachute Frankenhopper
Gray Drake (*Siphlonurus occidentalis*)	#12-16 Lawson's Paradrake, Hare's-Ear Nymph, Parachute Adams, Pheasant-Tail Nymph
Green Drake (*Drunella grandis*)	#10-12 Quigley Cripple, Lawson's Green Drake Paradrake, Nealley's Green Drake
Salmonfly (*Pteronarcys californica*)	#4-8 Bitch Creek Nymph, Stimulator, Rogue Foam Stone, Pat's Rubber Legs
Golden Stonefly (*Hesperoperla pacifica*)	#6-12 Stimulator, Elk-Hair Caddis, Pat's Rubber Legs, Bitch Creek Nymph, MFC Extended Body Foam Stone

The Lower Flathead

The Flathead exits Flathead Lake at the Kerr Dam near Polson and enters the tribal land of the Flathead Nation. Anglers need to obtain a tribal fishing permit in addition to a state-issued fishing license before hitting this section of river. From this point the river rolls through a series of white-water chutes—rough water that fly anglers should approach with caution and possibly avoid altogether, depending on the flows.

NorthWestern Energy manages Kerr Dam for power production, not the potentially vibrant trout fishery it could support downstream. There are trout below Kerr, but not many of them. "There are big browns in there from Kerr down to almost Dixon. Every year the fishing is a little different, but on years when it's not raging hot, and the water doesn't get really warm, we go in there in the summer and catch some big fish on Chernobyl Ant–style patterns. There's not a ton of fish per mile, but most all of them are nice 18-inch, healthy fish. They don't see many fishermen, so they eat big dry flies," Lanier says. "You can float at about 10,000 or 9,000 cfs and avoid all the white water. Buffalo Rapids is really nasty, but it's not really difficult to skirt around it. You have to pull out and go through this little bucket on the side and then drag over the rocks a little," Lanier says.

Depending on the flows, the lower Flathead is often easier to wade than the main stem above the lake. However, access is an issue. Because the surrounding land is tribal, and much of the water flows through a steep canyon, there aren't any state-managed access points like there are on other rivers. Between Kerr Dam and Dixon, there are only a few places to launch, making the lower river a good place for diehards willing to spend long days floating.

Reach Kerr Dam from US 93 by taking Minesinger Trail Road west near Pablo Reservoir, and then Beck Road north. Kerr Dam Road intersects from the west. Follow Kerr Dam Road to the access area beneath the dam. To reach the Buffalo Bridge take-out, drive west on Valley View Road from the dam area. After several 90-degree turns, it intersects with Buffalo Bridge Road, which leads to the access.

The distance between the dam and Buffalo is not far, but floating all the way to Sloan Bridge, a small county bridge in the middle of a canyon and the next take-out, may be too long. To reach Sloan, turn west from US 93 on Round Butte Road in Ronan. Several miles later, turn south (left) on Sloan Road, and follow it to the bridge. The access is on the southwest side of the river.

Some river rats make the trip from the dam to Sloan Bridge or down to Dixon in two or three days and camp along the shoreline at night. Fishing and camping on the lower Flathead requires a tribal permit, the cost of which varies depending on whether you are a tribal member or have residency status. The Confederated Salish and Kootenai Tribes also heavily regulate both activities, especially along the lower Flathead River, so consult the tribal recreation regulations before firming up your plans. For more information on tribal fishing and camping regulations, the cost of a permit, or where to buy a permit, visit cskt.org or call (406) 675-2700.

As the Flathead heads south toward Dixon from Buffalo Bridge, it slows and turns warm, which is less-than-ideal habitat for salmonids and better suited for bass and pike. In fact, mention the Flathead River to locals and most will instantly think you're referring to the backwater sloughs and soft pockets of the lower river as opposed to the upper river's trout habitat.

In Dixon the Flathead meets the Jocko River—a nice, small stream with limited access but worth fishing if you can find a place to jump in the water. While the cold-water contribution from the Jocko is welcomed, it's mostly too little too late. The fishery from this point down is slow, clear, and warm, but the pike and bass love it. There are a few islands, side channels, and sloughs, but the size of the water makes them tough to reach unless you have a boat or canoe.

Pike are incredible on a fly rod. They are aggressive attackers that ambush flies. The downside to their presence in the Flathead is their voracious appetite. Since their introduction, their distribution into Flathead Lake and the upper river has corresponded with the decline of native cutthroat and bull trout.

Northern Pike are one of the most aggressive fish you can pursue with a fly rod, and the lower Flathead River is full of them. Look in pools, backwaters, and other nearly-stagnant portions of the river off the main stem, especially if there is cover like weeds or vegetation where these fish can camouflage themselves and ambush prey. CHRIS McCABE/RIVER OTTER FLY SHOP PHOTO

Combined with another exotic, the lake trout in Flathead Lake, the two predators consume millions of pounds of wild trout each year.

For the most part, pike prefer to stay out of the main current and hunker down in the backwaters and sloughs of the lower river. Sometimes you can see fish in the shallow water in the early season when they try to find warmer waters and jump-start their systems in preparation for spawning. Jig big streamers in front of their faces—try large rabbit-strip ties, Lefty's Deceivers, Barr's Meat Whistles, and Clouser Minnows.

MT 200 bumps into the lower river near Dixon and follows the southern bank until it merges with the Clark Fork River close to Paradise. There are a few pull-offs along MT 200, but private-property fences make foot access nearly impossible. There is a boat ramp in Dixon (take 2nd Street north across the railroad tracks to the river), but the next take-out (Camas Creek Bridge on MT 382) near Perma is over 15 miles downstream. Plan on either a long day or an overnight trip. This is one of my favorite areas on the lower Flathead. There are dozens of small islands, sloughs, and structures that are perfect for anglers who like to fish structure.

Bass, another exotic introduced to the lower river, have gained some fanfare over the years, though there are more smallmouth in the system than largemouth. In fact, one of the two fish that hold the state's smallmouth record (it's a tie) is from the lower Flathead River. The other is from Fort Peck Reservoir. The bass bite typically begins in late spring as water temperatures increase and the bass start getting in the mood to spawn. Most of the action will be between Dixon and Paradise since the water conditions upstream from here favor pike and trout.

The closer the water gets to 60 degrees, the more the bass will move up into the shallows. Before and after the spawn, the fish are most aggressive and easiest to target with fly rods. Look for dropoffs between shallow ledges and pools 4- to 6-feet deep. You won't catch many lunkers, but plenty of fish up to 3 pounds will take Clouser Minnows, large streamers tied with bunny strips, and Deceiver-type patterns. There are plenty of large food items like crayfish and minnows, so if something isn't working, experiment with another pattern or color.

You can fish the last portion of the Flathead by floating from Camas Creek Bridge to Paradise. This stretch is a little wider and slower than the water upstream with fewer channels and islands, but there are still plenty of bass and pike. After connecting with the Clark Fork, look for the access on the northeast side of the MT 200 bridge.

Barr's Meat Whistle

Hook:	#1/0-3/0 Gamakatsu 90-Degree Jig
Thread:	Black 140-denier Ultra Thread
Head:	Large brass or tungsten cone
Body:	Blue Sparkle Braid
Tail/Wing:	Black rabbit strip
Collar:	Black Sili Legs, Flashabou, and marabou

Parachute Frankenhopper

Hook:	#6-10 Tiemco 5263
Thread:	Orange 3/0 monocord
Eyes:	Black permanent marker
Dubbing:	Fiery amber Scintilla
Legs:	Smoke/Green/Crystal Fish Scale rubber legs
Body:	Gold foam colored with black permanent marker
Underwing:	Pearl and red Krystal Flash
Wing:	Ginger hen saddle lightly lacquered and trimmed to shape
Post:	Fluorescent orange Antron
Hackle:	Grizzly

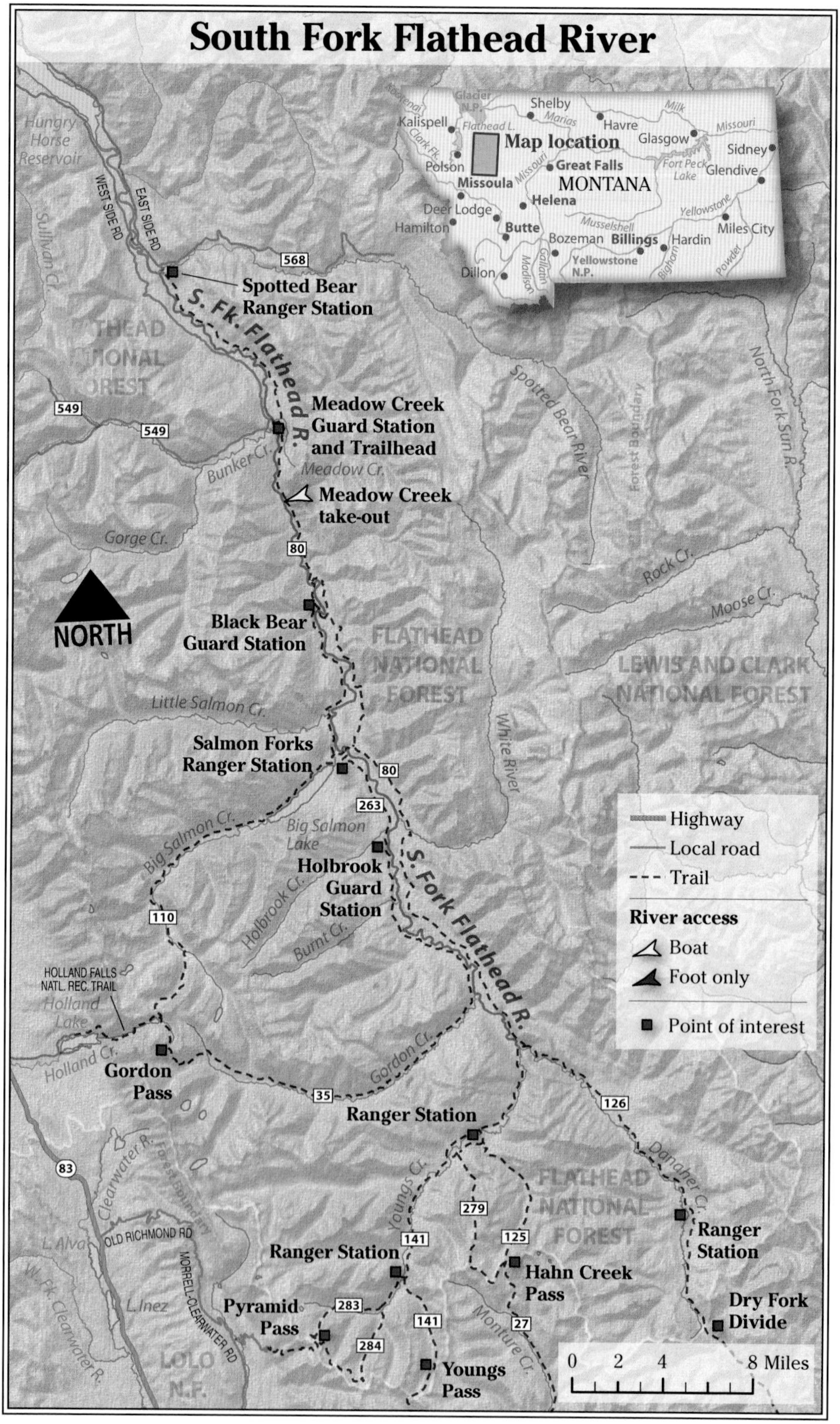
South Fork Flathead River
Map location
MONTANA
Glacier N.P.
Shelby
Kalispell
Flathead L.
Havre
Glasgow
Missouri
Sidney
Polson
Great Falls
Fort Peck Lake
Glendive
Missoula
Helena
Deer Lodge
Hamilton
Butte
Miles City
Bozeman
Billings
Hardin
Yellowstone N.P.
Dillon
Hungry Horse Reservoir
WEST SIDE RD
EAST SIDE RD
568
Spotted Bear Ranger Station
S. Fk. Flathead R.
Meadow Creek Guard Station and Trailhead
549
Bunker Cr.
Meadow Cr.
Meadow Creek take-out
Gorge Cr.
80
Black Bear Guard Station
NORTH
Spotted Bear River
North Fork Sun R.
Rock Cr.
Moose Cr.
FLATHEAD NATIONAL FOREST
LEWIS AND CLARK NATIONAL FOREST
Little Salmon Cr.
Salmon Forks Ranger Station
White River
263
Big Salmon Cr.
Big Salmon Lake
Holbrook Guard Station
Holbrook Cr.
Burnt Cr.
S. Fork Flathead R.
110
Highway
Local road
Trail
River access
Boat
Foot only
Point of interest
HOLLAND FALLS NATL. REC. TRAIL
Holland Lake
Holland Cr.
Gordon Pass
Gordon Cr.
35
Ranger Station
126
Danaher Cr.
83
Clearwater R.
Youngs Cr.
279
Ranger Station
OLD RICHMOND RD
141
125
L. Alva
Ranger Station
Hahn Creek Pass
MORRELL-CLEARWATER RD
Pyramid Pass
283
Dry Fork Divide
L. Inez
141
27
Monture Cr.
W. Fk. Clearwater R.
284
LOLO N.F.
Youngs Pass
0 2 4 8 Miles

CHAPTER 16

South Fork of the Flathead

If there is a better fly-fishing adventure in Montana than the South Fork of the Flathead, I don't know about it. A foray there means returning to the basics of fly fishing and soaking in the most important, though sometimes overlooked, facet of the sport—the experience. A federally designated Wild and Scenic River, the South Fork is buried deep in the Bob Marshall Wilderness and is the most untrammeled river in the state. Reachable only by foot or horse, the river is loaded with hungry, aggressive, and native westslope cutthroat in a wilderness setting that most people only see in photographs. It's also one of the few places in the state where anglers have a short season to legally pursue bull trout, of which there are plenty.

"With the possible exception of the Middle Fork of the Salmon River in Idaho, there is not a better wilderness experience in the Lower 48 than the South Fork of the Flathead," Westslope Troutfitters co-owner Justin Lawrence says. "I've guided in Alaska, and I'm still in awe at the fishing and scenery on the South Fork."

The river begins along the peaks that make up the Bob Marshall's southern borders. Youngs Creek, the western fork of the river, begins on the southwestern fringe near Pyramid Pass. Danaher Creek, the eastern fork, starts in a drainage only a few peaks to the east—not far from the North Fork of the Blackfoot. Both tributaries are fun cutthroat fisheries in their own right and a prelude to the fishing on the South Fork if you're camping on their banks.

The main stem of the South Fork begins at the merger of the two creeks and flows over 60 miles where it empties into Hungry Horse Reservoir with all but the last few twists and turns outside the wilderness boundary. The first mile or two of the South Fork has good wade fishing, but in a normal year it's too full of logjams and other debris to make floating an option. Most groups that pack-in boats journey downstream along the main stem before settling on a launch site. This doesn't mean there aren't any other obstacles as you head downriver, so pay attention around every bend for possible hazards.

For those hiking in, or wade-fishing from a raft, there are trails along the banks, and once you're in the water, you can move freely up- or downstream and find plenty of fishable water. TR 80 (north shore) and TR 263 (south shore) neighbor the heart of the main stem and intersect with numerous other

The South Fork is one of the few places in Montana where you can legally pursue bull trout. The season is short, and you must obtain a catch card from the MDFWP, but catching one of these brutes is something you won't soon forget. FLY FISHERMAN *MAGAZINE* PHOTO

trails and creeks that offshoot into valleys, meadows, and alpine lakes. The area has become a popular destination in the last decade, so don't be surprised to see other campers, hikers, or pack strings while on your trip.

"The crowds come and go. It's never as bad as on other rivers, but if you pick a high-traffic week and you go in the same time as other groups, then it feels a little crowded. But on most days, you won't hardly see anybody," outfitter Steve Hawkins says. "As popular as it's become, I still don't feel it's as crowded as it was in the late 1970s and early 80s when the backpacking fad hit. We still see some backpackers but only a fraction of what we used to see. Horse use has been about the same. Some years there's more traffic; other years, less."

Downriver the South Fork continues to gain volume from larger tributaries like Burnt Creek, Holbrook Creek, and the White River. The Salmon Forks Ranger Station is downstream of the White River near the outflow from Big Salmon Lake. This area is a good spot to camp, fish for bull trout, and hike uphill to the lake itself. It's just under a mile from the river along TR 110, which then follows the lake along the northern shoreline. It connects with Holland Lake (just outside the wilderness boundary), so it's a well-traveled route. Little Salmon Creek is Big Salmon's neighbor to the north and dumps a considerable amount of water into the South Fork. So if you miss Big Salmon, look on the western shore downstream for Little Salmon.

Little and Big Salmon creeks are somewhat of a halfway point to the Meadow Creek take-out and a good place to gauge your progress. From here the river and valley open up a little bit, and there are more braids and side channels perfectly suited for wade fishing or a riverside lunch break. You may not see the Black Bear Guard Station from the water, but a pack bridge spanning both shorelines (just past the inflow of Hungry Creek) is a good landmark and makes it easy to pinpoint your location on a topographical map.

Knowing your location from this point on is crucial unless you're with someone familiar with the river. The corridor gradually constricts as you head downriver, picking up in pace and creating a few small white-water chutes.

The upper South Fork is much more intimate than the lower river, and many of the fishable areas are better tackled on foot. In some areas, you can see the trout suspended in the current, waiting for a meal to pass by, so approach with stealth and wear polarized sunglasses to help spot fish. FLY FISHERMAN *MAGAZINE PHOTO*

Getting in and out of the Bob Marshall Wilderness is what prevents many anglers from enjoying the South Fork of the Flathead; however, a reputable outfitter can help you with travel arrangements for a fee. FLY FISHERMAN *MAGAZINE PHOTO*

Some places are barely wide enough for a raft and oars, so use caution and keep a sharp eye looking ahead.

Look for signs signaling the Meadow Creek take-out. It's a sloping rock face (much like a boat ramp) on the eastern side of the river with a small lagoon at the base. This is one pit stop you can't miss. The water in the gorge downstream is beyond dangerous—even for white-water enthusiasts. Be mindful of others taking out, and slip your boat into the holding water until your turn. Once out of the water, move off to the side while disassembling your gear and deflating the boat.

From this point, it's a short hike out along the upper rim of the river canyon to the Meadow Creek Station, but too far to carry gear and deflated rafts—hence the importance of making arrangements with an outfitter beforehand to pack you out. There are a few corrals and a large parking lot, but it's a popular place for hikers since so many trails into the Bob Marshall begin at this point, so expect a full lot.

After the Meadow Creek Gorge, the South Fork is again accessible to anglers for a little more than 15 miles before entering Hungry Horse Reservoir. Given that this is the only portion of river reachable via automobile, it receives significantly more pressure than the remote reaches upstream. Still, the area around the Cedar Creek and Spotted Bear access is worth a shot if you have some downtime before or after making your way into the wilderness.

"The lower river isn't as remote or tough to access. It gets a little more pressure, but not much. The fish are still very aggressive. They are a little smaller, and a little smarter, but the populations are healthy and the water is beautiful," Westslope Troutfitters co-owner Brendan Friel says. "They still allow you to keep fish in that lower stretch, and that's something we hope changes."

I will say this, it's easy to get tunnel vision and focus on the South Fork's fishing and nothing else—the cutts, bulls, and river have that kind of magnetism. But don't shortchange an adventure in this area. It's one of the largest wilderness landscapes in the Lower 48 and packed with scenery, wildlife, and treasures you will regret missing if you don't take your eyes off the water now and again.

Cutthroat trout are the name of the game on the South Fork of the Flathead. Foam attractors and hopper-style patterns tend to catch the larger fish, while beetle, ant, and small caddis patterns attract smaller fish. FLY FISHERMAN *MAGAZINE PHOTO*

BEARS IN THE BOB

The Bob Marshall Wilderness is one of the few places in the continental United States containing a population of grizzly bears, so bear encounters in forested areas can, and do, occur. For the most part, bears try to avoid humans, but every turn on a trail presents a legitimate chance of bumping into one.

The best way to avoid confrontations is to be smart. Keep your eyes and ears alert at all times when you're on trails or relaxing in camp, and if you see a bear don't approach it. Give it space and try to leave the area undetected if possible. Always carry bear spray, but don't use it as a shield or put yourself into a situation where you have to use it. Here are some other tips to keep in mind while in bear country:

- Store your food in trees at night and minimize any odors that would signal a meal to a hungry bruin with his nose in the wind.
- Stay away from dead animal carcasses—bears sometimes feed on them for days and remain close by.
- Make noise on the trail when approaching blind corners.
- Try to avoid traveling alone.
- Use caution when walking away from camp at night.
- Keep dogs under control—bears sometimes see barking canines as a threat. ■

Packing In

Do-it-yourself, backcountry-loving anglers with a flare for multiday pack trips love the South Fork of the Flathead because it combines the best of both worlds. But it doesn't come easy, and depending on the route and point of entry, hiking can take two days or more to reach your destination. With the exception of the Meadow Creek trailhead where the South Fork main stem neighbors the trails heading south, all other routes have more than a fair share of ascensions, descents, switchbacks, and fords through tributaries. Needless to say, being in prime physical shape is a requisite. Of course, there is always the four-legged option. Most trips into the Bob and the upper reaches of the South Fork take either one terribly long day or two shorter days on horseback, depending on where you're starting and where you're going.

Whether you're doing it yourself or traveling with an outfitter, the trailhead near the North Fork of the Blackfoot is a popular starting point. Follow Trail (TR) 31 to TR 32 along the river to Dry Fork Divide. From there you can drop down into the Danaher drainage and follow the creek (TR 126) to the junction with Youngs Creek. It's a considerable distance to walk, but there are some great camping areas, you'll be close to fresh water (process through a portable water-filtration system before consuming), and the grade is not as steep as some other routes.

Pyramid Pass, another access point, will take you to the Youngs Creek drainage. The initial climb from the trailhead to the wilderness boundary is steep, but at the top of the pass you'll collide with Pyramid Lake, which is a good spot to filter water, catch your breath, and spot a few cruising trout. Drive on Forest Road (FR) 477 from Seeley Lake, and then FR 467 and FR 4381 to the trailhead. Trails 283, 141, and 125 go along Youngs Creek to the Danaher junction.

Also near Seeley Lake, the Holland Gordon Trail will take you to the edge of the wilderness. From there you can enter the Bob and follow the Gordon Creek Drainage (TR 35) or Big Salmon Creek past Big Salmon Lake (TR 457 and 110)—both deposit you close to the middle of the South Fork's main stem. These are heavily traveled routes, so expect company. Turn on Holland Lake Road from MT 83 just north of Seeley Lake and follow the signs to the trailhead. It's a few miles from the trailhead to the wilderness border, but the ascent isn't terribly tough.

The trailhead near Monture Creek is a third option. Turn north on FR 89 from MT 200 and drive 8 miles to the trailhead. From this point, the trail winds through Hahn Creek Pass, past the Hole-in-the-Wall Cave, and into the South Fork Valley. Expect horse traffic and other users, especially heading into the September hunting season.

Wherever you elect to camp, take the necessary precautions to dispose of food and pack-out any garbage. The Bob Marshall Wilderness is a remarkable area, and one way to ensure future generations can enjoy it is to leave the areas as pristine as you find them.
FLY FISHERMAN *MAGAZINE PHOTO*

Floating the South Fork of the Flathead is a once-in-a-lifetime experience for most anglers. I'd go every season if I could, but the logistics, planning, and expenses that go into organizing and executing a float trip are immense. Horses and mules are by far the easiest way to get in and out of the Bob Marshall Wilderness with floating equipment. But unless you know someone with a team of animals you're likely going to need an outfitter to transport your gear to the river and then arrange a day to be picked up at the Meadow Creek take-out. If you already own rafts and gear, then the outfitter's cost is typically a few hundred dollars per animal. The more people and gear that needs to be transported, the more animals it takes to complete the task. Talk to an outfitter for a better estimate as you plan.

"For the guys that want to do it themselves, there's always the option of a drop camp. You don't get to float the river, but outfitters can drop a party off with camp gear, then come back in a few days and ride out," Hawkins says. "If you're going to float it, you'll probably have to hire two outfitters—one to drop you off and one to pick you up. It would be too costly for someone to drop you off, pack-out, then drive around, pack-in again and haul you out. You're better off finding someone local near where you want to go in and take out. That's the expensive part. But once you're on the water, it's worth it."

Limit each person to one pack for clothes and personal items, and leave heavy or extraneous items like plastic boat seats and huge camp kitchens at home. Pack as though you have to carry it—it reduces the loads that need to be transported over the mountains and in your boats once on the water. Also discuss with your group whether a boat devoted to just carrying gear is needed. A gear boat leaves more room in the fishing boats for the task at hand but means an additional load for horses and mules, which increases your cost.

If you are doing it yourself, don't forget to bring the essentials. Things like a GPS, USGS topographical maps, compass, first-aid kits, a water-filtration system, raincoats, and fire-starting devices are just a few. You never know what Mother Nature is going to throw at you. Create a checklist of all the things you need and, to avoid forgetting something critical, add, subtract, or substitute items—depending on their importance—as you mull and plan in the months prior to packing. What's more, learn how to use everything before you go. Don't wait until you're at the trailhead to crack open your GPS instruction manual or figure your route on a topographical map.

Also, camp relatively close to the Meadow Creek take-out area the night before your final day. Trying to finish the last few miles of the float, disassemble and pack the gear at the take-out, hike to the trailhead, and drive the 60-plus miles on the dirt road around Hungry Horse Reservoir and back to civilization soaks up most of the day. Reaching the take-out before the lunch hour ensures you get the job done and move out with time to spare.

Option number two is to hire an outfitter that furnishes everything from animals to tents, rafts, food, and other camp luxuries. "Most pack trips are limited on space, so we tell people they have to limit what they bring to about 50 pounds. This includes a few changes of clothes—both for around camp and for fishing—some rain gear, and anything else. It should all fit in a small

If you plan on floating the South Fork, allocate one boat, or large portions of the other boats, for gear. Tents, food, and other necessities add weight and take up space, but proper planning can help you travel prepared for most situations. FLY FISHERMAN *MAGAZINE PHOTO*

duffel bag," Hawkins says. "We provide everything else like sleeping gear, tents, and even some fishing gear."

Of course, these types of trips are considerably more expensive, but you're also paying for the outfitter's knowledge along the way. Most reputable outfitters know the Bob Marshall like the back of their hand: what essentials to bring and other intricate details you might not consider. If you don't have the time or the inclination to properly coordinate a trip to the South Fork, consider this option. The Montana Board of Outfitters maintains a list of licensed, legal outfitting operations and is a good starting point if you're unfamiliar with any operations. They're also a terrific resource for background checks to make sure the outfit you're hiring is reputable.

Depending on the snowfall amounts, the South Fork could be fishable as early as mid to late June. When I talked to McCoy about his 2008 season, he said snow pounded their camp on June 14. If you want to play it safe, don't plan a trip until the first week of July or later. At this time, you can expect the water to be somewhat high and fast, but clear and fishable. Floating may be difficult in the upper river as the season progresses and the levels continue to drop. By mid-August, the upper river may be suited best for wade angling and not floating. If this is the case, consider putting in a few miles downstream to avoid dragging or making portages over the shallows.

Hatches and Flies

South Fork hatches are not as prolific as on some of the state's other rivers, but the fish are so keyed up on feeding, even the slightest activity has fish strapping on their dinner bibs. Golden Stones appear as the high waters of runoff are receding around late June and early July and stick around for a few weeks after—more than enough time for the cutts to become addicted. Foam patterns withstand more abuse and continue to float longer than patterns tied with all-natural materials. Rogue Foam Stones, a golden Thing From Uranus, and Montana Fly Company's Extended Body Foam Golden are a few of my favorites. Pale Morning Duns also appear on the river in the height of the season, though you can use parachute mayfly imitations just about any time with success.

Hoppers and beetles are two other patterns I like to fish. On one particular day a friend of mine landed what may have been the largest cutthroat of the trip on a simple beetle tied with a peacock-herl body, deer-hair legs, and a strip of black closed-cell foam for a shellback. The fish was feeding on the surface, possibly on caddis or mayflies, but didn't hesitate to rush the beetle when he saw it; further proof South Fork fish are eager, opportunistic feeders. Place a fly next to structure or under overhanging brush and grass to mimic a bug stumbling into the water and you'll see what I'm talking about. General nymphs like Beadhead Pheasant-Tail Nymphs, Prince Nymphs, Hare's-Ear Nymphs, Copper Johns, and San Juan Worms work great. Tie one on as a dropper if you're so inclined, but the dry-fly fishing is so good, I'd rather fish two dry flies.

What it boils down to is if it looks like food, the fish will eat it. It's true for stoneflies, mayflies, and especially caddis. In fact, if you're looking for one of the best all-around fly patterns on the South Fork, a plain Elk-Hair Caddis may just be it. I've seen fish ascend the water column and rise for this fly when it was sloppily floating right next to the oar blades of our raft. "A black ant and an Elk-Hair Caddis is something I'll use until the day I die," Hawkins says.

If you're fishing for bull trout (catch-and-release season is open from the third Saturday in May through August 15), think big, heavy, and furry. These fish are more interested in the cutthroat dancing on the end of your line than a foam stonefly twitching in the current. Use streamers like Double Bunnies, large Marabou Muddler Minnows, Woolhead Sculpins, or anything else that looks enticing to a 26- to 36-inch fish that eats meals half its size.

Whatever streamer you select, make sure you're getting it in front of the fish. A short, stout leader and sinking-tip line are good starting points. Try to cast and retrieve the fly so it swims perpendicular or slightly upstream in the

Cutthroat are king on the South Fork of the Flathead, and because their feeding season is so short, they're not ultraselective when feeding. Use foam patterns if possible—they float longer than flies tied with natural materials, which often sink after you catch a few fish on them. FLY FISHERMAN *MAGAZINE PHOTO*

current. This is easier in the deep, slow pools where most bull trout hang out, though I have caught one or two in shallower water.

Undercut banks, sharp dropoffs after riffles, and the junctions of tributaries are all likely bull-trout holding areas. The water of the South Fork is so clear you should have no trouble spotting fish in some places—look for white-tipped fins hovering above the bottom of the stream. In some cases, you can float over a pool and spot bulls from above, shore the boat at the tailout, walk upstream with a streamer rig, and fool the same fish into striking. They're aggressive, territorial, and a great break from netting cutthroat all day.

When it comes to South Fork fish, leave grandiose expectations at home—chances are slim you're going to find your next 22-inch-plus trophy in these waters (with the exception of bull trout). Most of the cutthroat range between 10 and 18 inches. A few make it to the 20-inch mark, but even fewer surpass it. But, I'd gladly trade several 14-inch feisty South Fork fish for one or two 20-inchers in any other river.

The feeding season for South Fork cutthroat is short, so they don't waste any time charging even poorly presented dry flies. One trick for steering your catch ratio from the small fish to the larger specimens is to size-up your fly-pattern selection. If you tie on caddis, ants, or anything else that's easy for small fish to wrap their jaws around, expect a majority of your time to be spent unhooking trout under 12 inches long. If you use Golden Stonefly patterns, Stimulators, Hoppers, or other patterns sized in the single digits, you'll keep the small fish at bay and see more of the river's larger residents. Five-weight rods and floating lines are just fine if you're chasing cutthroat, but if you have bull trout in your sights, a 6- or 7-weight rod with a sinking-tip line is a better bet.

Deep pools, especially those near tributary mouths, are great places to search for bull trout. Use a sinking-tip line and weighted fly with an across-stream presentation to trigger a strike. FLY FISHERMAN *MAGAZINE PHOTO*

South Fork Bull Trout

Designated as "threatened" throughout the Northwest under the Endangered Species Act, this char is off limits in other strongholds like the Blackfoot River. In the South Fork of the Flathead, however, between the third Saturday in May and July 31, you can tie on 2 feet of 12-pound tippet, a yellow/natural or white/natural Double Bunny, get it as low as it will go, and hold on. Most bulls strike with full force and drag out the ensuing battle until your forearm goes numb. You must release all bull trout that you catch.

If you plan on fishing for bull trout in the South Fork of the Flathead, you must obtain a free bull trout catch card from Montana Department of Fish, Wildlife, and Parks. Applications are available at the Region One office in Kalispell or online (fwp.mt.gov). They are not available at license outlets.

After the close of the season, you must return the completed catch card to the address below—even if you didn't catch one. MDFWP uses the information to gauge management objectives, and if you do not submit it at the end of the season, you will not be eligible to obtain a card the following season.

Whether you catch a bull in or out of season, it is legal to photograph the fish. Try to have your equipment ready to take the shot, don't squeeze the fish, and keep it in the water as much as possible to help it recover. Release the fish quickly after snapping the photograph.

Return completed catch cards to:
Montana Fish, Wildlife and Parks
490 N. Meridian Road
Kalispell, Montana 59901

MFC Double Bunny

Hook:	#2-6 MFC 7030
Thread:	Tan Nymo thread
Weight:	1 mm lead wire
Eyes:	Lead dumbbell eyes
Wing:	Natural brown rabbit strip over white rabbit strip
Fins:	Mottled brown rooster saddle
Collar:	Fibers from red saddle hackle feather

Schlotter's Foam Flying Ant

Hook:	#14-18 Tiemco 101
Thread:	Camel 8/0 Uni-Thread
Body:	1/8" black closed-cell foam
Wing:	Plastic wing material
Outriggers:	White poly yarn
Hackle:	Brown rooster saddle

Romans' Thing From Uranus

Hook:	#6-12 MFC 7030
Thread:	Tan 6/0 Uni-Thread
Body:	Tan foam
Legs:	Speckled tan Centipede Legs (#2)
Dubbing:	Golden Stone Wabbit Dubbing
Wings:	Natural cow elk
Head:	Tan foam

Middle Fork Flathead River

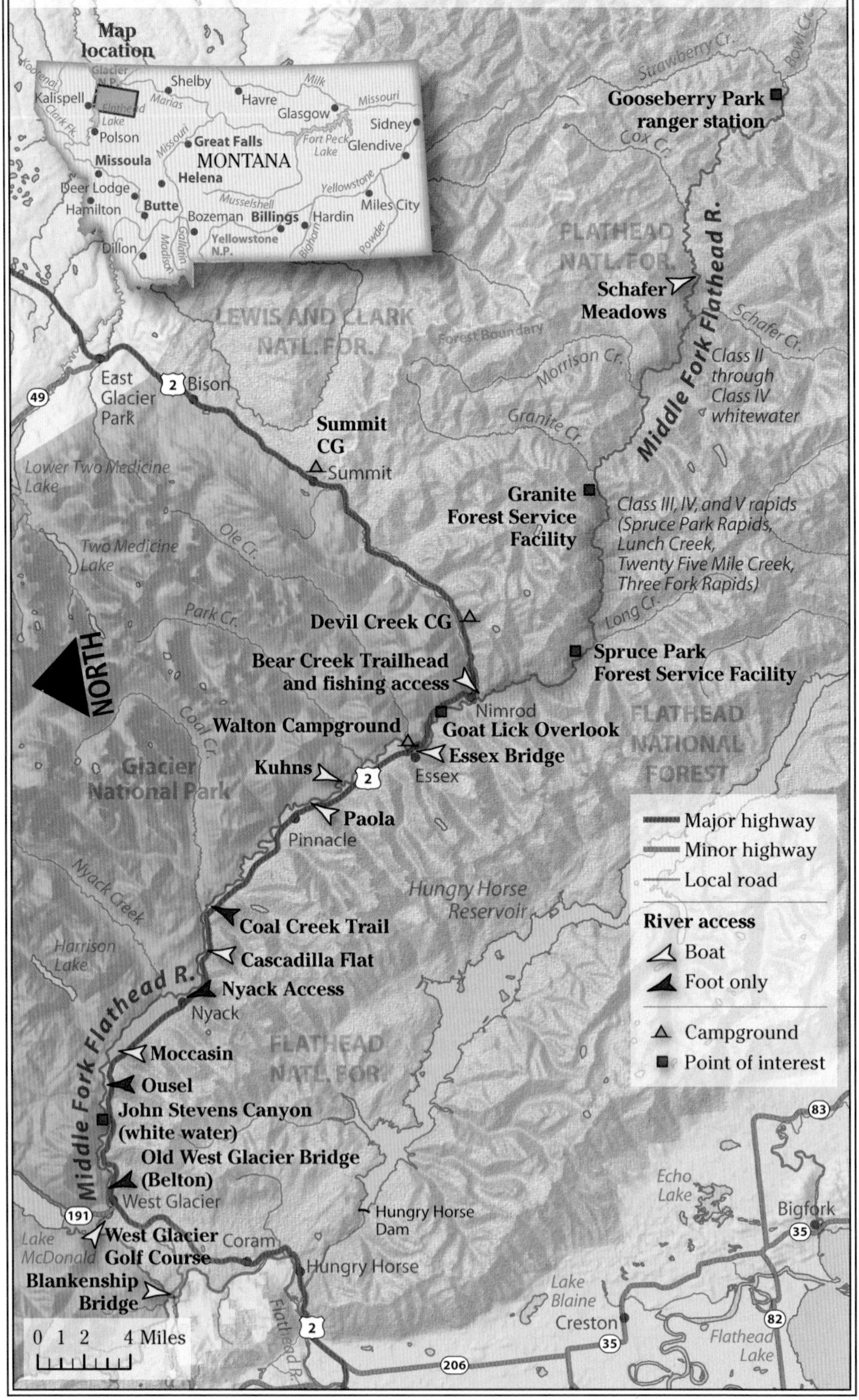

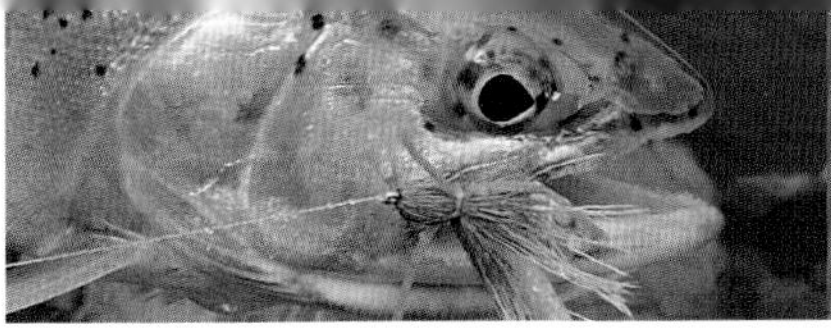

CHAPTER 17

Middle Fork of the Flathead

The Middle Fork of the Flathead doesn't garner as much attention from the fly-fishing community as other rivers in Montana. Known more for its scenery and wilderness white-water runs than its fishing, it's overlooked and overshadowed by other tourist attractions in the northwest corner of the state and Glacier National Park. "We get a lot of incidental business from people coming to Glacier in July and August that want to fly-fish one day, drive through the park on another, and then squeeze in a round or two of golf," Westslope Troutfitters co-owner Brendan Friel says. "The Middle Fork is suited for that because it gives them a taste of the scenery, the cutthroat are eager to hit a fly even if a beginner is struggling with casting or something, and it's fun for a family."

The average size of Middle Fork fish is smaller than in other Montana rivers, but I've found them to be somewhat larger than an average fish on the North Fork of the Flathead. Like the North Fork, the food supply in this system is fickle, and when you combine that with a short feeding season and extremely cold water temperatures in the off-season, it's hard for fish to pack on the pounds. Most specimens you encounter are cutthroat, but there is a growing rainbow population (and a correlating increase in the number of cuttbows). Bull trout are also present, but once again, they are a no-no.

One unique feature of the Middle Fork is its clarity. It is wholly made up of high-elevation snowmelt and at some angles glimmers with the hue of a fine and rare jewel. The Middle Fork is a beautiful river where you have to trade any elevated fly-fishing aspirations and expectations for a day when the aesthetics and experience outweigh your catch.

When and Where

The Middle Fork of the Flathead begins at the confluence of Bowl and Strawberry creeks in the Great Bear Wilderness, not far from the South Fork of the Flathead drainage. It flows in a northwesterly direction for approximately 40 miles and is a designated Wild and Scenic River until reaching the Bear Creek trailhead—the uppermost point where you can access the river via automobile.

Though most fish in the river rarely stretch past 16 inches, it is possible to find larger fish. Seek less pressured areas that are away from public access points by walking farther from the access point, or use a boat to shuttle you to different pools and riffles as you work downstream. JAY NICHOLS PHOTO

There are two options for reaching the headwaters. Hikers and horseback riders can move upstream from the Bear Creek Trailhead (TR 155). There is a large parking lot where the Middle Fork, Bear Creek, and US 2 meet. Follow the trails upstream along the river and you will eventually intersect with areas like Spruce Park and Schaefer Meadows. This route takes some planning, but it offers a backcountry experience for anglers willing to mix some backpacking with their fishing.

If hiking isn't your game, you can fly into Schafer Meadows, a popular access point for kayakers and rafters fond of the upper river as runoff subsides in late June through early July. Some outfitters pack in sportsmen on horseback, but a backcountry airstrip makes it easy for bush pilots and rafting companies to shuttle equipment and clients in less time. If you decide to float this reach, stay in touch with any of the fly shops or rafting companies around Kalispell and West Glacier regarding flow levels and conditions. Then, when you're on the water, watch for logjams or other obstructions as runoff levels drop and expose hazards. A steep canyonlike corridor envelops much of the upper river and contains Class III and IV rapids. A few charter aircraft companies in Kalispell can drop you and your party off at Schafer Meadows for around $350 (per two people with gear).

The second half of the river between Bear Creek to Blankenship Bridge makes up the southern border of Glacier National Park and follows US 2 where access is more abundant than on the North Fork. There are fewer private property buffers between the road and the water, more pull-offs, and a string of managed access sites. In a few areas, the river isn't visible from the road because of the steep shoulder, so some points are easier to climb down than others.

The river downstream of Bear Creek is also popular with floaters, but as the water levels decline through the season, the white-water rafting and

The glacier-fed waters of the Middle Fork are extremely clear, so the river's cutthroat have no problem spotting dry flies, even in fast water. That said, bring patterns tied with foam or other floating, lightweight materials because they stay on the surface longer than those tied with dubbing or yarn. JAY NICHOLS PHOTO kayaking crowds thin somewhat and the river morphs into a place better suited for wading anglers, fishing rafts, and personal pontoon boats. By mid-July, the Middle Fork is clear and easier for fishermen to navigate. Keep in mind also that fishing is closed within a 100-yard radius of this tributary's mouth. Watch flow levels before you decide to rig up and make the trip. In years with low snow levels, some portions of the river are too low to float the last third of the season. For overnighters, Devil Creek Campground is just a short jaunt along Bear Creek and a solid option if you're fishing in the neighborhood.

Between Bear Creek and the Goat Lick access (a popular tourist pit stop where exposed natural salt minerals attract wildlife such as mountain goats), the river is sandwiched between steep hillsides and all but invisible from the road. A few fast-water chutes and riffles in this short stretch house fish, but because it's so difficult to reach, I recommend moving farther downstream if you're a wading angler. If you're floating, you can put in at Bear Creek and take out at Essex Bridge. Just make sure to get out and work some of the good-looking water on foot. Watch for Goat Lick Rapids. An experienced oarsman should not have trouble passing through.

About five miles downstream from Goat Lick is Essex Bridge, a popular put-in area for both anglers and rafters (it's sometimes called Walton Bridge because it neighbors Walton Ranger Station). There is a modest parking area reachable from the northwest side of the bridge (US 2), a public restroom, and

White-water rafters and kayakers like the Middle Fork in the early season when flows are high, but as levels drop, boulders and riffles become better suited for fly anglers. Areas with plentiful structure and soft-water breaks generally hold the most cutthroat.
JAY NICHOLS PHOTO

some nice-looking water that is easy to reach on foot. But the convenience of this site is also its curse. Anglers hit the 100 yards up- and downstream from the bridge often, and it's entirely possible to not move a single fish.

It's a full-day float from Essex Bridge to Paola (approximately 10 miles), but it's probably one of the best stretches to fish. This water is incredibly scenic, not difficult to row, and there's good-looking water around every turn. I can't say enough good things about it. Just be sure to get out of the boat and hit some of the riffles and pools on foot. Some of the best fishing is at the head of the riffles and around tributary mouths—stuff that's sometimes out of reach if you don't anchor up the boat and shuffle your feet. Pace yourself—there are some miles to cover before the day is finished.

"I think it takes a bigger, stronger fish to hang out in some of the faster water from the mid to lower river," Friel says. "We find fish in really fast water where you wouldn't think they'd be. The Flathead system is one of the last strongholds for the westslope cutthroat, but there are a few nonnative rainbows vying for the same food source, which is not abundant. So when a fly is put in front of their nose in fast water like that, it's a race."

Paola is a large, rocky bar along the west side of the river. There is a parking lot along the road if you plan to walk to the water, but if you're loading or unloading a boat, a four-wheel-drive vehicle with clearance is a good choice since the rocks are somewhat loose along the water.

A short distance downstream is a foot access near Stanton Creek. It's part of the Coal Creek Trail, which after fording the river, continues into Glacier National Park. The trail is unmarked from the road and virtually overgrown with brush later in the summer, but there is a pull-off approximately five miles south from Nyack near the railroad tracks, and you can follow the trail northwest to the water.

Cascadilla Flat is 2 miles south from Nyack on the north side of the road. If you want a taste of white-water action on the Middle Fork, put in here and float to Moccasin Creek. Most of the water is relatively easy to navigate with the exception of a few Class II chutes, and you can avoid a majority of the white-water crowd that head downstream from Moccasin.

Moccasin Creek marks the beginning of the river's infamous white-water stretch. It's sometimes tough to reach because a flowing side channel separates it from the main river. Because of this, most floaters fear floating past the channel (or don't know about it) and use Moccasin as a put-in rather than a take-out. Anglers fishing this area are also noticing an increase in the number of rainbow and cuttbow hybrids latching on to the end of their lines. While some welcome their presence, MDFWP encourages harvests to preserve the river as a cutthroat stronghold.

Downstream is John Stevens Canyon and rough water (reaching Class III white-water levels). This area drops an average of 35 feet per mile over the course of 5 miles, so the water is speeding downstream. But as the levels drop, there is some fishing to be had. Because of the danger, it's better to first work this section with a guide before ever attempting to do it on your own. Those

Though the makeup of the Middle Fork makes it difficult to produce epic hatches, a smattering of stoneflies, mayflies, and caddis appears. However, don't be worried about matching the hatch. The cutthroat are opportunistic feeders and are just as likely to hit an attractor pattern as hard as anything else. JAY NICHOLS PHOTO

with experience know the safest chutes and can devote themselves to what's ahead while you pound the water.

"The white-water stretches combine some excitement and what I consider some of the best fishing on the Middle Fork," Friel says. "The downside is there might be 80 rafting trips going down past you in the summer. So I wait until the water is lower and the rafting companies slow things down. Aside from that, it doesn't get a lot of angling pressure because it's not great water for hard drift boats, and other guides don't always want to work that hard. I just tell my clients that they have to be prepared to tie their own flies on because I can't let go of the oars."

After the white water, it's a short trip to either West Glacier (near the entrance to the park) or Blankenship Bridge. After West Glacier, the river flow slows considerably, and it makes the last few meanders before meeting the North Fork of the Flathead near Blankenship Bridge. Most floaters take out well before this point, though, as the fishing action often tapers off the last few miles. Local kayakers take out and tourists hang out and jump into the river off the old steel bridge heading into the park. The best boat ramp is near the West Glacier Golf Course a mile or so downriver.

If you're interested in hitting the lower white-water portions of the river on foot later in the season when flows drop, there are several pull-offs along US 2 between West Glacier and Moccasin Creek. Some are near gated railroad access roads, but roads run down to the water so you can park and walk down the road to different points along the river. You can also park near the old West Glacier Bridge about a mile upstream from the West Glacier park entrance (follow Old Bridge Road east before entering the park). At one time, this bridge was the entrance to the park, but it is now a footbridge. Park on the south side, cross the bridge, and take a trail that follows the river upstream along the boundary of the park for a few miles.

Hatches and Flies

Moderately sized (#6-12) foam nasties such as Fat Alberts or Stimulator-style dry flies often work better than any realistic imitations because they float well and are easy to see. Target some of the river's heavier water in addition to the soft-edge seams, eddies, and dropoffs. Cutthroat hang out in the chip-chop and are ready to pounce on a fly. Allowing food items to pass is not something Flathead cutts are known for. "One of the problems I think people have on the Middle Fork is they use small flies like Parachute Adams in the fast water," Friel says. "In some of that faster water, the small flies sink, so you have to get the big foam stuff that stays up. A lot of this fishing isn't so much of what you're throwing, but where you're throwing it."

The deep pools scattered through the Middle Fork's length are also something to marvel. The clear water lets you see to the bottom, where on occasion you may see some larger fish hovering close to the bottom of the stream. If you decide to throw small streamers, I strongly advise using a sinking-tip line. A weighted fly alone may have a tough time getting in the fish's face at these depths, and having the extra driving power from a sinking tip should give you just the push you need to get down. Of course this technique will also make your flies susceptible to a strike from lurking bull trout, but

Start at the head of pools, just below the riffles. Middle Fork cutthroat often hang close to the faster, more oxygenated water in relatively shallow areas. From there, work downstream through the rest of the pool systematically so you cover all likely holding areas. JAY NICHOLS PHOTO

The Middle Fork of the Flathead makes up the southern border of Glacier National Park and offers some terrific views of the area's mountain peaks. Bring a camera to document your catch as well as some of Montana's best scenery. JAY NICHOLS PHOTO

as long as you don't fish for them intentionally, and immediately release any incidental catches, you shouldn't have anything to worry about.

Strong leaders in the 2X to 3X range keep fish from breaking off and don't twist when casting heavier foam attractors like they do on 4X. The fish are not leader shy, so don't put yourself at a disadvantage by going too light. The same goes for rods. I like a fast-action 4- or 5-weight when fishing dry flies and a stout 6-weight if I'm sinking streamers.

Don't be in a rush to get on the water at first light. The Middle Fork is suited for bankers' hours because of the cold water and the cool nights that keep it that way. Depending on weather patterns and the time of year, it may take a few hours for the river to warm and bring out the bugs and the trout that follow.

Directions

US 2 follows the Middle Fork from West Glacier until the river splits off into the Great Bear Wilderness—it's just one reason why you can expect to see more anglers and floaters on this water than on the North Fork. Paved roads and easy access make it a snap to get on and off the water, and that's always a factor when you're on vacation (as so many are in the Glacier National Park area). Some access points are marked better than others, so if you're unsure about an area, ask a local shop for info.

Because many of the tributaries draining into the Middle Fork are off limits to angling, if you're seeking smaller water, consider parking at the Bear Creek junction and hiking into the wilderness portion of the river. If you have the time and the money, you can also hire an outfitter or charter a plane to reach the upper river.

Rogue Foam Stone (Golden)

Hook:	#8-10 Tiemco 200R
Thread:	Yellow 3/0 Danville
Body:	Yellow foam colored with brown marker
Underwing:	Twelve strands of root-beer Krinkle Flash
Wing:	1 mm polystyrene foam colored with brown marker
Overwing:	Light natural cow elk
Collar:	Cow elk dyed golden
Legs:	Pumpkin/pepper flake Sili Legs
Head:	Cow elk dyed golden

Lawson's Green Drake Paradrake

Hook:	#10-12 Tiemco 100
Thread:	Yellow 3/0 Uni-Thread
Wing:	Dark gray elk hair
Body:	Olive elk hair
Tail:	Black moose mane
Hackle:	Yellow dyed grizzly

Taylor's Fat Albert

Hook:	#6-14 MFC 7027
Thread:	Dark brown 6/0 Uni-Thread
Underbody:	Yellow foam
Overbody:	Brown foam
Legs:	Speckled tan Centipede Legs (#2)
Underwing:	Pearl High Voltage
Wing:	White Gator Hair
Indicator:	Yellow foam

North Fork Flathead River

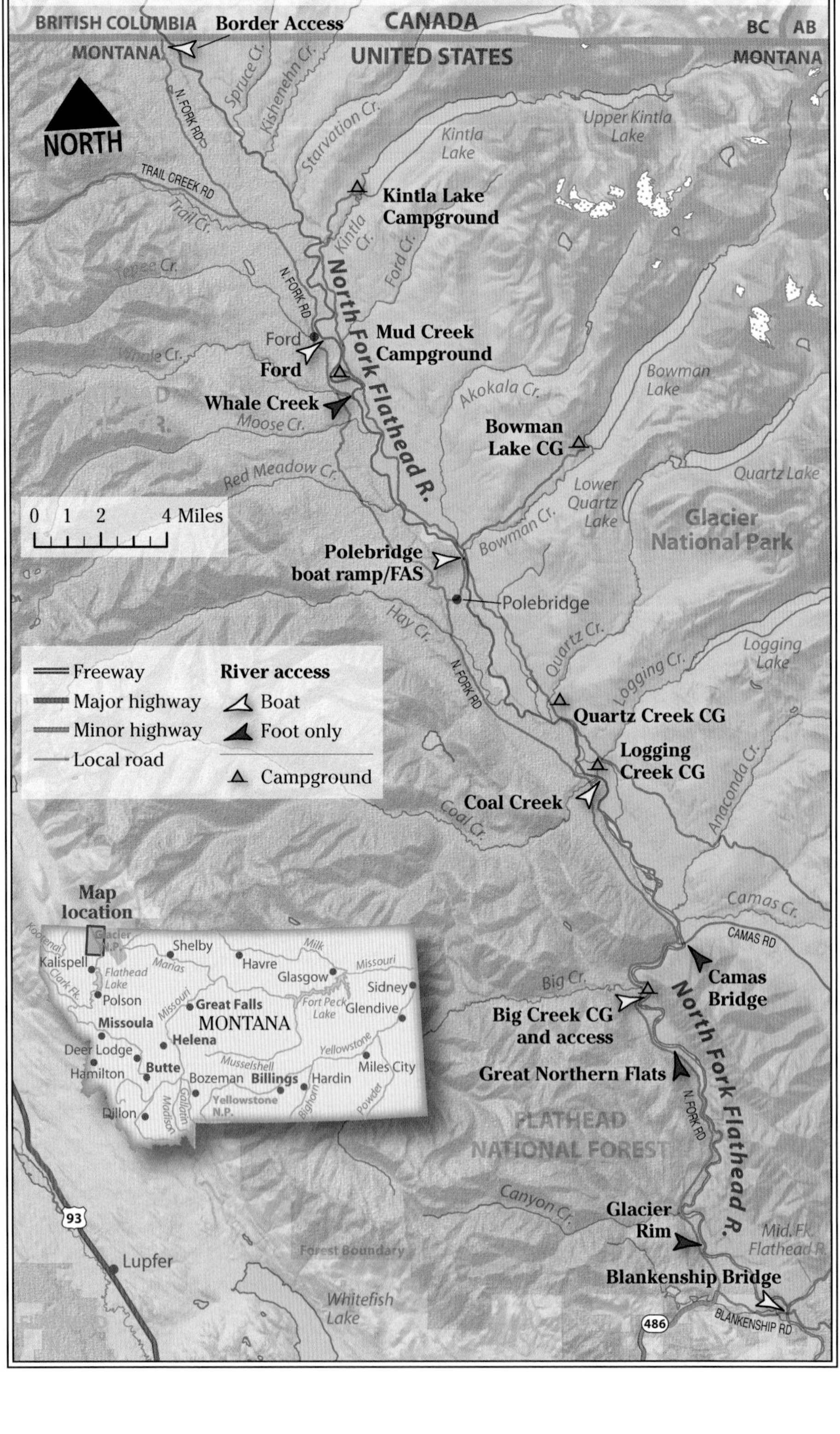

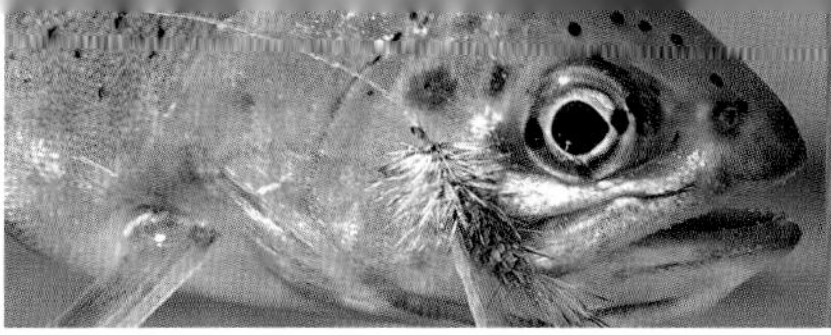

CHAPTER 18

North Fork of the Flathead

The North Fork of the Flathead's beginnings are rooted deep within Canada, but the second half of the river flows over U.S. soil and after crossing the border, makes up the western boundary of Glacier National Park. The scenery alone supplies an incredible angling backdrop and is worthy of a visit. "Any other state would be begging for a system like this, but in Montana we have so much great trout water that few people pay attention to it." Westslope Troutfitters co-owner Justin Lawrence says.

I've read other articles and books that say the North Fork is dead—sterile water with little bug activity and few trout. I disagree. The fishing is good on the North Fork of the Flathead. Wild cutthroat and a few rainbows, though far below trophy proportions, are plentiful, and while most of the fish average 8 to 12 inches, you may catch a few larger individuals in lightly fished areas or the lower half of the river (many fish make their way up from Flathead Lake). If you stress size and quantity over the overall experience, the North Fork of the Flathead may not be for you. If you enjoy the company of wildlife, relative solitude, unspoiled scenery, and crisp, clear water, then by all means, wade farther.

One reason for the stunted growth of North Fork trout is that the system lacks some of the natural elements required to nurture aquatic insect life. "Being glacial-fed water, it takes a long time for these fish to get big," Lawrence says. "It's not the nutrient-rich water you have in other rivers in Montana. These are massive freestone river systems, but the average fish is smaller than what you would find on proportionately sized water elsewhere."

Cutthroat spawn in the spring, and most of the fish make their way up from Flathead Lake at that time. After the spawning season, plenty of resident fish remain in the system throughout the summer. "The fish use the North Fork as a thoroughfare between the lake and their spawning grounds. Biologists have tagged fish that go way up into Canada and spawn and then end up back in Flathead Lake. Those that stay in the system average 12 inches

The North Fork of the Flathead makes up the western border of Glacier National Park, so wildlife like elk, deer, moose, and bear frequent the area. Proceed with caution when walking through dense areas along the river to avoid spooking dangerous wildlife. JAY NICHOLS PHOTO or so," Westslope Troutfitters co-owner Brendan Friel says. "There are certain areas that have big fish, but I think catching them is a timing [of the year] issue and [more] a matter of knowing where to fish than anything else. But you can fish blind anywhere on the North Fork and catch a lot of small fish."

The river is also home to bull trout, and like many of the state's other rivers, they are protected under the Endangered Species Act. You may catch one accidentally, or see one chasing a cutthroat on the end of your line, but it is illegal to intentionally fish for them. In fact, many of the tributaries of the North Fork of the Flathead (and their mouths) also have special closed seasons to protect spawning fish, so be sure to check the regulations book before you head out to make sure you're heading to open water.

Where and When

The North Fork of the Flathead forms from snow, springs, and other sources deep in the Rocky Mountains of British Columbia and flows just shy of 50 miles to the Montana border. After crossing into the state, it is a designated Wild and Scenic River until the Big Creek junction (just downstream of Camas Bridge). This is one of the few rivers in the United States to neighbor a well-traveled road and still receive such a high accolade.

The water is void of man-made dams, which makes it easier to float and wade, but it also makes it vulnerable to the nuances of Mother Nature. It encompasses an immense drainage, and spring runoff makes the river look

North Fork of the Flathead cutthroat aren't large or difficult to catch on the surface with small attractors and terrestrial patterns, so they are perfect targets for anyone learning to fly-fish.

like the muddy Colorado. Running high, brown, and often carrying whole trees downstream, it's a raging torrent you don't want to mess with. Any other time of the fishing season it flows with cold, clear water.

"There is some good fishing before the snowmelt, maybe three weeks worth, but once the water starts moving, it doesn't come back into shape until early July at best," Lawrence says. "With that, the river channels change every single year."

The North Fork Road (MT 486) runs along the base of the Whitefish Range and through Flathead National Forest along the western edge of the river from the international border to the junction with the Middle Fork of the Flathead (Blankenship Bridge) near West Glacier. Be prepared for several miles of bumpy, dusty, and harsh driving over a dirt road that can shake a car to pieces. It lets the air out of a fair number of tires, so carry a spare and tools, and know how to change a flat.

Despite its rough nature, the North Fork Road is the best course for accessing the river. Be mindful of private land in some areas as it's inter-

Though the lower river is popular with white-water enthusiasts, the upper river near Polebridge has ample opportunities for wading anglers. If you float, plan a shuttle in advance. The area lacks services, and shuttle rates from companies in West Glacier are expensive. JAY NICHOLS PHOTO

The North Fork has stoneflies, mayflies, and caddis, but because the river lacks crucial nutrients, hatches are often less than explosive. Still, the river's cutthroat feed with gusto and will rise to hatch-matching patterns even when the naturals aren't present. JAY NICHOLS PHOTO

spersed along the national-forest boundaries, and avoid steep hillsides when accessing the water. The rocks and soil are loose in some spots, and it's better to find a gentler slope up- or downstream and then work to wherever you'd like to fish.

The river between Blankenship Bridge and Camas Bridge (a western entrance to Glacier National Park) sees the most traffic. Between these two points, there are a few access areas that are good for angling, but it's mostly popular with recreational floaters because of white-water chutes like Fool Hen Rapids. Glacier Rim and Big Creek Campground are two of the most notable pull-offs for floaters (Big Creek Campground with a dump station, toilets, water, and picnic tables is one of the only campgrounds suited for both tents and RVs on the North Fork Road). There are a few other parking areas and places where you can dump or load a personal pontoon boat like the Great Northern Flats access, but because of the steep embankments (and other obstructions like boulders) I don't advise trying to load or unload anything larger.

Camas Creek Bridge is another good access point barely a mile upstream of Big Creek Campground. If you're willing to pay the park's entrance fee, you can drive from West Glacier (Glacier Route 8) and bypass the dusty, rough lower portion of North Fork Road. Most of the water upstream is flat and somewhat featureless, but downstream there is a string of pools, riffles, and

OUTFITTER PERMITS

While wade fishing on the North Fork of the Flathead is a good way to go, floating the river offers an exceptional fishing experience. Recreational floaters are free to use the river at their leisure, but commercial floats are a little tougher to come by. The Forest Service sold four commercial floating permits for the North Fork system in the 1970s, and they aren't issuing any more.

Many guides and outfitters skirt the issue by simply working for those outfitters with the permits. This allows some outfits to organize small-group, overnight floats for the second half of the season when the water is lower.

"We work with several great outfitters that put on wilderness trips that basically run from the U.S. border to Big Creek," Westslope Troutfitters co-owner Justin Lawrence says. "We have two gear boats that go along with us. They set up camps and do all the cooking. We provide all the gear needed, and all clients worry about is floating and fishing."

Glacier Raft Company (406) 888-5454
Glacier Wilderness Guides (406) 387-5555
Great Northern Raft Company (800) 735-7897
Wild River Adventures (800) 700-7056 ■

fast-water chutes. If you're camping at Big Creek, ask someone to drop you off at Camas Creek Bridge and spend the day nudging your way downstream.

Upstream of Camas Creek Bridge, steep hillsides, fallen trees, brush, tall grass, and other good cover for bears to hide in separate the river and road. This changes near Coal Creek, however. As you head north on North Fork Road, take the last turn right (east) just before the bridge over Coal Creek. There are some good wade-fishing areas here, and some use it as a launch for a float to Big Creek Campground. Not only is this area one of the most scenic on the river, several braids and side channels can make for some interesting fishing. Beware of logjams and other hazards, though.

Farther upstream is the community of Polebridge, an outpost in the truest sense of the word. People from all over the world make the trip to the Polebridge Mercantile (406-888-5105), a tiny general store that is surrounded by history, a perfect meeting place for travelers, and the scene for weddings, music festivals, and dogsled races. A word to the wise—call ahead to find out if there are any scheduled events if you want to avoid crowds on the water and traffic on North Fork Road.

There is a bridge, campground, ranger station, and river access about one mile north of Polebridge. Turn right (east) on Polebridge Loop Road from North Fork Road. It angles north and intersects with Glacier Drive briefly before eventually connecting with Glacier Route 7. After a few miles, Glacier Route 7 veers northeast toward Kintla Lake and away from the river. If you head downstream, the road bumps into the river now and again but not with as much regularity.

Much of the land along the road around Polebridge up to the Canadian border is private. Ford is the next major pit stop north of Polebridge (though there is a small unmarked access between Whale Creek Road and Moose Creek Road), but don't expect anything in the way of facilities or conveniences. There is a small river access road (FR 308) to the east just north of Whale Creek Road (FR 318). For the adventurous souls willing to do their own shuttle, the water between Ford and Polebridge is an option. "The road gets worse north of Polebridge," Friel says. "It might be part of the reason this system stays uncrowded and wild. They've talked about paving the road for years, it's just never come to fruition."

North from Ford, the North Fork Road once again wanders away from the river. They neighbor one last time near the international border. There, there is an access (the last one in the United States), and despite the remoteness of the area, border patrol officers mind the fences, so abstain from working upstream and concentrate on wading or floating with the current to avoid any hassles.

Like the other forks of the Flathead, the North Fork is a favorite among white-water enthusiasts. Rafters, tubers, and recreational floaters—not anglers—make up most of the traffic on the lower few miles of the North Fork Road. There are a few Class II and III rapids, but the most turbulent (and popular) runs are between Big Creek and Glacier Rim. Downstream from Glacier Rim, the river settles with only a few Class I chutes until the Blankenship Bridge take-out.

If you're feeling especially adventurous, plan and pack for a multiday trip on the upper half and see lengths of the river that rarely get fished. Be prepared to do your own shuttle. You can inquire about established shuttle services at some of the rafting companies in West Glacier, but they are expensive. A bike, moped, or hitchhiker's thumb are some of the best shuttle options on this particular river.

Hatches and Flies

Walk along the shoreline and you'll see shucks from stoneflies, mayflies, and other critters trout are more than willing to eat. Just don't daydream about blizzard hatches. While this comes as a blow to match-the-hatch anglers, it works to the advantage of those willing to throw attractors and old standbys like Stimulators and Elk-Hair Caddis. "There's not a lot of food in the system, so we fish dry flies 99 percent of the time. These are hungry fish willing to eat on top. For first-time fly fishers, it's an excellent place to learn the sport," Lawrence says.

Mayflies like PMDs, a handful of caddis, Golden Stones, Salmonflies, Yellow Sallies, and terrestrials are some of the most prevalent species. Cutthroat are not fussy feeders, which is why some fly anglers regard them as one of the least-technical fish to pursue. To them, a meal is a meal and if it looks good, they'll eat it. You can get away with attractor patterns and other flies that don't resemble anything on the fish's present-day menu.

"We have great Golden Stone and Green Drake hatches just postrunoff for about a month," Lawrence says. "Even though the stoneflies are a nocturnal hatch, you can fish a Golden Stone or big Stimulator (or whatever your favorite stonefly pattern is) through most of July and August and catch fish. Attractors like Wulffs, Humpies, and others work well too."

For North Fork cutthroat, the feeding season is short, and they're not the type of fish that's going to pass over any morsel. One day last summer Jay Nichols and I had good fishing with a #10 Lawson's Green Drake Paradrake when there weren't any Green Drakes present, let alone any mayflies. Carry Stimulators, hoppers, ants, beetles, parachute mayfly patterns, and small foam Chernobyl Ant–style flies, and you'll have it covered.

Streamers also have their place. They represent larger-than-average meals for these fish, and the heftier cutties will certainly give chase if one passes in front of their nose. Woolly Buggers, small Muddler imitations (a Marabou Muddler is one of my favorites), and anything else that looks like a small leech or baitfish work well. Just remember that this is serious bull-trout country (especially the upper half of the river near the mouth of the tributaries), so don't break the law and start plunking #2/0 rabbit-strip creations when you see white fins suspended over the streambed.

Don't come to the North Fork gunning for large game. There are some decent-size fish, but a 3- or 4-weight rod, or a lightweight, slow-action 5-weight, will be better matched to the average fish. If you're chasing the larger

North Fork cutthroat are opportunistic feeders, so don't be afraid to throw patterns that represent hatches already past their prime.

Many cutthroat in the North Fork reside in Flathead Lake and use the river to travel to and from their spawning grounds. Treat anything you catch with care as the health of the fishery depends on a strong breeding population of fish.

fish and swinging streamers through the deep holes, use a fast-action 6-weight rod with a sinking or sinking-tip line.

The North Fork is slippery. Rock Creek is probably the only piece of water I can think of that is greasier. Wear cleats or studded soles on your wading boots if possible. Felt soles seem to slide over the slimy rocks. Because the water in the North Fork is so cold, and temperatures can plummet at a moment's notice, be prepared to combat hypothermia should someone go for a swim. If you're shuttling along the river in your car, keep a towel and warm change of clothes set aside. Floaters should carry a dry bag with one or two changes of clothes and other emergency items like a first-aid kit. Hypothermia can set in fast, even in the middle of summer, so take the necessary precautions to avoid it.

Directions

The North Fork Road (MT 486) intersects with US 2 in the center of Columbia Falls (Nucleus Avenue). Head north out of town and then northeast on Railroad Street. It changes to the North Fork Road after the railroad overpass and collides with the lower river approximately 10 miles later. Soon after, the pavement ends and the dusty washboard road begins.

Unless you're exploring the neighboring national forest lands or scouting a feeder creek, there's no need to leave the North Fork Road. It is the best way to get to the few access points there are on this river, and should an accident happen (flat tires are common), you'll be in a better position for getting assistance.

Big Creek Campground is clearly marked from the road, but there are fees both for camping and using the river access area (even if you're wade-fishing). You can elect to veer off the North Fork Road into the forest on one of the many unmarked dirt roads if you're looking for a campsite with solitude, but you'll be missing out on the conveniences of fresh water and public restrooms, which are nice after cruising on such a dirty, rough road for so long.

Aside from the camping, the Ford, Schnaus, and Ben Rover cabins are available for rent from the U.S. Forest Service—check recreation.gov or the Hungry Horse District Office at (406) 387-3800 for availability—or visit a couple bed-and-breakfasts. Polebridge Mercantile also has a few rooms if you're too tired to set up camp, but the rental cabins are one of the best deals. There are a few in Polebridge available for reservation through Vacation Rental by Owner (vrbo.com).

Other campgrounds on the eastern side of the river within the borders of Glacier National Park are reachable through the West Glacier, Camas Creek Bridge, or Polebridge entrances. I don't recommend RVs and trailer rigs given the rough terrain and somewhat primitive nature of some campgrounds. Glacier Route 7 (inside the North Fork Road) or Camas Road (Glacier Route 8) run through the western portion of the park and connect near Apgar and the southern intersection of Going-to-the-Sun Road.

Unfortunately, most of Glacier's western campgrounds (Logging Creek, Quartz Creek, Bowman Lake, and Kintla Lake) aren't on the banks of the North Fork, so it's tougher to reach the river. But if you're willing to drive to and from the river, they're base-camp options. Plus, if you plan on exploring Glacier, these campgrounds are near trails that lead into some of the park's lakes that contain trout. A copy of the park's fishing regulations serves as a license, but become familiar with the strict angling regulations before wetting a line.

Hikers need to exercise caution, however. Over the years, several fires have rolled through Glacier and portions of the Flathead National Forest, leaving swaths of standing, burned timber that present a hazard for anglers and campers. They can topple over without a moment's notice. Take care when walking in burned areas when the wind is blowing and stay away from charred trees that are already on their way over.

For other services, lodging, or cold drinks, stop by the Home Ranch Bottoms tavern, store, and campground just south of Polebridge; call (406) 888-5572. There are several signs along the North Fork Road, so you can't miss it. Comforts don't come cheap in this part of the state due to the overhead costs of running a business off the grid. Expect to spend a few bills for things like a six-pack of beer ($13 or more) and camping ($35 a site for two people and $7 for every person after that). Other than that, you're on your own, so stock up before heading upriver.

Lastly, it shouldn't come as a surprise to know an abundance of wildlife make their way down to the water, including moose and bears. Exercise caution when you're walking along the banks or through especially brushy areas with poor visibility.

In the end, it won't be about big fish, blizzard hatches, or any other ego-driven vernacular that circulates through the fly-fishing community like a flu epidemic. A trip to the North Fork is a return to what excited most people about the sport in the first place—a simple grassroots fly-fishing adventure. If you feel like recapturing that feeling again, the North Fork of the Flathead is worth exploring.

Stimi Chew Toy (Royal)

Hook:	#6-16 MFC 7002
Thread:	Orange 6/0 Uni-Thread
Tail:	Natural cow elk
Rib:	Copper wire
Abdomen:	Peacock herl and fluorescent-red Antron Body Wool
Underwing:	Mottled web Etha-Wing
Wing:	Natural cow elk
Overwing:	White calf tail
Thorax:	Orange Wing N' Flash
Legs:	Speckled red Centipede Legs (#2)
Hackle:	Grizzly saddle hackle

Schroeder's Hi-Vis Parachute Ant

Hook:	#14-18 Tiemco 100
Thread:	Black 8/0 Uni-Thread
Body:	Black or tan Superfine dubbing
Post:	Yellow poly yarn
Hackle:	Grizzly saddle

Wilcox VW Hopper

Hook:	#6-14 Dai-Riki 280
Thread:	Orange 8/0 Uni-Thread
Abdomen:	Fluorescent chartreuse Midge Diamond Braid
Underbody:	Gold foam
Overbody:	Brown foam
Hackle:	Furnace or grizzly dyed brown
Underwing:	Pearl Rainbow Thread or pearl Krystal Flash
Wing:	Natural elk hair
Eyes:	Yellow 3D adhesive eyes
Indicator:	Psychedelic Foamicator

APPENDIX A

Fly Shops, Outfitters, and Lodging

Bighorn River

Fly Shops

Bighorn Angler (866) 925-8337 bighornangler.com
Bighorn Fly and Tackle (406) 666-2253 bighornfly.com
Bighorn Trout Shop (406) 666-2375 bighorntroutshop.com
Fort Smith Fly Shop and Cabins (406) 666-2550 flyfishingthebighorn.com

Outfitters

Angler's Edge Outfitters (406) 666-2417 anglersedge.com
Big Sky Fly Fishers (406) 690-4752 bigskyflyfishers.com
Bighorn River Fly Fisher (866) 658-7688 bighornriverflyfisher.com
Two Leggins Outfitters (406) 665-2825 twolegginsoutfitters.com

Lodging

Bighorn Fly and Tackle (406) 666-2253 bighornfly.com
Bighorn River Fly Fisher (866) 658-7688 bighornriverflyfisher.com
Bighorn Trout Shop (406) 666-2375 bighorntroutshop.com
Eagle Nest Lodge (406) 665-3711 eaglenestlodge.com
Forrester's Bighorn River Resort (800) 665-3799 forrestersbighorn.com
Riverbend Angler Resort (877) 558-7688 bighornrivercabins.com
The Bluffs on the Bighorn (406) 666-2255 bighornbluffs.com

Yellowstone River

Fly Shops

Greater Yellowstone Fly Fishers (406) 585-5321 gyflyfishers.com
Jacklin's Fly Shop (406) 646-7336 jacklinsflyshop.com
Montana Troutfitters (406) 587-4707 troutfitters.com
George Anderson's Yellowstone Angler (406) 222-7130 yellowstoneangler.com

Outfitters

Matson Rogers' Angler's West (406) 333-4401 montanaflyfishers.com
Montana Fly Fishing Guides LLC (406) 223-2488 montanaflyfishingguides.com
Montana Trout Wranglers (866) 456-6889 or (406) 580-6050 troutwranglers.com

Yellowstone River (continued)

Lodging

Dome Mountain Ranch (800) 313-4868 domemountainranch.com
Hubbard's Yellowstone Lodge (406) 848-7755 hubya.com/hyl
Rivers Bend Lodge and Cabins (800) 541-4113 riversbendlodge.com
Yellowstone Valley Ranch (406) 333-4787 yellowstonevalleyranch.com

Gallatin River

Fly Shops

Matson Rogers' Angler's West (406) 333-4401 montanaflyfishers.com
Bozeman Angler (406) 587-9111 bozemanangler.com
East Slope Outdoors (888) 359-3974 eastslopeoutdoors.com
Fins and Feathers of Bozeman (406) 586-5373 finsandfeathersonline.com
Gallatin Riverguides (406) 995-2290 gallatinriverguides.com
George Anderson's Yellowstone Angler (406) 222-7130 yellowstoneangler.com
Montana Troutfitters (406) 587-4707 troutfitters.com

Outfitters

Matson Rogers' Angler's West (406) 333-4401 montanaflyfishers.com
Big Sky Anglers (406) 581-6059 bigskyanglers.com
East Slope Outdoors (888) 359-3974 eastslopeoutdoors.com
Gallatin Riverguides (406) 995-2290 gallatinriverguides.com
TroutChasers (406) 763-9049 montanatroutchasers.com
Montana Trout Wranglers (866) 456-6889 or (406) 580-6050 troutwranglers.com
Wild Trout Outfitters (800) 423-4742 wildtroutoutfitters.com

Lodging

320 Ranch (800) 243-0320 320ranch.com
Big River Lodge (406) 763-5504 bigriverlodge.com
Gallatin River Lodge (406) 388-0148 grlodge.com
Lone Mountain Ranch (406) 995-4644 lonemountainranch.com
Rainbow Ranch Lodge (406) 995-4132 rainbowranchbigsky.com
TroutChasers (406) 763-9049 montanatroutchasers.com

Madison River

Fly Shops

Arrick's Fly Shop (406) 646-7920 arricks.com
Beartooth Fly Fishing (406) 682-7525 beartoothflyfishing.com
Blue Ribbon Flies (406) 646-7642 blueribbonflies.com
Bud Lilly's Trout Shop (406) 646-7801 budlillys.com
Fins and Feathers of Bozeman (406) 586-2188 finsandfeathersonline.com
Galloup's Slide Inn (406) 682-4804 slideinn.com
Greater Yellowstone Fly Fishers (406) 585-5321 gyflyfishers.com
Jacklin's Fly Shop (406) 646-7336 jacklinsflyshop.com
Madison River Fishing Company (800) 227-7127 mrfc.com
Montana Troutfitters (406) 587-4707 troutfitters.com

The Bozeman Angler (406) 587-9111 bozemanangler.com
The River's Edge (406) 586-5373 theriversedge.com

Outfitters
Eaton Outfitters (800) 755-3474 eatonoutfitters.com
Glenn Bell Fly Fishing (406) 640-1490 flyfishwestyellowstone.com
Lost Fork Outfitters (406) 581-9113 lostforkoutfitters.com
Madison River Outfitters (406) 646-9644 madisonriveroutfitters.com
Matson Rogers' Angler's West (406) 333-4401 montanaflyfishers.com

Lodging
Beartooth Fly Fishing (406) 682-7525 beartoothflyfishing.com
El Western Resort (800) 831-2773 elwestern.com
Fan Mountain Inn (877) 682-5200 fanmountaininn.com
Galloup's Slide Inn (406) 682-4804 slideinn.com
Madison Valley Ranch (800) 891-6158 madisonvalleyranch.com
Moonlight on the Madison (866) 210-7481 moonlightonthemadison.com
Papoose Creek Lodge (406) 682-3030 papoosecreek.com
Rainbow Valley Lodge (800) 452-8254 rainbowvalley.com
West Fork Cabin Camp (406) 682-4802 wfork.com
Wilderness Edge (866) 226-7668 wedgeretreat.com

Jefferson River

Fly Shops
Four Rivers Fishing Company (888) 474-8377 4riversmontana.com
Frontier Anglers (406) 683-5276 frontieranglers.com
Great Divide Outfitters (406) 267-3346 bigholetrout.com
Montana Fly Company (406) 835-2621 montanaflyco.com
Montana Trout Stalkers (406) 581-5150 montanatrout.com
Sunrise Fly Shop (406) 835-3474 sunriseflyshop.net
The StoneFly Fly Shop (406) 494-0707 thestonefly.com

Outfitters
Flatline Outfitters (406) 684-5639 kingsflatline.com
Four Rivers Fishing Company (888) 474-8377 4riversmontana.com
Greg Lilly (406) 684-5960 hwlodge.com
TroutChasers (406) 763-9049 montanatroutchasers.com
Stonefly Inn and Outfitters (406) 684-5648 thestoneflyinn.com

Lodging
Big Hole C4 Lodge (877) 684-5760 bigholec4lodge.com
Crane Meadow Lodge (406) 684-5773 cranemeadow.com
Five Rivers Lodge (800) 378-5006 fiveriverslodge.com
Healing Waters Lodge (406) 684-5960 hwlodge.com
Iron Wheel Guest Ranch (406) 494-2960 ironwheel.com
Jefferson River Guest Ranch and Campground (406) 684-5225 thejeffersonrivercamp.com
Stonefly Inn and Outfitters (406) 684-5648 thestoneflyinn.com
The Old Hotel (406) 684-5959 theoldhotel.com
TroutChasers Lodge (406) 763-9049 montanatroutchasers.com

Beaverhead River

Fly Shops

Backcountry Angler (406) 683-3462 backcountryangler.com
Four Rivers Fishing Company (888) 474-8377 4riversmontana.com
Frontier Anglers (800) 228-5263 frontieranglers.com
Montana Fly Company (406) 835-2621 montanaflyco.com

Outfitters

Anderson and Platt Fly Fishing (828) 773-3730 anderson-platt-flyfishing.com
Bloody Dick Outfitters (406) 681-3163 goldwest.visitmt.com
Craig Fellin Outfitters (406) 832-3252 flyfishinglodge.com
Flatline Outfitters (800) 222-5510 kingsflatline.com
Four Rivers Fishing Company (888) 474-8377 4riversmontana.com
Frontier Anglers (800) 228-5263 frontieranglers.com
Greg Lilly (406) 684-5960 hwlodge.com
Stonefly Inn and Outfitters (406) 684-5648 thestoneflyinn.com

Lodging

Armstead Campground (406) 683-4199 goldwest.visitmt.com
Backcountry Angler Inn (406) 683-3462 backcountryangler.com
Best Western Paradise Inn (406) 683-4214 bestwestern.com
Big Trout Ranch (406) 684-5995 bigtroutranch.com
Broken Arrow Lodge (406) 842-5437 brokenarrowlodge.com
Five Rivers Lodge (800) 378-5006 fiveriverslodge.com
Frontier Anglers (800) 228-5263 frontieranglers.com
Goose Down Ranch (406) 683-6704 goosedownranch.com
Guest House International Inn and Suites (406) 683-3636 guesthouseintl.com
Healing Waters Lodge (406) 684-5960 hwlodge.com
Comfort Inn Dillon (406) 683-6831 comfortinn.com
Rivers Edge Lodge Bed and Breakfast (406) 693-6214 riversedgelodgebb.com
Sundowner Motel (406) 683-2375 goldwest.visitmt.com
Super 8 Motel of Dillon (406) 683-4288 super8.com
Stonefly Inn and Outfitters (406) 684-5648 thestoneflyinn.com

Big Hole River

Fly Shops

Four Rivers Fishing Company (888) 474-8377 4riversmontana.com
Frontier Anglers (800) 228-5263 frontieranglers.com
Great Divide Outfitters (406) 267-3346 bigholetrout.com
Montana Fly Company (406) 835-2621 montanaflyco.com
Sunrise Fly Shop (406) 835-3474 sunriseflyshop.net
The StoneFly Fly Shop (406) 494-0707 thestonefly.com
Tom Smith's Backcountry Angler (406) 683-3462 backcountryangler.com
Troutfitters (406) 832-3212 bigholetroutfitters.com

Outfitters

Beavertail Outfitters (406) 683-6232
Big Hole River Guide (406) 782-0567 montanatroutflyfishing.com

Craig Fellin Outfitters (406) 832-3252 flyfishinglodge.com
Stonefly Inn and Outfitters (406) 684-5648 thestoneflyinn.com
Troutfitters (406) 832-3212 bigholetroutfitters.com

Lodging

Big Hole C4 Lodge (877) 684-5760 bigholec4lodge.com
Big Hole Lodge (406) 832-3252 flyfishinglodge.com
Canyon Creek Guest Ranch (877) 518-2407 canyoncreekguestranch.com
Complete Fly Fisher (866) 832-3175 completeflyfisher.com
Crane Meadow Lodge (406) 684-5773 cranemeadow.com
Five Rivers Lodge (800) 378-5006 fiveriverslodge.com
Great Waters Inn (406) 835-2024 greatwatersinn.com
Jackson Hot Springs Lodge (406) 834-3151 jacksonhotsprings.com
Nez Perce Motel (406) 689-3254 goldwest.visitmt.com
Pioneer Mountain Lodge (406) 689-3229 goldwest.visitmt.com
Sportsman Motel (406) 835-2141 sportsmanmt.com
Stonefly Inn and Outfitters (406) 684-5648 thestoneflyinn.com

Rock Creek

Fly Shops

Flint Creek Outdoors (406) 859-9500 flintcreekoutdoors.com
Grizzly Hackle Fly Shop (800) 297-8996 grizzlyhackle.com
Kesel's Four Rivers Fly Shop (406) 721-4796 fourrivers.net
The Kingfisher (406) 721-6141 or (888) 542-4911 kingfisherflyshop.com
Missoulian Angler (406) 728-7766 missoulianangler.com
River Otter Fly Shop (406) 273-4858 riverotterflyfishing.com
Rock Creek Fisherman's Mercantile (406) 825-6440 rcmerc.com

Outfitters

Blackfoot River Outfitters (406) 542-7411 blackfootriver.com
Classic Journey Outfitters (877) 327-7878* classicjourneyoutfitters.com
Complete Fly Fisher (866) 832-3175* completeflyfisher.com
Dixon Adventures (406) 240-6306 dixonadventures.com
John Perry's Montana Fly Fishing (406) 825-2997* johnperryflyfishing.com
Montana Fly Fishing Connection (406) 370-2868 mtffc.com
*Outfitters with permits to float Rock Creek

Lodging

Bighorn Bed and Breakfast (406) 859-3109 bighornmontana.com
Blue Damsel Lodge (406) 825-3077 bluedamsel.com
Rock Creek Fisherman's Mercantile (406) 825-6440 rcmerc.com
Rock Creek Trout Bums (406) 825-6146 rockcreektroutbums.com

Blackfoot River

Fly Shops

Blackfoot Angler (406) 793-3474 blackfootangler.com
Grizzly Hackle Fly Shop (800) 297-8996 grizzlyhackle.com
The Kingfisher (406) 721-6141 or (888) 542-4911 kingfisherflyshop.com
Missoulian Angler (406) 728-7766 missoulianangler.com

Blackfoot River (continued)

Outfitters

Blackfoot River Outfitters (406) 542-7411 blackfootriver.com
Dixon Adventures (406) 240-6306 dixonadventures.com
John Perry's Montana Fly Fishing (406) 825-2997 johnperryflyfishing.com
Montana Fly Fishing Connection (406) 370-2868 mtffc.com
PRO Outfitters (406) 442-5489 prooutfitters.com
WTR Outfitters (406) 793-5666 wtroutfitters.com

Lodging

Doubletree Edgewater (406) 728-3100 doubletree1.hilton.com
Holiday Inn Parkside (406) 721-8550 himissoula.com
Paws Up Resort (406) 244-5200 pawsup.com
Red Lion Inn (406) 728-3300 redlion.rdln.com
Rich Ranch (406) 677-2317 richranch.com

Clark Fork

Fly Shops

Grizzly Hackle Fly Shop (800) 297-8996 grizzlyhackle.com
Kesel's Four Rivers Fly Shop (406) 721-4796 fourrivers.net
The Kingfisher (406) 721-6141 or (888) 542-4911 kingfisherflyshop.com
Missoulian Angler (406) 728-7766 missoulianangler.com
Rock Creek Fisherman's Mercantile (406) 825-6440 rcmerc.com

Outfitters

Backdoor Outfitters (888) 330-3861 backdooroutfitters.com
Blackfoot River Outfitters (406) 542-7411 blackfootriver.com
Carl Mann's Montana Experience Outfitters (406) 777-1687 carlmannoutfitting.com
Clark Fork River Outfitters (800) 745-3933 flyfishbigsky.com
Classic Journey Outfitters (877) 327-7878 classicjourneyoutfitters.com
Dixon Adventures (406) 240-6306 dixonadventures.com
John Perry's Montana Fly Fishing (406) 825-2997 or (800) 580-9703 johnperryflyfishing.com
Montana Fly Fishing Connection (406) 370-2868 mtffc.com

Lodging

C'mon Inn (406) 543-4600 cmoninn.com
Days Inn & Suites, Lolo (406) 273-2121 daysinn.com
Doubletree Edgewater (406) 728-3100 doubletree1.hilton.com
Holiday Inn Parkside (406) 721-8550 himissoula.com
John Perry's Clark Fork River Lodge (800) 580-9703 johnperryflyfishing.com
Rock Creek Fisherman's Mercantile (406) 825-6440 rcmerc.com

Bitterroot River

Fly Shops

Chuck Stranahan's Flies and Guides (406) 363-4197 chuck-stranahan.com
Grizzly Hackle Fly Shop (800) 297-8996 grizzlyhackle.com

Kesel's Four Rivers Fly Shop (406) 721-4796 fourrivers.net
Missoulian Angler (406) 728-7766 missoulianangler.com
River Otter Fly Shop (406) 273-4858 riverotterflyfishing.com
The Kingfisher (888) 542-4911 kingfisherflyshop.com

Outfitters

Backdoor Outfitters (888) 330-3861 backdooroutfitters.com
Dixon Adventures (406) 240-6306 dixonadventures.com
John Perry's Montana Fly Fishing (406) 825-2997 or (800) 580-9703 johnperryflyfishing.com
Montana Fly Fishing Connection (406) 370-2868 mtffc.com
Renegade Fly Fishing Outfitters (406) 880-7221 flyfishmissoula.com
Wapiti Waters (800) 254-5311 wapiti-waters.com

Lodging

Angler's Roost (406) 363-1268 anglersroost-montana.com
Best Western, Hamilton (406) 363-2142 bestwestern.com
Bitterroot River Inn (406) 363-9700 bitterrootriverinn.com
Bitterroot River Lodge (406) 363-0708 bitterrootriverlodge.com
Days Inn & Suites, Lolo (406) 273-2121 daysinn.com
Flying R Guest Cabins (406) 821-4631 montanaflyingrcabins.com
Triple Creek Ranch (406) 821-4600 triplecreekranch.com

Missouri River

Fly Shops

Big R Fly Shop (406) 761-7441 bigrflyshop.com
CrossCurrents (406) 235-3433 crosscurrents.com
Headhunters Fly Shop (406) 235-3447 headhuntersflyshop.com
Montana Fly Goods (406) 442-2630 or (800) 466-9589 montanaflygoods.com
Prewett Creek Inn and Fly Shop (406) 468-9244 prewettcreekinn.com
The Trout Shop (800) 337-8528 thetroutshop.com

Outfitters

Eagle Creek Outfitters (406) 468-9171
Falls Outfitters (406) 868-1951 fallsoutfitters.com
Fishy Expeditions (509) 733-9055 fishyexpeditions.com
Missouri River Expeditions (406) 449-6446 missouririverexp.com
Montana Fishing Outfitters (406) 439-4545 dragfreedrift.com
Montana River Guides (406) 235-4360 montana-river-guides.com
Montana River Outfitters (406) 761-1677 montanariveroutfitters.com
Montana Trout Syndicate (406) 439-5194 mtsyn.com
Osprey Expeditions (800) 315-8502 osprey-expeditions.com
Wolf Creek Outfitters (866) 688-7688 wolfcreekoutfitters.com

Lodging

Blacktail Ranch (406) 235-4330 blacktailranch.com
Craig Trout Camp (877) 379-3597 craigtroutcamp.com
End of the Line Sportsman's Retreat (406) 468-9111 sportsmansretreat.com
Missouri River Lodge (406) 468-2224 missouririverlodge.com
Prewett Creek Inn and Fly Shop (406) 468-9244 prewettcreekinn.com

Smith River

Fly Shops

Big R Fly Shop (406) 761-7441 bigrflyshop.com
CrossCurrents (406) 235-3433 crosscurrents.com
Montana Fly Goods (800) 466-9589 montanaflygoods.com

Outfitters

Big Sky Expeditions (406) 442-2630 or (800) 466-9589 montanaflygoods.com
Blackfoot River Outfitters (406) 543-6528 blackfootriver.com
Blast & Cast Outfitters (406) 682-4420 montanaoutfitters.org
Complete Fly Fisher (866) 832-3175 completeflyfisher.com
Glacier Wilderness Guides (800) 521-7238 glacierguides.com
High Plains Drifter (406) 721-2703 highplainsdrifter.com
Lewis and Clark Expeditions (406) 449-4632 lewisandclarkexpeditions.net
Montana Fly Fishing Connection (406) 370-2868 mtffc.com
PRO Outfitters (406) 442-5489 prooutfitters.com

Lodging

Heaven on Earth Ranch (406) 866-3316 heavenonearthranch.com
Tenderfoot Motel (406) 547-3303 tenderfootmotel.com

Shuttle Services

Amy's Think Wild Shuttle Service (406) 547-2215
Budget Shuttle Service (406) 293-1146
Smith Shuttle Service (406) 866-3522

Kootenai River

Fly Shops

Dave Blackburn's Kootenai Angler (406) 293-7578 or (800) 322-9339 montana-flyfishing.com
Kootenai River Outfitters (406) 295-9056 kroutfitters.com

Outfitters

Dave Blackburn's Kootenai Angler (406) 293-7578 or (800) 322-9339 montana-flyfishing.com
Kootenai River Outfitters (406) 295-9056 kroutfitters.com
Linehan Outfitting (406) 295-4872 fishmontana.com

Lodging

Dave Blackburn's Kootenai Angler (406) 293-7578 montana-flyfishing.com
Evergreen Motel (406) 293-4178 libbyevergreenmotel.com
Kootenai River Outfitters (406) 295-9056 kroutfitters.com
Linehan Outfitting (406) 295-4872 fishmontana.com
Sandman Motel (406) 293-8831 sandmanmotel.us
Sandman Motel Down-Under (406) 293-7795 sandmanmotel.us
Swanson Lodge (406) 295-8909 swansonlodge.com

Flathead River (Main Stem)

Fly Shops

Arends Fly Shop (406) 892-2033
Bigfork Anglers (406) 837-3675 bigforkanglers.com
Lakestream Fly Shop (406) 862-1298 lakestream.com
Stumptown Anglers (877) 906-9949 stumptownangler.com

Outfitters

Channel Outfitters (406) 325-7496 channeloutfitters.com
Glacier Anglers (406) 888-5454 or (800) 235-6781 glacierraftco.com
Northern Rockies Outfitters (406) 756-2544 northernrockiesoutfit.com
Westslope Troutfitters (406) 250-6119 westslopetroutfitters.com

Lodging

Averill's Flathead Lake Lodge (406) 837-4391 flatheadlakelodge.com
Best Western White Oak Grand Hotel (406) 857-2388 bestwestern.com
Glacier Pines RV Park (406) 752-2760 glacierpines.com
Glacier Ridge Suites (406) 752-4333 glacierridgesuites.com
The Great Bear Inn (406) 250-4577 thegreatbearinn.com

South Fork of the Flathead

Fly Shops

Arends Fly Shop (406) 892-2033
Glacier Anglers Fly Shop (406) 888-5454 or (800) 235-6781 glacierraftco.com
Lakestream Fly Shop (406) 862-1298 lakestream.com
Stumptown Anglers (877) 906-9949 stumptownangler.com

Outfitters

Big Salmon Outfitters (406) 676-3999 bigsalmonoutfitters.com
Bob Marshall Wilderness Ranch (406) 754-2285 wildernessranch.com
Cheff Guest Ranch (406) 644-2557 cheffguestranch.com
Diamond R Guest Ranch (800) 597-9465 diamondrranch.com
Hawkins Outfitters (406) 296-2642 hawkinsoutfitters.com
Paws Up Outfitters (406) 244-5363 pawsupoutfitters.com
Rich Ranch (406) 677-2317 richranch.com
Salmon Forks Outfitters (800) 228-7806 salmonforks.com
Spotted Bear Ranch (406) 755-7337 spottedbear.com
WTR Outfitters (406) 793-5666 wtroutfitters.com

Lodging

Double Arrow Resort (800) 468-0777 doublearrowresort.com
Holland Lake Lodge (406) 754-2282 hollandlakelodge.com
Paws Up Resort (406) 244-5200 pawsup.com
Rich Ranch (406) 677-2317 richranch.com
Spotted Bear Ranch (406) 755-7337 spottedbear.com

Middle Fork of the Flathead

Fly Shops
Arends Fly Shop (406) 892-2033
Glacier Anglers Fly Shop (800) 235-6781 glacierraftco.com
Lakestream Fly Shop (406) 862-1298 lakestream.com
Stumptown Anglers (877) 906-9949 stumptownangler.com

Outfitters
Glacier Raft Company (406) 888-5454 glacierraftco.com
Glacier Wilderness Guides (406) 387-5555 glacierguides.com
Great Northern Raft Company (800) 735-7897 gnwhitewater.com
Westslope Troutfitters (406) 250-6119 (a booking agent) westslopetroutfitters.com
Wild River Adventures (800) 700-7056 riverwild.com

Lodging
Glacier Mountain Shadows (406) 892-7686
Glacier Peaks RV Park (406) 892-2133 glacierpeaksrvpark.com
Glacier Raft Company (406) 888-5454 glacierraftco.com
Holiday Inn Express, Kalispell (406) 755-7405 hiexpress.com
LaSalle RV Park and Campground (406) 892-4668 or (877) 894-4178
Meadow Lake Resort (406) 892-8700 meadowlake.com
Stanton Creek Lodge (406) 888-5040 stantoncreeklodge.com

North Fork of the Flathead

Fly Shops
Arends Fly Shop (406) 892-2033
Glacier Anglers Fly Shop (800) 235-6781 glacierraftco.com
Lakestream Fly Shop (406) 862-1298 lakestream.com
Montana River Anglers (406) 261-2033 montanariveranglers.com
Stumptown Anglers (877) 906-9949 stumptownangler.com

Outfitters
Glacier Raft Company (406) 888-5454 glacierraftco.com
Glacier Wilderness Guides (406) 387-5555 glacierguides.com
Great Northern Raft Company (800) 735-7897 gnwhitewater.com
Westslope Troutfitters (406) 250-6119 (a booking agent) westslopetroutfitters.com
Wild River Adventures (800) 700-7056 riverwild.com

Lodging
Glacier Mountain Shadows (406) 892-7686
Glacier Park Super 8 (406) 892-0888 super8.com
Glacier Peaks RV Park (406) 892-2133 glacierpeaksrvpark.com
Glacier Raft Company (406) 888-5454 glacierraftco.com
Home Ranch Bottoms (406) 888-5572 homeranchbottoms.com
LaSalle RV Park and Campground (406) 892-4668 or (877) 894-4178
Meadow Lake Resort (406) 892-8700 meadowlake.com
Polebridge Mercantile (406) 888-5105

APPENDIX B

Special Floating Regulations

Beaverhead Regulations

In the late 1990s, fishing pressure on Montana's rivers was at an all-time high. This was most apparent on small rivers like the Beaverhead, where even the slightest increase in the number of anglers made the water feel crowded. Reacting to the cry of outfitters, guides, and visiting fishermen, Montana Department of Fish, Wildlife and Parks created a new set of regulations in 1999 that allowed certain people on different reaches of the river depending on the day of the week and time of year. After a two-year trial period, the new guidelines were set in place.

Some anglers cried foul—that the new regulations restricted visiting anglers and deterred tourism. Others said it dealt a blow to the outfitting industry. Attitudes have changed somewhat since then, but there is still a common misconception about what the regulations mean, particularly to nonresidents. Below is a list of the regulations and a brief synopsis of how the regulations affect anglers and outfitters. Coupled with the map of the river, you should have a good idea of where, when, and how you can fish the Beaverhead.

Clark Canyon Dam to Anderson Lane

Creel limit: Three daily and in possession, only one over 18 inches, and only one rainbow trout. Aside from the seasonal closures, there are no regulations between the dam and High Bridge, so anyone can wade- or float-fish it any day of the week.

Clark Canyon Dam to Pipe Organ Bridge

Open the third Saturday in May through November 30. Because of low flows, spawning fish, and other issues, fishing is not allowed on this portion of the river other than these dates.

High Bridge FAS to Henneberry FAS

Closed to float fishing by nonresidents and float outfitting on each Saturday from the third Saturday in May through Labor Day. Residents, outfitters, guides, and nonresidents can fish these waters during this time; nonresidents and outfitters cannot do so with the aid of a boat. This includes using a boat to shuttle between wade-fishing areas.

Henneberry FAS (near Henneberry Bridge) to Pipe Organ Bridge

Closed to float fishing by nonresidents and float outfitting on each Sunday from the third Sunday in May through Labor Day. Feel free to wade-fish to your heart's content.

Downstream from Pipe Organ Bridge

Open entire year.

US 91 South Bridge (Tash Bridge) to Selway Bridge

Closed to float outfitting from the third Saturday in May through Labor Day. Nonresidents and residents can float- or wade-fish this section.

Anderson Lane Downstream to Mouth (Near Twin Bridges)

Creel limit: Five daily and in possession, one over 18 inches, only one may be a rainbow trout.

Regulations change yearly. Check with the most current Montana fishing regulations book for more information, or check the Montana Fish, Wildlife and Parks website for up-to-date information and possible closures.

Big Hole Regulations

Like the Beaverhead, angling days on the Big Hole River grew exponentially in the late 1990s, prompting the Montana Department of Fish, Wildlife and Parks to explore a strategy that mitigated conflicts and fostered a pleasant experience.

The result was a list of regulations that dictated when, where, and how anglers could enjoy the Big Hole depending on their residency, profession (guides and outfitters), day of the week, and time of the year. Implemented in 1999, the new regulations confused and angered most anglers and outfitters, but as the pressure on the river dispersed, attitudes changed.

"The regulations spread people out a little bit," Stonefly Inn and Outfitters owner Dan "Rooster" Leavens says. "The thing I hate hearing from people is 'darn it, I can't float the canyon today.' Well, there are 120 miles of water. Surely, you can go catch fish somewhere else. It's really not a big deal. People just don't like it when someone tells them where they can't go."

However, many that visit the Big Hole remain confused on what the regulations mean to them. Below is a list of the regulations, and some brief notes to help with interpretation. Many of the restrictions are only in force between the third Saturday in May and Labor Day—not the entire year. Coupled with the map of the river, you should have a good idea of where, when, and how you can fish the Big Hole.

Entire River

Extended season for whitefish and catch-and-release for trout opens December 1 to the third Saturday in May with artificial lures and/or maggots only. All float users are limited to a total of two launches at or near each official access site each day (i.e., one party, two boats = two launches). Three boats or more and someone has to go elsewhere. See the Big the Hole River map for official access sites.

Headwaters to North Fork Big Hole River

Open the entire year to the harvest of brook trout.

Headwaters to Mudd Creek FAS

Closed to float outfitting from the third Saturday in May through Labor Day. Outfitters and guides cannot launch commercial float trips on this stretch during this time period. However, commercial wade-fishing trips are permitted. Residents and nonresidents can also fish this area.

Headwaters to Dickie Bridge

Combined trout: Five daily and in possession, no size restriction during open season. This is also grayling habitat, so take extra care of your catch until you identify what's on the end of your line.

Mudd Creek FAS to Fishtrap FAS

Closed to float outfitting on each Tuesday from the third Saturday in May through Labor Day. Outfitters and guides cannot launch commercial float trips on this portion on Tuesdays during this part of the season. However, commercial wade-fishing trips are permitted. Residents and nonresidents can float or wade-fish this area.

Fishtrap FAS to East Bank BLM FAS

Closed to float outfitting on each Thursday from the third Saturday in May through Labor Day. Outfitters and guides cannot launch commercial float trips on this portion on Thursdays during this part of the season. However, commercial wade-fishing trips are permitted. Residents and nonresidents can float- or wade-fish this area.

East Bank BLM FAS to Jerry Creek FAS

Closed to float outfitting on each Wednesday from the third Saturday in May through Labor Day. Outfitters and guides cannot launch commercial float trips through this portion on Wednesdays during this part of the season. However, commercial wade-fishing trips are permitted. Residents and nonresidents can float- or wade-fish this area.

Dickie Bridge to Divide Bridge (Divide FAS)

Artificial lures only. Bait is not permitted.

Jerry Creek FAS to Divide FAS

Closed to float fishing by nonresidents and float outfitting on each Saturday from the third Saturday in May through Labor Day. Montana residents are the only ones allowed to float on Saturdays during this part of the season. However, nonresidents, outfitters, and guides can wade-fish—they simply cannot do so with the aid of a boat. This includes using a boat to shuttle between wade-fishing areas.

Divide Bridge (Divide FAS) to Melrose Bridges (Salmon Fly FAS)

Artificial lures only. Closed to float fishing by nonresidents and float outfitting on each Sunday from the third Saturday in May through Labor Day. Montana residents are the only ones allowed to fish this portion from a boat on Saturdays during this part of the season. However, nonresidents, outfitters, and guides can wade-fish—they simply cannot do so with the aid of a boat. This includes using a boat to shuttle between wade-fishing areas.

Melrose Bridges (Salmon Fly FAS) to Glen FAS (bridges)

Closed to float outfitting on each Monday from the third Saturday in May through Labor Day. Outfitters and guides cannot launch commercial float trips on this portion on Mondays during this part of the season. However, commercial wade-fishing trips are permitted. Residents and nonresidents can float- or wade-fish this area.

Glen FAS (bridges) to Notch Bottom FAS

Closed to float outfitting on each Friday from the third Saturday in May through Labor Day. Outfitters and guides cannot conduct commercial float trips on this portion on Fridays during this part of the season. However, commercial wade-fishing trips are permitted. Residents and nonresidents can float- or wade-fish this area.

INDEX